The View from Here

The View from Here

Conversations with Gay and Lesbian Filmmakers

MATTHEW HAYS

ARSENAL PULP PRESS
VANCOUVER

THE VIEW FROM HERE
©2007 by MATTHEW HAYS

ARSENAL PULP PRESS
Suite 200, 341 Water Street
Vancouver, BC
Canada V6B 1B8
arsenalpulp.com

The publisher gratefully acknowledges the support of the Canada Council for the Arts and the British Columbia Arts Council for its publishing program, and the Government of Canada through the Book Publishing Industry Development Program and the Government of British Columbia through the Book Publishing Tax Credit Program for its publishing activities.

Efforts have been made to locate copyright holders of source material wherever possible. The publisher welcomes hearing from any copyright holders of material used in this book who have not been contacted.

Cover photograph of Divine from *Pink Flamingos* directed by John Waters ©1972 Lawrence Irvine / New Line Cinema
Text design by Shyla Seller

Printed and bound in Canada

Library and Archives Canada Cataloguing in Publication:

Hays, Matthew, 1965-
    The view from here : conversations with gay and lesbian filmmakers / Matthew Hays.

Includes bibliographical references.
ISBN 978-1-55152-220-3 (pbk.)

    1. Homosexuality in motion pictures. 2. Gays in motion pictures.
3. Gay motion picture producers and directors—Interviews.
4. Screenwriters—interviews. 5. Independent filmmakers—Interviews.
I. Title.

PN1995.9.H55H39 2007   791.43′653   C2007-902271-5

CONTENTS

For my parents
(who probably took me to too many movies)

and

for Steve
(who I've probably dragged to too many movies)

Acknowledgments

First and foremost, I must thank all of the filmmakers who participated in the creation of *The View from Here*. The book is meant as a celebration of their work and a tribute to their creative spirit. The time they granted me for all of the interviews is greatly appreciated.

The team at Arsenal Pulp Press were simply incredible throughout every stage of this book's creation. Thanks to Robert Ballantyne and Brian Lam for having faith in me and the book (and for their patience when deadlines were missed, which seemed to be constant). They have assembled a superb team, among them Bethanne Grabham, Shyla Seller, and Janice Beley. I cannot thank this group of people enough for their hard work and dedication to the project.

I must also thank the Canada Council for the Arts, which supplied me with a much-needed grant that provided crucial financial support during the initial stages of research and writing.

Tim Lawrence, a former student of mine, provided his skills transcribing most of the interviews for this book, and with them came his insights and critiques.

The View from Here was born as the thesis project for my Master's degree at Concordia University. My advisor, Dennis Murphy, gave me invaluable support and insight, and without him, I can honestly say I would not have finished my degree. Thanks must also go to the members of my defence committee, Martin Allor and Thomas Waugh. Thomas Waugh merits special acknowledgment for all of his valued help in contacting various queer filmmakers who ultimately appear in the book, not to mention his valued words of wisdom and support. As well, I would like to thank Chantal Nadeau, who chaired my defence.

For their unconditional support and assistance in putting the bits and pieces of this book together, I'd also like to thank Michael Debbané, Kelly Hargraves of First Run Features, James Harvey-Kelly, Stacey Johnson, Don Lobel, Alison Machum, Erik Schut of TLA, Bonne Smith, Carole Zucker, and Mario Falsetto.

I need to thank numerous editors who encouraged me with this book and who understood when I needed to take time away to write it, including Mark Dillon and Sean Davidson at *Playback*, Marc Glassman at *Montage* and *POV*, and Wyndham Wise at the (sadly now-defunct) *Take One*. At the *Montreal Mirror*, the weekly with which I've been associated since 1993, thanks must go to Rupert Bottenberg, Simon Briscoe, Annie Ilkow, Joanne Latimer, Patrick Lejtenyi, Sarah Musgrave, Genevieve Paiement, Pierre-Marc Pelletier, Philip Preville, Nathalie Rabbat, Annarosa Sabbadini, Chris Sheridan, Mireille Silcoff, Mark Slutsky, Alastair Sutherland, Juliet Waters, Matthew Woodley, and Chris Yurkiw.

Finally, I would also link to thank my students, an ongoing source of inspiration and insight who have allowed me to continue my education. Stephen Sondheim once called teaching "the sacred art." He was right.

Introduction

*It is difficult enough to be queer, but to be queer in the cinema
is almost impossible. Heterosexuals have fucked up the screen so
completely that there's hardly room for us to kiss there.*
—Derek Jarman, filmmaker

The roots of this book go back to the year I took off from school to travel through Europe; it was in London that I saw my very first John Waters films at the Institute of Contemporary Arts. There were three Waters films in particular—*Pink Flamingos*, *Female Trouble*, and *Desperate Living*—that I can say, without exaggeration, changed my life. Waters' sheer audacity and over-the-top, hyperbolic representations of character and plot were all just so perfectly, shockingly, unapologetically *queer*.

Since then, I have worked extensively for the alternative press (in particular, for the *Montreal Mirror*, a news and entertainment weekly, as a critic, reporter, and editor) and for various mainstream publications, while completing two degrees—in film studies and media studies—at Concordia University in Montreal. *The View from Here* reflects the intersection of my areas of specialization as a journalist and student: queer identity and the cinema.

Looking at the thirty-two interviews in this book (thirty-three if you include the legendary Divine), it is impossible not to be thunderstruck at the evolution of queer-authored cinema over the past fifty years. Finding a common thread to link the filmmakers profiled here at times appeared to be a futile exercise, given the depth and variety of their work. Indeed, *The View from Here* is a tribute to the broad range of films created by gay and lesbian artists: the experimental works of Kenneth Anger, the gritty documentaries of Janis Cole and Holly Dale, the playful formalism of John Greyson, the brash musicals of Bill Condon, the erotic performance art of Annie Sprinkle, and beyond.

Mirror, mirror

One cannot read these interviews without reflecting on the broad and rigorous writing that's been done on the relationship between queers and the big screen. Certainly, I've been influenced by various takes on the subject, such as Vito Russo's plea for positive cinematic images in his 1981 book *The Celluloid Closet*, Richard Dyer's defence of the use of stereotypes, B. Ruby Rich's landmark 1992 essay "The New Queer

Cinema" denouncing the idea that queer directors should necessarily portray "positive" images on screen, and Thomas Waugh's radical rethinking of pornography.

Russo's *The Celluloid Closet*, in particular, had a profound impact on how audiences view gays and lesbians in the movies. The book carefully documents the litany of negative gay and lesbian images on film perpetuated by Hollywood studios; Russo punctuates this point with a ghoulish yet insightful Necrology: a list of numerous gay and lesbian characters in Hollywood films and the manner in which they die on screen. It is dismaying, to say the least. He summed up his opinion at the end of his book: "Hollywood is too busy trying to make old formulas hit the jackpot again to see the future. Hollywood is yesterday, forever catching up tomorrow with what's happening today." Although Russo's tome was criticized for numerous reasons—his omission of many European directors and his Hollywoodcentricism, in particular (Thomas Waugh described *The Celluloid Closet* as "lite, but essential")—the book set in motion, in Hollywood and elsewhere, a chain of reactions toward the negative cinematic stereotyping he exposed so well.

Russo died from AIDS-related causes in 1990, and I wish he were still around to see how things have changed, especially the massive independent film movement that would follow *Celluloid's* publication, encouraged by new institutions like the Sundance Film Festival and Miramax Films. Suddenly, being an outsider potentially became a hugely profitable proposition for filmmakers. As a result, a new breed of queer auteurs started making their own films, on their own terms. Documentary filmmaker Robert Epstein told me that when he and co-director Jeffrey Friedman were putting together their documentary based on Russo's book, they originally included interviews with these up-and-coming gay and lesbian directors, which unfortunately, due to the sheer size of the project, had to be edited out. In a sense, I feel like this book helps to fill the gap between where Russo left off—a critique of Hollywood from the outside—and where we are now: autonomous creators of our own cinematic universes.

If there is a common thread to these interviews, I would suggest it is the self-consciousness many gay and lesbian filmmakers feel about their work. Given the ongoing debates surrounding gay and lesbian representations on screen, how can queer filmmakers not feel a heavy burden every time they pick up a camera? When I screen their work, I get a sense that, as the filmmakers look upon the world through their lenses, they are acutely aware that they too are being watched, an affect that B. Ruby Rich refers to as "Homo Pomo." As John Cameron Mitchell told me, there is a distinct advantage to being both queer and a filmmaker: "You know that things aren't what they seem. You are aware of surface and then reality because you have to hide something so basic about yourself—about who you're attracted to. Everything has a surface, and it's like, 'What's really behind there?' You're aware of code, you're aware of camp, which means exaggeration of surface." This self-consciousness connects many of the filmmakers in the book: it is present in copious Hollywood romantic comedy references made by Ian Iqbal Rashid in *Touch of Pink*, the tabloid reflections of Fenton Bailey and Randy Barbato, the recycling of film culture of Bruce LaBruce, the reflections on voyeurism of Patricia Rozema, and the camp outrageousness of John Waters.

Labels

For most of the people I spoke with for *The View from Here*, the idea for the book seemed a no-brainer. Many expressed shock that such a project hadn't already been done, given the vast amount that has been written about queer theory and cinematic representations of gays and lesbians. But still others seemed to resist the idea of such a book. Some filmmakers declined to be a part of it—some politely (like the Hollywood director who sent me a massive bouquet of flowers to apologize), some not so politely (like the one who hung up the phone on me as I was requesting an interview). Those who didn't like the idea of the book most frequently stated that they didn't see the point in being labelled as a gay or lesbian filmmaker. I've encountered this argument numerous times over the years, and it was perhaps best articulated by director Joel Schumacher in 2003 on the occasion of the release of his film *Phone Booth*: "I'm a big opponent of labels. African-American judge, Jewish vice-presidential candidate, lesbian congresswoman, transgendered military officer, whatever. I don't recall anyone referring to Bill Clinton as our Caucasian, heterosexual, WASP, male ex-president. In other words, he's normal and everyone with a label isn't." This struck me as a fascinating perspective, certainly in part because I've always thought of Clinton as an icon of heterosexuality (not to mention the fact that many referred to him as the first black president of America, due to his affinity with the African-American community—but that's another book).

It's an intriguing argument, but I'm not sure how much sense it ultimately makes. When people analyze the work of playwright Harold Pinter, for instance, biographical analysis is frequently offered: Pinter grew up in post-World War II Britain when anti-Semitism ran rampant, and as a Jew, suffered at the hands of racist bullies who repeatedly beat and tormented him. Many Pinter biographers, critics, and academics have pointed to these formative experiences as the reason for the heavy strain of anxiety that runs throughout much of Pinter's work. When these points are made, no one would suggest that the label of Jew is irrelevant to this analysis of Pinter's oeuvre. Then why should an analysis of one's sexual orientation be any different? Undermining stereotypes, resisting labels, or at the very least questioning their implications, is crucial, but to deny them is, well, to be in a state of denial. At the same time, I remain sensitive to the artist's right to personal privacy. I have spoken to many film icons who said that, once they'd publicly acknowledged that they are gay, felt like they had a rainbow flag indelibly stamped on their foreheads.

Exclusions

Some readers will note, quite correctly, that there are absences in this list of filmmakers. *The View from Here* reflects certain biases on my part that must be noted: as a critic working for a weekly newspaper, my primary focus has always been feature-length films. While a number of the filmmakers included have made short films, most of the works discussed are feature-length, and only one director, Kenneth Anger, has never made a feature. As well, the book is undeniably North America-centric, with a large number of American and Canadian directors. This again reflects my vantage point as a Montreal-based critic, where my work focuses primarily on films that play in repertory and arthouse cinemas (as well as some multiplexes) in North America.

As I wrote this book, it pained me to know that there is a dearth of filmmakers from developing nations, and that there are too few people of color and too few women represented. The question of gender equity was one that struck me especially hard, and remains an enigma. In many areas of the film business, women have made huge inroads, but the director's chair remains overwhelmingly occupied by men (two female filmmakers included in this book, the team of Janis Cole and Holly Dale, addressed this gender gap specifically in their 1988 documentary film and accompanying book *Calling the Shots*). For some reason, film remains a male-dominated medium, despite the large presence of female directors now working in television.

There are also interviews that I could not arrange for the book—for example, Todd Haynes filmed his Bob Dylan biopic in Montreal during the summer of 2006, but he was too busy to grant me an interview, despite being in the same city—and despite the huge number of queer directors in the UK, I got but one—the delightful Ian Iqbal Rashid. As for other Brits, Nicholas Hytner declined, Terrence Davies did not reply to my request, and Isaac Julien was in the midst of a film project and didn't have time. All of this being said, I must state that one of my strategies for staying sane as I worked on this project was knowing there would one day be a second volume. Oversights, omissions, and scheduling conflicts can all be rectified, provided huge numbers of queer cinephiles rush out and buy this book, safely ensuring that I can do a sequel.

Stand and Deliver

Finally, at the risk of sounding like a talking float at a gay pride parade, I really want *The View from Here* to stand as a celebration of the work of all the filmmakers included. Years ago, when I interviewed Chris Smith, Britain's first openly-gay Member of Parliament, about his very public coming out, he said that if he'd made one gay person's life better by what he'd done, then that would have made it all worth it. Clearly, each of the films discussed in this book are in their own way brazen, bold acts of defiance, attempts to push the envelope of representation in a world that, in many cases, would rather render us invisible.

From where I stand, the view has never looked better.

Pedro Almodóvar, courtesy Sony Pictures Classics/Photofest

Pedro Almodóvar: Auteur of Desire

In person, director Pedro Almodóvar is as confounding and contradictory as any one of his films—he appears to shun the limelight when it is common knowledge that he has fostered a public persona, and has put as much work into promoting his films as he has making them. He is also unapologetically queer, but at the same time says he feels no special identification or affinity with the gay community.

And yet, there are his films, with their unmistakably, unquestionably queer sensibilities. Full of drag queens, women on the verge of nervous breakdowns, and hot men played by the likes of the young Antonio Banderas (who owes his career to Almodóvar). Each of his films is surprising and unusual in its own right, yet they all share Almodóvar's flair for passion and melodrama. Now in mid-career, his work keeps getting better and better, challenging audiences while remaining hugely entertaining. Acknowledged as the most important Spanish director since Luis Buñuel, Almodóvar has also had a significant impact on his own national culture while engaging international audiences at the same time. It is a tribute to his defiantly singular perspective that he has never been lured to America to make a film in English—despite the massive amounts of money Hollywood has reportedly offered him. Sensibly predicting that the road to Hollywood is paved with compromise, Almodóvar has continued to make films on his own terms in his native Spain.

Born in the village of Calzada de Calatrava, Spain, in a region known as La Mancha (made famous by Don Quixote), Almodóvar, the son of a gas-station attendant, grew up in a strict Catholic family. He was drawn to the arts early on, winning an essay competition when he was ten years old. He moved to Madrid when he was a teenager, where he worked through the 1970s in various jobs for the phone company—work he considered drudgery, but which paid the bills.

To satiate his creative appetites, Almodóvar wrote for a number of publications, both underground and mainstream, drew comic strips, and authored a soft porn novel under a pseudonym. He soon got involved in the theater, working with an avant garde stage troupe, Los Goliardos. He also began to experiment with the Super 8 camera, making several short films.

Mark Allinson points out in his 2001 book, *A Spanish Labyrinth: The Films of Pedro Almodóvar*, that it is fitting that the name Almodóvar means "place of freedom" or "freeing of slaves," because, he says, Almodóvar's rise to international superstardom coincided with Spain's transition from fascism to democracy. Indeed, this sense of euphoric freedom—a rejection of the repressive ways of the past—runs through Almodóvar's films. His second feature, *Pepi, Luci, Bom y otras chicas del montón* [*Pepi, Luci, Bom and Other Girls Like Mom*] (1980), sets the standard for many of the flamboyant, over-the-top characters who populate Almodóvar's cinematic universe. It also marks the beginning of Almodóvar's long collaboration with actress Carmen Maura, who in *Pepi* plays a woman who plots her revenge after being raped by a police officer. Almodóvar's reputation grew in 1982 with *Labyrinth of Passion*, a strange and hilarious parody of Freudian psychology in which the characters attempt to comprehend their twisted libidinal drives (and sexual limitations). This period saw Almodóvar's star rise on the international film-festival circuit, where he unleashed several dark and raw comedies: *Dark Habits* (1983), *What Have I Done to Deserve This?* (1984), *Matador* (1986), and *The Law of Desire* (1987).

But it was in 1988 that Almodóvar gained a new level of international attention when he released *Women on the Verge of a Nervous Breakdown*. Here, many of Almodóvar's quintessential elements are brought together—insane yet sympathetic characters; vivid, almost comic-book-like art direction; and outlandish plot twists—in a critically acclaimed film that drew crowds to arthouse cinemas worldwide. Almodóvar followed it with what is arguably his most controversial film, *Tie Me Up! Tie Me Down!* (1989), in which heartthrob Antonio Banderas—who plays it butch and mean—kidnaps Victoria Abril (as a naughty actress relegated to lurid B-movies), who in turn falls for Banderas despite the fact that he binds her and beats her. Some critics cried foul: was this a case of gay male fantasy, or flat-out misogyny? Watching *Tie Me Up! Tie Me Down!* today, it all seems glaringly obvious that the filmmaker employed comedy as a means of social commentary—but tell that to the pundits of 1989.

In the 1990s, Almodóvar continued to create surprising, intelligent, and unusual comedies—films that didn't match the box-office success of *Women on the Verge*, but repeatedly confirmed his status as one of the world's most talented filmmakers. In *High Heels* (1991), a mother and daughter attempt to reconcile after the daughter marries one of Mom's old boyfriends. In one of my favorite Almodóvar films, the under-appreciated *Kika* (1993), the Spanish auteur delves into themes of voyeurism and tabloid culture, making his Hitchcock fetish perfectly clear (Almodóvar samples part of the *Psycho* musical soundtrack at one key moment in the film). Then came *The Flower of My Secret* in 1995, about an unhappy novelist, and *Live Flesh* in 1997, about the unusual and often cruel tricks of fate.

In 1999 Almodóvar released *All About My Mother*, which led to universal critical acclaim as well as a Best Foreign Language Film Oscar. With nods to everyone from film pioneer John Cassavetes to Tennessee Williams, *All About My Mother* is a beautiful film about redemption and the rebuilding of hope after devastating personal loss, featuring a dead son with a transsexual father, an HIV-positive nun, and countless cultural references (in particular *All About Eve* and *A Streetcar Named Desire*).

Almodóvar's incredible roster of films continued: *Talk to Her* (2002), about two men who become friends while taking care of their comatose girlfriends; *Bad Education* (2004), about two men who grapple with abuse they suffered as children; and *Volver* (2006), about a woman who disposes of the body of her abusive husband after her young daughter inadvertently kills him, then finds herself confronted by the apparent ghost of her mother. All of these films reflect Almodóvar's expansive hallucinogenic imagination: it isn't surprising that actors no less than Lauren Bacall, Gena Rowlands, and Jeanne Moreau have expressed their strong desire to work with him, given his unique ability to create three-dimensional roles for women.

I met Almodóvar in September 2006 at the Toronto International Film Festival, where he was in attendance with Penélope Cruz to promote *Volver*. Unfortunately, Almodóvar's schedule was so tight that I could only speak with him as part of a roundtable with several other critics. What follows is an edited transcript of Almodóvar's responses to questions from myself and Martin Bilodeau, a film critic for the French-language Montreal newspaper *Le Devoir*, who kindly granted me permission to include his questions.

What did it mean to you to have your entire cast of women in *Volver* [2006] win the best actress prize at the Cannes Film Festival?

I feel like the mother of all of them—very proud. I thought it was a very smart idea on the part of the jury to give that prize to the women because it was a movie about women characters and they represent the mother, and so they should be honored. To award a family of actresses is fitting, because it is also a movie about family. I think they did a good thing.

Did working with Carmen Maura again in *Volver* after so many years remind you of your work of the 1980s?
No, because in *Volver* the character is very different, and it's been eighteen years since *Women on the Verge of a Nervous Breakdown* [1988], the last movie that we did together. Carmen Maura is the perfect kind of actress for me. She has solid qualities that I really love in an actress. And in *Volver* we discovered that we had the same chemistry as before, which was very moving.

Your recent film *Bad Education* [2004] reminds me of *Law of Desire* [1987]. Was making *Volver* a deliberate reflection of the films you've made before?
When I wrote *Volver*, I was thinking more about my childhood. There is no child [the youngest is a teenager] in the movie, but it is based on my childhood memories in my little village in which I was surrounded by all these types of women, my mother and the neighbors. In fact, this memory is one of the only moments I look back on because I never looked back to my childhood. It is a door that I closed because I suppose that I didn't like it. Now, these recent movies tell me something about the strong women who educated me.

In the 2004 Italian film, *Don't Move*, by filmmaker Sergio Castellitto, Penélope Cruz was cast as a figure clearly inspired by neo-realist films. Did that inspire her with this role in *Volver*?
No, the characters are very different. I was inspired by the housewives of neo-realism of the 1950s—Sophia Loren, Anna Magnani—those wonderful actresses. That was the similarity with Castellitto's film, but the characters are very different.

Do you identify yourself as a Spanish filmmaker?
I try not to think about it. I am Spanish and this is something I can't help. I don't need to make any effort to be faithful to my culture. What I try to do is not to be more international, but to be better understood. I am faithful to myself and the culture in which I was born, but I do not want the responsibility of representing my country. I represent myself and I am Spanish. Spain is a very

dynamic country and there are aspects of Spain that I don't represent and that I don't want to represent.

Do you feel any responsibility as a gay filmmaker?

When I write and direct, I am very honest and I give everything that the story demands from me. I don't feel the responsibility to demonstrate anything or defend anything, I am just trying to be myself. Even though there are very important elements of my character—being gay or being Spanish, or being born in a democracy—these circumstances come together in my work unconsciously.

Will you ever work in Hollywood?

You never know. But it seems to me that the production system of Hollywood is the opposite of what I am used to in Spain, and I don't think that Hollywood fits me because I am very independent with all my movies. Also, I don't dream of making a big, bad movie. That is something that I absolutely want to avoid—it's not my cup of tea. My ambition is to be completely involved in the story that I am telling. It is not a question of power, but I am the owner of the game. I invent it, I write the story. A film needs an author. In Hollywood, there are so many people giving their opinions, powerful opinions, and the director is one of fifteen people making the decisions in one movie. I don't know how to work in that situation. Perhaps I could see myself making a film in the US, but not in the Hollywood system.

What was it like to return to La Mancha, the region where you grew up?

I was very surprised because I didn't realize that it could be such a strong experience for me. Also, to go back to La Mancha was to go back to my mother, not in my memory, but [in the] landscape. It was incredibly moving and gave me an inner peace that I never felt before during a shoot. A shoot is very crazy, and peace is the last feeling that you have when you are shooting. Being in the same places where my mother had lived and the same places I had lived when I was a child was like a spiritual journey that I didn't expect. It was very healing.

Many of your earlier films have been re-released on DVD recently. What do you expect audiences will learn seeing your films grouped together like that?

Penelope Cruz in Volver *(2006), Sony Pictures Classics/Photofest*

Cast of Volver *(2006), Sony Pictures Classics/Photofest*

When I was younger, I made my movies with a crazy sense of humor. The passing of time is especially hard on movies. I don't know if I'm making a mistake with these re-releases, but I think the films have stood the test of time. It's a good way for people to get a comprehensive idea about my work.

It's interesting that *Volver* evokes neo-realism, because it's a film in color and not black and white. Also the colors in *Volver* are less saturated than they have been in previous films.
They are less saturated. I'm changing. The palette of my movies is always colorful, but it's true that in the last four movies the palette is darker and less colorful than my earlier films. This has to do with the type of story and how I feel toward it.

You were raised by a group of women. How did that influence you as a filmmaker?
Definitely my filmmaking is very influenced by the women who have surrounded me, those who were strong and were willing to face obstacles. The younger women, who flourished in Spain in the late 1970s and early '80s, inspired me too, but on a more unconscious level.

The Catholic Church emerges as a theme in *Bad Education* and many of your other films. What are your thoughts on Catholicism in Spain?
The Church in Spain is the only institution that hasn't evolved in the last fifty years. It is the only institution that doesn't operate according to the contemporary reality in Spain, which creates lots of problems. There are fewer and fewer Catholics in Spain. The Church is facing difficult situations and making lots of mistakes and behaving as a political party would—a political party of the extreme right. When Spain passed the laws on same-sex marriage, all the bishops and representatives of the Church protested alongside the right-wing political party of that time. They had never demonstrated like that before.

The Pope has just condemned Canada for legalizing same-sex marriage.
Don't listen to him!

People consider you a pivotal figure in changing attitudes toward gay people in Spain. Do you ever acknowledge that you are a hero in Spain in this respect?
I don't think that I am a hero and I am certainly not the only one [who is changing attitudes]. Of course, when things were more difficult, I would talk openly about these issues. I suppose that has helped. It was really the Spanish society itself that has progressed quickly on its own in the last twenty-five years, and it has been wonderful to witness that.

FILMOGRAPHY

Pedro Almodóvar is director and writer of the following films which are features unless otherwise noted:

Volver, 2006
La mala education (Bad Education), 2004
Hable con ella (Talk to Her), 2002
Todo sobre mi madre (All About My Mother), 1999
Carne trémula (Live Flesh) (director and co-writer with Jorge
    Guerricaechevarría and Ray Loriga), 1997
La flor de mi secreto (The Flower of My Secret), 1995
Kika, 1993
Tacones lejanos (High Heels), 1991
Atame! (Tie Me Up! Tie Me Down!), 1989
*Mujeres al borde de un ataque de nervios (Women on the Verge of
    a Nervous Breakdown)*, 1988
La Ley del deseo (Law of Desire), 1987
Matador (director and co-writer with Jesús Ferrero), 1986
*Tráiler para amantes de lo prohibido (Trailer for Lovers of the
    Forbidden)* (TV short film), 1985
*Qué he hecho yo para merecer esto! (What Have I Done to Deserve
    This?)*, 1984
Entre tinieblas (Dark Habits), 1983
Laberinto de pasiones (Labyrinth of Passion), 1982
*Pepi, Luci, Bom y ostras chicas del monton (Pepi, Luci, Bom and
    Other Girls Like Mom)*, 1980
Folle... folle... fólleme Tim!, 1978

Salomé (short film), 1978
Sexo va, sexo viene (short film), 1977
Muerte en la carretera (short film), 1976
Sea caritativo (short film), 1976
Who's Afraid of Virginia Woolf? (trailer for TV), 1976
Blancor (short film), 1975
La Caida de Sodoma (short film), 1975
Homenaje (short film), 1975
El Sueno, o la estrella (short film), 1975
Dos putas, o historia de amor que termina en boda (short film),
    1974
Film politico (short film), 1974

Kenneth Anger, from the documentary Anger Me, *courtesy Elio Gelmini*

Kenneth Anger: The Experimenter

Though Kenneth Anger is far from a household name, he has been a remarkably influential filmmaker. Indeed, Anger has never made a feature-length film, but rather has forged a career in the cinematic underground, creating an oeuvre of unforgettable and disparate short experimental films.

Though his films are about as far away from the Hollywood aesthetic as one could imagine, Anger was born into the belly of the beast, growing up in a wealthy Los Angeles home. As a toddler, Anger appeared in William Dieterle and Max Reinhardt's 1935 film adaptation of *A Midsummer Night's Dream*, a fitting start for a filmmaker who delves into the rich tapestry of his own subconscious. As an adolescent, his parents disapproved of his filmmaking aspirations, but his grandmother encouraged such a path, buying him a used 16mm camera for a birthday gift.

Although Anger began making films at a young age, sadly, his early work has been lost. Only one of his early films, *Fireworks*—and a brilliant one at that—has been properly maintained. Anger made *Fireworks* at the age of seventeen over one weekend in 1947 while his parents were away; it is a truly astonishing film, and one any serious queer film buff must see to believe. In it, Anger depicts a homoerotic dream, one populated by muscle-bound sailors who beat up the young filmmaker (he plays the lead role) when he asks them for a light for his cigarette. Awash in body fluids and soaked in Freudian and Jungian symbolism, this alternately disturbing and hilarious dreamscape is easily one of the most astonishing films I have ever seen. Experimental film expert and author Scott MacDonald points out that *Fireworks* holds a place in history as "the first openly gay American movie ever." Despite working in the experimental milieu, the film drew broad attention. In fact, the first print of *Fireworks* ever sold went to famous sex researcher Alfred Kinsey, who was apparently fascinated by its bold, carnal imagery. It won a film award in France in 1949 from a jury headed by Jean Cocteau, who then invited Anger to Paris, where Anger would live for a dozen years before returning to the US.

Anger has continued to make films since *Fireworks*, but his output has been uneven due to various funding problems. From *Rabbit's Moon* (1950), a film that was inspired by Anger's own suicide attempt, to *Lucifer Rising* (1972), Anger has consistently employed symbolism drawn from the occult to create his own unique and bizarre cinematic visions. Arguably his most influential film is *Scorpio Rising* (1964), in which a group of leather-clad bikers are juxtaposed with religious images (culled from a religious film that Anger claims was delivered to his house by mistake). Anger has attracted famous fans during his long career; Mick Jagger composed and recorded music for *Invocation of My Demon Brother*, Anger's 1969 short, and Anaïs Nin appears in his 1954 film *Inauguration of the Pleasure Dome*. Martin Scorsese has cited Anger's work, in particular *Scorpio Rising*, as deeply influential.

Aside from his films, Anger is also infamous for his notoriously gossip-laden books, *Hollywood Babylon* and *Hollywood Babylon II*. The first volume, published in French in 1959, is rife with sordid tales ripped from the tabloids about Hollywood's lurid underbelly. *Hollywood Babylon* was then published in English in 1974 and followed by *Hollywood Babylon II* in 1984.

Anger continues to make films to this day. In 2004, he made *Mouse Heaven*, a droll short in which he uses pre-*Fantasia* Mickey Mouse memorabilia to create a toy dreamscape. He is currently working on a film about the suicide of his friend, Elliott Smith, a Los Angeles-based rock musician. As I wondered how I could get an interview with the elusive Anger for this book—he does not have a phone in the Los Angeles hotel room in which he lives, calling the idea "a nuisance"—I was given a gift from the movie gods. Toronto-based filmmaker Elio Gelmini, as it turned out, had just completed his incisive and thoughtful feature documentary on the legendary filmmaker, *Anger Me*. The film would be screening at Montreal's Festival du Nouveau Cinéma in October of 2006, offering me a rare opportunity to talk with Anger.

He phoned me from his hotel lobby, collect, almost a week before his Montreal appearance. He was particularly happy that he was being interviewed on a Friday the 13th, as he suggested that "there are only two of those a year. I get more energy out of those witchcraft-connected things." I had been warned that Anger tends to talk about whatever subject he wants to, for as long as he wants to. Still, he was lovely and gracious to speak with, and very generous in sharing his stories with me.

A few days later, I received a call from Richard Kerr, head of the film department at Concordia University in Montreal, asking me to moderate a master class by Anger himself. So one week after our phone interview, Anger shook my hand, looked directly at me, and said, "I didn't know you'd have blue eyes"—a quintessential Anger statement, both disarming and amusing.

At the master class, we screened two of his films, *Fireworks* (at my insistence), and *Mouse Heaven* (at his). Anger then told wild stories about the film business for an hour, pausing occasionally to opine about current events. At one point, he conceded that he struggles with mental illness, citing a history of being bipolar. "You know, Francis Ford Coppola is bipolar, and so am I," he told the crowd. "I refused to take lithium. He [Coppola] took lithium and I said, 'Well, look what it's turned you into, Francis. It's turned you into a fucking wine grower!'"

Our original phone conversation took place on October 13, 2006. Coincidentally—or could it have been occult luck?—earlier that day, I had interviewed Joan Collins.

Are you happy with *Anger Me* [2006], the feature-length documentary that has been made about you?

I'm as happy as I'll ever be with a film made by somebody else about me. Aside from that, it was all right. It doesn't thrill me, but it doesn't feel like an obituary either. I've got projects on the front burner, not the back burner. I haven't been on *Oprah* yet—I don't think she's ever heard my name—although I don't have ambitions to break through to the TV public.

I find it interesting that you began your filmmaking career in Hollywood, because your films seem so anti-Hollywood.

No, I'm not anti-Hollywood, not at all. And my films aren't anti-Hollywood. My godfather, Edmund Goulding, directed *Nightmare Alley* [1947], which starred Tyrone Power. Have you seen it? That was a great film noir.

But you did leave Hollywood for Europe at quite an early stage in your life.

In the late 1940s when I graduated from Beverly Hills High School, the red menace thing [McCarthy era] had already begun. They were persecuting some friends who had belonged to a labor youth group during the 1930s. They had worked with Columbia Pictures as dancers, but as teenagers they had also been involved with the free lunch program and linked with the Communist Party. It was more grotesque than terrifying. So my friends quit Columbia Pictures and were moving to Paris. They said, "Why don't you come along and be our mascot?" I had studied French and got an A and wanted to meet Jean Cocteau. I had a very convenient entrance

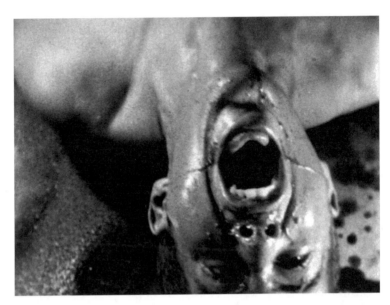

Anger in Fireworks *(1947), courtesy Fantoma Films*

Still from Rabbit's Moon *(1950), courtesy Fantoma Films*

into Paris. My duty was to walk my friends' poodle around the Arc de Triomphe and, out of respect for the city, make sure to clean up after the dog.

Do you recall the first film you ever saw?
When I was three years old, I could walk and talk. I was a smart kid. The next year, I was acting in *A Midsummer Night's Dream* [1935]. The first movie I ever saw, my grandmother took me to: *Thunder Over Mexico* [1933] by [Sergei] Eisenstein, which during filming, the film's socialist producer, Upton Sinclair, got cold feet and stopped the money flow, and Stalin ordered Eisenstein back to Russia [for desertion]. It was about the grandeur of the very bloody history of Mexico. Its images, photographed by Eduard Tisse, were so powerful that they were seared into my brain. There's a scene where the peasants are captured and punished for rebelling against the Spanish. They are buried up to their necks and then the conquistadors run across them with their beautiful horses until the peasants' brains are bashed out with the hooves. This had such an impression on me as a child, and it was quite some time until anyone could get me on a horse, although I was more afraid of the oppressors. Eisenstein, who was gay, used a lot of violence in his films. He was a great influence on me. He knew how far to go without going too far. Jean Cocteau also told me that that was something you must learn. It's a truism that's been forgotten in Hollywood. People just get blasé. There's all this gratuitous violence. I haven't seen *The Departed* [2006] yet, which I've heard is full of blood. Which is fine, it's a gangster film, but after a certain point it all just becomes camp, and then you have to say, well, how many gallons was the order on that fake blood?

***Fireworks* [1947] is one film that I always show to my film history students.**
Where do you get the print?

I sometimes rent it from a local video store.
I hate to inform you, but that is probably a pirated print. I don't get any royalties from it, which is pretty painful, because I live on the edge. These copies are often visually degraded. But I don't have the energy to get into a long-distance dispute with them.

Every time I watch *Fireworks* I'm shocked at how brazen it is.

It's easy to be brazen when you're seventeen, know what you want to do, and barely have the means to do it. My model is Arthur Rimbaud; he wrote magnificent poems when he was a teenager, then went to Africa and became an arms dealer and never wrote another poem. Rimbaud was always my model.

But you never became an arms dealer.

No, in spite of the rumors.

Back to *Fireworks*.

I didn't have any microphones, so it was a silent movie. Silent movies are a great art form, but it meant that I couldn't rely on speech. My favorite film in the whole world is *Sunrise* [*Sunrise: A Song of Two Humans*, 1927], by F.W. Murnau. It's an extremely Germanic film— the set designer, cinematographer, and director were all German. In a daring move by the producer William Fox, who was a genius despite the fact that he went to prison for tax evasion, brought these Germans over and gave them freedom to use all the state-of-the-art technology of the studios at the time. That's why *Sunrise* is so beautiful. They made the whole thing in the studio; there were no actual exterior shots.

What inspired *Fireworks*?

An event happened in Los Angeles in the summer of 1943 called the Zoot Suit Riots, involving some Mexican cool cats and American Sailors. The Mexicans were dressed in silk and satin zoot suits. The American sailors were antagonistic toward them because they were slackers. There was a girl who was supposed to go with a sailor but ended up with a zoot suiter, so the sailors descended on them. I happened to be in the neighborhood at the time, and watched the riot from about a block away. The sailors in their summer whites and little round hats chased down the Mexican zoot suiters and ripped them and their suits to shreds, until the Mexican guys were practically naked. No one was killed but some were badly hurt, and it was the front page story in the *LA Times*. I still have the newspaper clipping somewhere. Later, I kept having dreams about the riots. They were at night, and these white uniforms would come out of the night and attack. Finally, the dreams evolved into people chasing me.

[Regarding the inspiration for *Fireworks*,] I have vivid dreams, which are like movies. And they're always silent. It's as if you're looking into a crystal ball. You know, crystal balls are like the first movies. People don't realize that people were seeing visions before movies. It's true: if you concentrate on a crystal ball and let your imagination flow, the various lights in the room will collect themselves into a picture or pattern. It's a scientific thing, something that happens in the optic nerve. Crystal balls shouldn't be scorned like some sort of cheap trick. You should try it some time. You could buy one for about forty or fifty dollars on Hollywood Boulevard. I think they're made of acrylic plastic now [*laughs*]. But they look about the same.

Fireworks is an intensely homoerotic film.
Yes, it's about being attracted to something you're afraid of. You're attracted to something that's particularly dangerous like a rough and tough man. I knew not to do what the young man in the film does, which is to ask them for a light for my cigarette. I never smoked, though I do in the film. Bette Davis smoked in all of her films like a furnace. That's where I learned to smoke like that, from watching her. Back in the '40s, asking for a light was an old pick-up line in subterranean gay culture. Gays still smoke more than any other minority group. That's why I don't go to gay bars. Full of smoke.

Did you feel any affinity at all with the gay movement?
I went to Europe in 1950 after _Fireworks_ won an award in 1949, given by Jean Cocteau. He handwrote me a letter in French which must be worth something by now. He said that my work came from the deep night from which all great works emerge, paraphrasing what Jung had said about artistic creation. Henri Langlois, the curator of the Cinémathèque Française, then took me in. At the Cocteau reception in Paris, I said I'd like to stay on in Paris, and he said, "Well, I need an assistant so I'll just hire you."

I was disheartened to learn that you're not really earning much in the way of royalties from your work. How can that be?
It's so easy to pirate things these days. But you know, I have never been a businessman. My father wanted me to be an aircraft engineer, like him. I said that I wanted to be an artist. He said no one can make a living from that. I gave him a list of people who had, including Picasso. He cut me out of his will—only left me one dollar.

What about publishing the third volume of *Hollywood Babylon*?
The publishers read it and said there are too many hot wires in it.
The Church of Scientology people are very prone to sue. But I said
if you cut the stuff out about John Travolta and Tommy Cruise,
you'll cut the heart out of the book.

So there aren't proper residuals from your earlier work?
People compare me to Andy Warhol. But he had the Midas touch.
He could take a piece of crap and sign his name to it and they'd sell
it for a fortune. That's not me.

FILMOGRAPHY

Kenneth Anger is director and writer of the following short films:

Anger Sees Red, 2004
Mouse Heaven, 2004
The Man We Want to Hang, 2002
Don't Smoke That Cigarette, 2000
Ich will!, 2000
Senators in Bondage, 1976
Lucifer Rising, 1972
Invocation of My Demon Brother, 1969
Kustom Kar Kommandos, 1965
Scorpio Rising, 1964
Inauguration of the Pleasure Dome, 1954
Eaux d'artifice, 1953
Rabbit's Moon, 1950
Puce Moment, 1949
Fireworks, 1947
Escape Episode, 1946
Drastic Demise, 1945
The Nest, 1943
Prisoner of Mars, 1942
Tinsel Tree, 1942
Who Has Been Rocking My Dreamboat?, 1941

Gregg Araki: Nowhere Man

Over the course of nine films, Gregg Araki has constructed his own strain of unique nihilistic cinema. His works depict a dark universe, reflected in many of their titles: *Nowhere* (1997), *The Doom Generation* (1995), *The Long Weekend (O'Despair)* (1989), and my favorite, for the doomed MTV pilot *This is How the World Ends* (2000).

Araki is an only child who grew up in Santa Barbara, California, and completed a Masters degree in film at the University of Southern California. His characters and plot lines, often soaked in cynicism and despair, reflect his background in music—Araki was part of the west coast punk scene in the late 1970s and '80s. In fact, before venturing into film turf, Araki was writing music reviews for the *LA Weekly*.

After his first two low-budget films in the late 1980s, Araki gained indie filmmaker notoriety with a controversial film that draws on the AIDS crisis for inspiration. *The Living End* (1992) chronicles the road trip of two gay men, both HIV-positive, who embark on a reckless journey of abandon across the American landscape, occasionally knocking off the odd homophobe along the way. The film's dark undercurrent drew repeated comparisons to the 1991 film *Thelma & Louise*, Ridley Scott's much more mainstream hit about two renegade women who also armed themselves for vengeance, although Araki has always rejected the comparison. Araki presciently dedicated *The Living End*, released at the end of George Bush Sr.'s presidency, to "the hundreds of thousands who've died and the hundreds of thousands more who will die because of a big, white house full of Republican fuckheads."

Araki's next project was his Teen Apocalypse trilogy: *Totally F***ed Up* (1993), *The Doom Generation* (1995), and *Nowhere* (1997). Here, a panoply of teen characters wade through various subplots involving rape, suicide, drugs, SM, and murder. This bleak chic is offset by Araki's quirky sense of humor and penchant for American pop culture. In *Nowhere*, Araki includes dreamlike cameos by various refugees from such staples of 1970s and '80s trash TV as *The Brady Bunch* and *The Facts of Life*. It also marks a period when Araki makes it clear he isn't interested in labels; despite the political anger expressed in *The Living End*, he has insisted that he is a filmmaker, "not a politician." He tagged *The Doom Generation* as "a heterosexual movie" as a way of mocking the very idea of a film being labelled gay. "I like to be thought of without any kind of adjective attached to it," he told me in a 1997 interview. "A gay film-

Gregg Araki on the set of Mysterious Skin *(2004), Sony Pictures Classics/ Photofest*

maker, a Gen-X filmmaker, an Asian-American filmmaker—I'd just like to be thought of as a filmmaker."

Araki's 2004 film brought him his greatest critical acclaim. Based on a novel by Scott Heim, *Mysterious Skin* was the first screenplay Araki adapted from another source. A shocking story of two boys and how they deal with getting over the child abuse they suffered at the hands of a pedophile, *Mysterious Skin* made numerous critics' top-ten lists. Grasping for meaning in their lives, one boy becomes fixated on UFO theories, while the other works as a hustler. Araki stated that the novel made such a big impression on him when he read it in 1995 that he had long envisioned bringing it to the big screen. Though Araki isn't wild about labels, he was very gracious about being a part of this book, and was generous with his time. Despite being tied up in post-production on his latest feature, *Smiley Face*, he granted me this interview in December 2006.

How did you first get into filmmaking?

I was always interested in art from a very early age. As a kid, I used to spend hours on my own drawing and I even wrote and illustrated my own series of comic books. I had a very active imagination and had ambitions to become a comic book artist. To this day, I draw simple storyboards of every shot and scene in my films. They serve as comic-book-like visualizations of my movies. I've always worked in this way since I made my first student films in college.

Your first two films, *Three Bewildered People in the Night* (1987) and *The Long Weekend (O'Despair)* (1989), seem autobiographical.

I've always said that all my movies reflect many parts of my life, though none of them are straightforward autobiography. They express my worldview and serve as a Polaroid snapshot of where my head is at a particular time in my life. That's why each film is a powerful artefact for me, a time capsule of how I moved through the world when I made them. I recently did high-definition remasters of both *Totally F***ed Up* [1993] and *The Living End* [1992]. The experience blew my mind because it was like watching movies that were made by somebody else, yet they were strangely and powerfully familiar to me. Remastering *The Living End*—due to be released properly on DVD for the first time in 2007—reminded me of how this little renegade movie that we made with no money captured something about being gay and being unapologetic about it at a time in history when it was dangerous to do so, and it turned out to be transformative—in the same way that the 1960s irrevocably changed race relations in this country.

The Living End really tapped into what was going on politically at that time, being released in the middle of the AIDS pandemic.
My work has always been more personal than political, but as we all know there is a huge crossover. *The Living End* and the whole "queer new wave" hooplah was the byproduct of the cultural zeitgeist of the late 1980s and early '90s—the same sociocultural climate that bred ACT UP, Queer Nation [both gay and lesbian organizations], broader gay and queer political visibility, and so on. The film was by no means created in a vacuum, but rather it came from a very real and very specific time and place and mood, where being gay felt like a political act in itself—in a much deeper and more radical way than today. There was very much that sense of AIDS being like a hostile genocidal warfare, and that being gay immediately made you an outsider and dangerous to society at large. Being heavily influenced by punk and post-punk music, I was comfortable living in this margin. And it was this "punk" aspect of *The Living End* that made the film so upsetting and so threatening in the more mainstream vanilla gay culture.

I was totally surprised by [the response when it was released]. Before *The Living End*, I had made two similarly small and raw black and white movies on 16mm that played a few festivals and aired on PBS. The impact and hubbub surrounding *The Living End* was totally an accident. The film just happened to be in the right place at the right time. It became the eye of this storm that no one expected. I remember hearing stories about fistfights breaking out in gay bars over the movie. It blew me away that our little film provoked such a passionate response in people. I've heard that it's being taught in queer studies courses in universities, even though the version that gets screened is a totally hellacious, inferior video transfer that I didn't even supervise. I cringe every time I think about that lousy transfer being viewed. Seeing it again in this sparkling version is like watching a whole new movie.

How much of your work is a political response to something?
I don't tend to be reactive, really. I just make the movies I want to make. I follow my gut instinct and don't do anything that I'm

not in love with. Every film is three years out of my life and I will not be able to make that many while I'm on this planet, so it's not worth it for me to do anything I am not truly passionate about. Gus Van Sant once told me to focus on making the movies that I want to see myself.

What did you think of the *Thelma & Louise* comparisons?
I didn't much like *Thelma & Louise*. I thought it was too preachy and heavy-handed. [The comparison] was easy for reviewers because the films came out around the same time, so lazy critics wrote *The Living End* off as the "gay *Thelma & Louise*," despite the fact that the film is more closely related to films like *Bonnie and Clyde*, *Gun Crazy*, or *They Live By Night*—the outlaw couple genre that *The Living End* aspired and subscribed to. My film is first and foremost a love story where sex, desire, and passion get mixed up with violence. It is much more interesting to talk about it in relation to a film like *Breathless* [*A bout de souffle*, 1960]—with its doomed, mismatched lovers and weird shifts in tone. Or even *Bringing Up Baby* [1938], with its uptight, repressed protagonist being simultaneously liberated and destroyed by a semi-deranged free spirit.

Much of your work maintains a heightened sense of irony. You've acknowledged Jean-Luc Godard as a major influence. In a review of *The Doom Generation*, Roger Ebert wrote: "Hey, if we're dumb enough to be offended by his sleazefest, that's our problem; Araki is, you see, a stylist who can use concepts like iconography and irony to weasel away from his material." Ebert suggests that you are using your style as a director to evade ethical and moral questions about what it is you're representing.
As a filmmaker, I just make the movie. People will interpret or misinterpret it however they see fit. That's the beauty of cinema: one person can see black, one can see white, and they can argue about it till the cows come home. As the filmmaker, I can only speak for my own original directorial intent, and what this critic said about *Doom Generation* is 180 degrees from what I intended. I'm always 100 percent committed to my characters and totally empathize with them, however ironic, satirical, surreal, or hallucinogenic the context. I wholeheartedly relate to [the characters] Jon and Luke in *The Living End*, and to Jane F, the stoner protagonist in my new film *Smiley Face* [2007]. No matter how flawed or damaged they might

seem to others, I love them all in a weird way, like my own children. It's a turn-off for me when I see a movie that has characters in it who are clearly despised by their creator. So to make a long answer short, I have to say I politely disagree, and that the moral and ethical issues are not evaded but to the contrary are embraced, and in my view, exposed and explored.

The Doom Generation is tagged "a heterosexual movie" in the opening credits. How much do you dislike the gay filmmaker label?

I hate labels as much as anyone. Does anybody really like to be called "African American" or "Jewish" or "WASP" or "differently-abled" or any other stereotyping descriptor? In my view, labels are meant to categorize and separate everybody and everything into convenient little pigeonholes. I don't get the point of it. Why is there this compulsion to segregate and neatly arrange and name everything? It's really not my perception of the world.

A critic said in a review of Nowhere [1997] that "in Araki's world, it's uncool to care about something like quality." How do negative reviews affect you?

As the creator of something that you devote years of your life to and pour your heart and soul into, obviously it's more pleasant to get a rave review than a bad one. But I learned very early on that cinema is a totally subjective experience and I have no control whatsoever over my film once it's out there. When I get a great review, I go, "Cool." When it's nasty or negative, I go, "Oh well, maybe next time." I don't make movies for a pat on the back. My reasons are much deeper and more personal than that. It goes back to the children analogy: the films are like my kids; they are born and raised with love, and just because one gets a bad report card doesn't mean you take it out into a field and shoot it.

Mysterious Skin [2004] was your first screenplay adaptation. How was the experience different from your other films?

Making and adapting Mysterious Skin was one of the most rewarding and rich experiences of my career. I found it somewhat easier to write the screenplay for Mysterious Skin than to write an original script because [the structure] was laid out in the novel. The "voice" of the novel, its structure, characters, narrative arc, poetic tone, etc., were all created by Scott Heim, the book's author. In that way,

Johnathon Schaech (as Xavier Red) in The Doom Generation *(1995), Trimark Pictures/Photofest*

Joseph Gordon-Levitt (as Neil McCormick), Brady Corbet (as Brian Lackey) in Mysterious Skin *(2004), Desperate Pictures/Tartan USA/Photofest*

the writing of the script was more like editing a film—taking this large amount of material and condensing and distilling it down to its cinematic essence. I'd love to adapt another book. I've already done a similar kind of [adaptation] on a couple of outside scripts which are projects I've got in the pipelines—the trick is finding material that I love as much as something of my very own.

How do you feel that you've evolved as a filmmaker?

I feel that over the course of twenty years and ten films [including the TV pilot], I've become much more technically skilled. Since I was a kid, I've been a fast learner who got good grades. With each film, I learn so much about image, sound, composition, rhythm, music, editing, color, design, and so on. Every film I make is more technically accomplished than the last, and I hope to always keep evolving. I don't ever want to stand still as a filmmaker or make the same movie twice. At the same time, I hope I never lose the passion and excitement for film that I had back when I was making movies on my own with a 16mm Bolex and getting pushed around in a shopping cart at two o'clock in the morning.

FILMOGRAPHY

Gregg Araki is director and writer of the following which are features unless otherwise noted:

Smiley Face, 2007
Mysterious Skin, 2004
This is How the World Ends (TV pilot), 2000
Splendor, 1999
Nowhere, 1997
The Doom Generation, 1995
*Totally F***ed Up*, 1993
The Living End, 1992
The Long Weekend (O'Despair), 1989
Three Bewildered People in the Night, 1987

Fenton Bailey and Randy Barbato: Beyond the Valley of the Tabloids

Filmmakers and life partners Fenton Bailey and Randy Barbato have a fascination with the sensational side of American popular culture. Indeed, their body of work stands as a strange ode to the tabloid lens that celebrates wayward stars, notorious criminals, and those whose fame has been achieved in bizarre, unexpected ways.

Taken together, their films offer an alternate, lurid history of America and the world. Bailey and Barbato based two of their films, a documentary (1998) and dramatic feature (2003) both entitled *Party Monster*, on the violent and subversive Michael Alig, founding member of the notorious Club Kids of the late 1980s and early '90s, who was involved in a grimacing murder. When the American religious right realized its full power in helping to elect President George W. Bush in 2000, Bailey and Barbato turned their cameras on the famous fallen Christian televangelist icon Tammy Faye Bakker in *The Eyes of Tammy Faye* (2000). That same year, they released *101 Rent Boys*, a documentary on various sex trade workers hustling on the strip near the filmmakers' Los Angeles offices. In 2002, they focused on the woman at the center of President Bill Clinton's sex scandal, Monica Lewinsky, in *Monica in Black and White*. A year later, they profiled another notorious female subject, Anna Nicole Smith, in *Dark Roots: The Unauthorized Anna Nicole*. The possibility that Adolf Hitler might have been gay was the subject of their 2004 documentary, *Hidden Fuhrer: Debating the Enigma of Hitler's Sexuality*. And most recently, in 2005, the filmmakers documented one of the most famous stories in American counter-cultural history, recounting the story behind a landmark porn epic in *Inside Deep Throat*.

On the surface, any one of Bailey and Barbato's films are a Warholian collision of scandal, crime, sex, tragedy, and celebrity. *Party Monster*, in particular the 1998 documentary version, is perhaps the best example: it explores the mythology of Michael Alig, a popular fixture in the 1980s New York nightclub scene. Alig was himself a Warhol wannabe, creating his own universe of celebrities, conjuring up spontaneous parties on subway platforms and at McDonald's restaurants. Sadly, even this seemingly small-scale celebrityhood proved too great for Alig, who went down in a spiral of drugs and violence; he ended up imprisoned for murder after an acquaintance showed up in a cardboard box in the Hudson River.

Fenton Bailey and Randy Barbato, photograph courtesy World of Wonder

But while the subjects are lurid and often ludicrous, Bailey and Barbato's talent as filmmakers distinguishes their work from the tabloid culture from which they cull their material. In each of their projects, the prolific directors find an essential humanity in their subjects. Arguably the best example of this is *The Eyes of Tammy Faye*, in which the former wife of the disgraced televangelist Jim Bakker discusses God, cosmetics, her battles with drugs, her children, her pet dogs, and the power struggles she and her former husband had with fellow televangelists Jerry Falwell and Pat Robertson. Prior to the film, Tammy Faye had been dismissed by most as a caricature, but in the film she emerges as a sympathetic character, someone who has overcome the insanity of her past and redeemed herself. I sincerely doubt that anyone ever predicted that Tammy Faye, the woman once called the first lady of America's religious right, would end up the subject of a documentary made by two gay men, narrated by a famous black drag queen (RuPaul), and accompanied by a chorus of sock puppets.

I spoke with Bailey and Barbato in the fall of 2006 at the Los Angeles offices of their production company, World of Wonder.

How did you meet?

RANDY BARBATO: We met at NYU film school. We were both doing graduate degrees there. We sort of hit it off right at the beginning and started working on each other's films, something we've continued to do for the last twenty years. Our thesis films were funny. Fenton's was called *Hi Mom I've Gone to Outer Space*, which was about a young alien boy, and it had a surgery scene where the boy's best friend was a monkey who operated on the boy's brain. Mine was *Such a Nice Neighborhood*, and it featured a drag queen who moves into a suburban New Jersey neighborhood.

Many of your film subjects are arguably lurid and fodder for the tabloids. How do you go about choosing them?

RB: We choose subjects purely out of personal obsession and most of them tend to straddle the line of bad taste. That's the stuff that we are most curious about, that turns us on or gets us thinking— from Tammy Faye to drag queens to rent boys to Monica Lewinsky. They are all, in some way, shape, or form, misunderstood, and that is probably the biggest common thread.

Do you think that being gay filmmakers draws you to these misunderstood characters?

RB: Yes, and I think it is so corny, especially now that that would still be the case. If you grow up being an outsider, you identify with outsiders and are more sensitive to people who seem on the fringe.

One of the things I like about your films is that you often deal with tabloid subjects in a zany yet sensitive way.

RB: We think that whether a film is a documentary or a narrative, it should entertain on a certain level. That is our job; we are filmmakers, and thus entertainers. With all of our work, we let the subject inform the style of the film. The more that we can immerse ourselves in the subject's world, the better we can understand the subject's point of view. But when it comes to documentary, some people frown upon that. They think it should be all about objectivity. However, I think once you pick up a camera, there is no longer any objectivity; you've got to point it somewhere, you've got to focus it, then you have to edit ... it's difficult to be objective as a result. For us, our most successful material comes when we create an atmosphere where people are comfortable enough to reveal themselves.

A number of other documentary filmmakers I have interviewed have also said that they can't make films without getting involved with their subjects.

RB: I think there are two different things here: making a film that takes you into the subject's world, and getting close to them; we experience both parts of the spectrum. But we create delineations in terms of how personally involved we get with our subjects.

What documentary filmmakers are your primary influences?

RB: The Maysles Brothers. I loved *Grey Gardens* [1975], [and] Errol Morris's *The Thin Blue Line* [1988] was a really important film for me and Fenton; we watched it many times. Those are two films that are very different; one is steeped in this authentic vérité approach and the other is completely stylized. I think our work goes both ways. We are bi in that sense.

The Maysles were accused of getting too close to their subjects [a reclusive heiress and her adult daughter living in a dilapidated

mansion in the Hamptons] in *Grey Gardens*, **and that the end product was deeply exploitative.**

RB: That sounds ridiculous to me. If you are going to pick up a camera and film someone's life, then that is what you are doing, and if that person is someone who is losing their mind and living [in squalor] in a house then that's what you're going to capture. You can't direct a documentary from next door.

The first documentary of yours that I saw was *Party Monster* [1998]. How did you come across the story of Michael Alig?

RB: He was a friend. We are a few years older than him—though he would like you to believe that we are decades older. After NYU, we stayed in New York and used to DJ at clubs. We both knew Michael when he first came to the city. This was before he was a big success and a big drug mess. He was very anti-drugs in the beginning and he was also incredibly ambitious. We watched his whole rise and fall. By the time he became both a big success and a big mess, Fenton and I weren't going out to clubs anymore. We weren't really a part of the disco 2000 scene anymore, but we knew it well enough.

Then you read about the murder in the newspapers?

RB: We had been trying to make a film about club kids for years before the murder, before the scene began to lose momentum; we had already shot some stuff. Most people think that we became interested in that story and Michael Alig after the murder, but the reality is that we were able to do it then because we were finally able to get financing.

Were there complexities about making a documentary on a friend who was implicated in murder?

FENTON BAILEY: That's what motivated us to make the film. Rather than just telling the story of a murder, we wanted to tell something about Michael. We weren't eyewitnesses, but we were ultimately involved, because what do you do when a friend of yours kills someone? We resolved that by concluding that the phenomena of Michael Alig and the Club Kids happened because they had a co-dependent relationship with their audience. The whole Club Kid thing and the Michael Alig thing depended on getting attention from people. It was like oxygen to them, whether it was press clippings or people being outraged by what they did, which in turn

Tammy Faye Bakker, courtesy World of Wonder

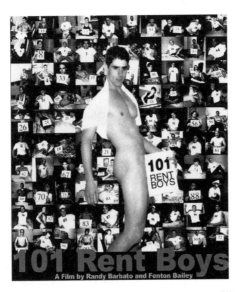

Poster from 101 Rent Boys *(2000), courtesy World of Wonder*

made Michael want to be more outrageous. I think that our film mimics that process by pulling the rug out from under the audience, making Michael likeable in the beginning so that by the time he turns monstrous, the audience has already bought the ticket for the ride.

Were you surprised by the reactions to the documentary?
RB: The documentary was very polarizing and I think that some people were really mean about it.

FB: I know that at Sundance [Film Festival] they were so nervous about it that they screened it along with a film about drunk driving to try to make the films look like public service announcements and to give them a moral weight.

Michael never felt that you were taking advantage of him?
FB: No, Michael never felt that way. Other people have and were quite vocal about it, but Michael, never. Our friendship has always been quite solid and honest. We told him, "You did this horrible thing, you should go to prison." As true friends, we tell him the truth, and he respects that.

In *The Eyes of Tammy Faye* [2000], you create a multi-dimensional portrait of Tammy Faye Bakker, with a lot of fun and camp. But at the same time, the film is very poignant. Was it difficult to strike that balance between her iconic camp status and the real person who is Tammy Faye?
FB: She is a real person. All we did was put her character on the screen. She has a great sense of fun about herself. We didn't ask ourselves, "Are we making fun of her?" We just filmed her as she is. Her sense of fun about herself is such an integral part of Tammy's personality and is one of the most wonderful things about her because it makes everyone so comfortable to be around her.

Whose idea was it to have the puppets reading the intertitles?
RB: Everybody loves puppets!

FB: It was Tammy's idea, because her whole ministry started with puppets. Tammy says, "Everybody loves puppets." That was the secret of their appeal. Randy and I to this day think that we should be doing more films with puppets.

Being gay filmmakers, did you have trouble getting Tammy Faye to agree to do the film?

FB: She said, "Let's go shopping!" No, she was reluctant.

RB: She was very reluctant. It is easy to forget now, but at the time we made that film she was so hated by virtually everyone. She was a national joke and the media had a field day with her on a daily basis. Her trust of the media was at an all-time low. She was living in Palm Springs, and Fenton and I would drive out for the weekend to talk her into letting us film. She agreed to the project after three or four trips. I think she was testing us out, deciding whether we were people she could trust, and we were doing the same with her.

When you decided to translate the documentary *Party Monster* into a feature film, what were some of the challenges you faced?

FB: Obviously it was very different. But I think there were more similarities than there were differences.

RB: Even though nobody made any money making [the dramatic version of] *Party Monster* [2003], it was great having a lot of people working on it.

FB: And having craft services—you don't have craft services on documentary shoots!

RB: When you are making a documentary, it is you and one or two other people.

FB: We never have enough money to make our projects. We were always looking at the clock and trying to make people perform or deliver. The difference with [the dramatic version of] *Party Monster* was that there were more people to take care of.

What drew you to *101 Rent Boys* [2000]?

RB: At the time, our offices [in Los Angeles] were right around the corner from Santa Monica Boulevard. The business of prostitution and hooking up hadn't exploded yet on the Internet. Hustlers worked the boulevard, and we saw guys every morning on our way to work.

FB: We were driving back from some pitch meeting at which we felt we had prostituted ourselves appallingly and we suddenly realized,

"We are them, they are us."

RB: Really, we felt so connected to them in a kind of "Up With Hookers" way. Our initial motivation was to make a film about the similarities we all have with people who turn tricks. It ended up being darker than we had intended.

Was any of it disturbing or alarming?

RB: A lot of it was. But more importantly, it was very moving. We were making some of [*101 Rent Boys*] during the production *The Eyes of Tammy Faye*.

It seems there's often a lot of overlap in your work. You always seem to be working on several documentaries at any moment.

RB: We have short attention spans.

FB: We call it the glamor of cable.

RB: You can't afford to do just one. We have many mouths to feed.

Do you ever worry as documentary filmmakers that people are bullshitting you?

FB: It's funny but maybe there is one case of a film we're making—I can't tell you who—where that is going on a bit, but generally the commitment to make a film about someone is so serious that you don't end up, for lack of a better word, in bed together unless they are taking it seriously.

Then you did *Dark Roots: The Unauthorized Anna Nicole* [2003]. You seem to be attracted to certain over-the-top, marginalized women.

FB: Love women. The whole Daniel thing is just awful. [Anna Nicole Smith's son Daniel died of an overdose.] He was such a nice kid. We admired him from afar. [This interview was conducted prior to Anna Nicole Smith's death.]

Then you switched gears and made a documentary about Hitler, *Hidden Fuhrer* [2004]. What led you to that?

FB: If Hitler had been gay, how interesting would that have been? I can understand that no one wants him to be gay because he is not a great role model, but just because an idea makes people uncomfortable is no reason to ignore it. The idea that Hitler might have been gay has been shoved under the carpet and ignored for precisely that reason. When the book [entitled *The Hidden Hitler*] came out, just before September 11, we were both fascinated by it. [The film's producer] Gabriel Rotello, an old friend of ours from New York, said that we should make a film about it. I think Hitler probably was gay.

RB: I don't.

FB: Some people say, "How could you make a film about Hitler being gay because he was a terrible person, then you are just playing into the anti-gay hand?" It is our feeling that gayness is something that just is; it is not an inherent moral value, and by saying that, we think that we are being very—

RB: Inclusive.

FB: What is so problematic about the whole gay debate is that the idea of being gay is cast in some sort of moral framework. "If you are gay, you are bad," and anybody who's grown up gay knows what that is all about, but in fact gayness just is what it is.

In 2005, you made *Inside Deep Throat* about a crucial moment in porn's evolution [the 1972 release and subsequent popularity of the porn film *Deep Throat*].
RB: I think that what attracted us to this subject was the fact that this moment in time was when porn crossed over into the mainstream. It was a tipping point that helps us understand where we as a culture are today. On one hand, it seemed at the time like we as a culture—I'm talking about American culture—might understand and embrace sexuality and sex in a mature and adult fashion. It was a time of hope, but it was also a depressing time because it was the beginning of the commodification of sex as we know it today. Our attraction to it had less to do with, "Let's make a film about the most popular heterosexual porno film ever made," but more, "What did this mean? How are our lives different today as a result of the success of that film?" We do genuinely believe that our lives are different today as a result of the commercial success of *Deep Throat*.

FB: Exactly, especially because the sexual revolution was a revolution of ideas. It wasn't just about getting laid as much as you could. It definitely had an ideological context. Those ideas are actually embedded in *Deep Throat*. It communicates powerful ideas about sexual ideology and yet the irony is that it ends up turning a revolution into commodification, into a consumer bonanza.

FILMOGRAPHY

Fenton Bailey and Randy Barbato co-directed the following:

Inside Deep Throat (feature documentary), 2005
Hidden Fuhrer: Debating the Enigma of Hitler's Sexuality (feature documentary), 2004
Dark Roots: The Unauthorized Anna Nicole (TV feature documentary), 2003
Party Monster (feature), 2003
Monica in Black and White (TV feature documentary), 2002
Out of the Closet, Off the Screen: The Life of William Haines (short documentary), 2001
101 Rent Boys (feature documentary), 2000
The Eyes of Tammy Faye (feature documentary), 2000
Juror #5 (TV feature documentary), 1999
Party Monster (short documentary), 1998
Shantay (short film), 1997
Drop Dead Gorgeous (A Tragicomedy): The Power of HIV Positive Thinking (TV short documentary), 1997
The Real Ellen Story (TV short documentary), 1997
America Undercover (TV series, various episodes), 1993

Holly Dale and Janis Cole, ca 1980, courtesy Janis Cole

Janis Cole and Holly Dale: Out From the Margins

Since their early collaborations as student filmmakers in the 1970s, Janis Cole and Holly Dale have exhibited a keen ability to capture the lives of outsiders. Drag queens, sex workers, hardened prisoners—these are just some of the subjects of Cole and Dale's compelling documentaries.

But while prisoners and those labelled sexually deviant had already been fodder for documentary filmmakers, Cole and Dale's approach was novel. Far from being academics or clinical sociologists, Cole and Dale often befriended and bonded with their subjects before or during filming. In their documentaries, Cole and Dale do not express themselves as objective, a claim that plagues so much of the mainstream media; instead, they are unapologetic advocates for their marginalized subjects, granting them the dignity and respect they deserved but were rarely granted. In return, their subjects gave them a remarkable gift: trust. As a result they have created a body of work that are indelible portraits of the disenfranchised.

Cole and Dale began working together while in the film program at Toronto's Sheridan College. Even with their early short films, they displayed an uncanny ability to empathize with their subjects. In *Cream Soda* (1975), for example, we meet various sex workers at a rub-and-tug parlor; in *Minimum Charge No Cover* (1976), the focus is on transsexuals and gays who made up a large part of Toronto's nightlife; and *Thin Line* (1977) provides a glimpse inside a maximum security prison for the criminally insane at Penetanguishene, Ontario, Canada.

In 1981, Cole and Dale again closely examined Canada's prison system in *P4W Prison for Women*, their first feature-length documentary, an unwavering look at inmates at an all-women's prison in Kingston, Ontario. The filmmakers' personal connection with the prisoners can be felt throughout the documentary; Cole and Dale have confirmed that they felt a sense of solidarity with the prisoners while making the film, given the dire conditions they faced on a daily basis. A flurry of publicity surrounded the release of *P4W*, and the ensuing discussions about Canada's prison system have since been credited with changes in public policy (in fact, the Kingston prison was ultimately shut down).

In 1984, Cole and Dale released what is arguably their most heart-wrenching and fascinating film, *Hookers on Davie*. With camera in tow, they set their sights on sex trade workers in Vancouver; the resulting film was one of the first to examine prostitution compassionately, allowing the subjects to speak candidly about their lives.

In 1988, Cole and Dale focused on another marginalized group: women filmmakers, a distinct minority in the business. The result, the feature-length *Calling the Shots*, was developed into a book of the same name (published by Quarry Press).

Cole and Dale continue to work in film and television, though their collaborations have become less frequent. Cole has continued to make documentary films and write for television, while also working as a cultural journalist. Dale made a horror feature, *Blood & Donuts*, in 1995, and has worked extensively directing episodic television and movies-of-the-week. We spoke by conference call in October 2006.

How did you first meet?
HOLLY DALE: We were both street kids and we met in the downtown scene.

JANIS COLE: This was in Toronto, when we were both about nineteen. We then went to film school together and started collaborating on short films. Holly started *Cream Soda* [1975] on her own, which was set in a body rub parlor where a lot of our friends were working. I worked with her on sound and editing, and I talked with her a lot about it conceptually. We then decided to do *Minimum Charge No Cover* [1976] together, which delved into the gay scene as well as transvestites, transsexuals, and female impersonators.

What drew you to that?
HD: We hung around the downtown scene—this is going back to the 1970s in the Yonge and Wellesley area. In film school the first thing our teacher told us was, "Make something that you know about." Since we hung out downtown, we knew people who worked in body rub parlors and also had a lot of gay friends and drag queen friends. So when other students would make films about their brother playing hockey, we made films about the street. It wasn't because we thought, "This would be a great film," it was more about us expressing our world.

Films featuring these kinds of subjects often get accused of being exploitative, but these were friends of yours, which is one of the reasons you got them to trust you.
JC: Our friends wanted to support our filmmaking because at that time a lot of our friends were not able to go to school. It was hard

to go to school. Both of us lived away from home, Holly from the age of fifteen and me from the age of sixteen, so we had to support ourselves. It was very difficult to put ourselves through film school, and because a lot of our friends didn't have the ability to go to school or to build a career like we were, they were really supportive.

HD: We were unconsciously making films that were trying to remove labels from people, which later became a very conscious thing for us when we started doing *[P4W] Prison for Women* [1981] and *Hookers on Davie* [1984]. We started out by giving a voice to our friends who weren't ashamed of who they were or what they did, such as being a prostitute, or being gay. Everybody was simply speaking out about who they were, and that became an inspiration for us and became the focus of what we wanted to do. It was a process of discovery rather than intention right from the beginning.

I an essay in the book *North of Everything* [University of Alberta Press, 2002], Kay Armatage suggests that your training at Sheridan College may have had a lot to do with shaping your aesthetic.
JC: I think so. We had the freedom of the 16mm film program where we both studied film in every capacity. We also had a teacher, Rick Hancox, who encouraged the students to delve into their own worlds. I would say that our world seemed to stand out as somewhat different, probably because of the world that we traveled in.

HD: I would say that Rick shaped us more than Sheridan College. He shaped us as filmmakers. He was very free and open and allowed people to do what they wanted to do.

I find your work compelling because you choose subjects whom some might dismiss as unsavory. And you present them very unapologetically, allowing them simply to tell their own story.
JC: When we made *Cream Soda* and *Minimum Charge No Cover*, we had no particular fascination with our subjects because they were just our friends, and it was our world. Also, when we were making those student films, we didn't know they would have a life [at seminars and festivals]. They still have a life now. But that wasn't our goal. Our goal was to learn filmmaking and use subjects who were close to us. By the time we took on the Penetanguishene prison with *Thin Line* [1977], we had the same feeling [as with our first

two films]: that we were just meeting people on their own terms.
We weren't afraid of them, yet we weren't overly fascinated; we
were very down to earth with them and they were with us as well.

**Do you feel that your sexuality influenced the way in which you
looked at your subjects?**

HD: I think that the fact that I left home when I was fifteen influenced me more. Ending up on the streets as a kid shapes your
perception of things. Being part of that world had a bigger effect
on my filmmaking than my sexuality. We are influenced by everything: our parents, our sexuality, our desires, our obsessions. I feel
like we were attracted to making *Thin Line, Hookers on Davie,* and
P4W because we were marginal people ourselves. So it was not only
our sexuality but also because we were street kids. As we moved
through these communities, we saw how they overlapped. We
would meet people who knew other people we knew.

JC: I grew up in a household with two brothers and I was the middle child. We were all very close in age and our parents treated us
all equally. From that, I had a really assured sense of ability about
myself. I didn't ever really go through that '60s phase of becoming
a feminist. I think I always was of feminist mind. I think there was
maybe the same confidence that comes from being able to embrace
your sexuality, and feel very confident about who you are.

How did you get access to the prison in *Thin Line*?

HD: It was hard. It took six months. There had only been one
film made there before, and that was just a segment for a television news program. With *P4W*, it took us five years to get into the
Kingston Prison for Women. The warden retired the same week
that they finally let us in. The assistant warden, who was afraid to
question our authority because he wanted to be appointed warden,
said, "I don't know what kind of freedom you're supposed to have
here." And we replied, "We have total freedom." Bev Whitney, the
girl who pops up in almost every scene and takes us on the journey
through the prison, was key in helping us. She was able to get us
into all the different cliques without any one clique isolating us
because of another. Today it is more common for media to have access to places like prisons and police stations, but back then it was
almost impossible to do.

Two inmates from P4W Prison for Women *(1981), courtesy Janis Cole*

Still from Minimum Charge No Cover *(1976), courtesy Janis Cole*

I understand you met with virtually every inmate there.
JC: Yes. There were about 100 inmates. We met with them maybe half a dozen times before we started to shoot. We really got to know a lot of the inmates, and we researched their crimes very well. There were about sixty women who wanted to be in the film; we narrowed the list to half a dozen people that we really wanted to focus on. They became the nucleus of the film, representing the prison, prison society, and the inmates.

Were there changes made at the prison as a result of the film?
HD: Maggie MacDonald got out of the prison [because of the film]. She was the double murderer who had been incarcerated for sixteen years and didn't know when her sentence would be over. The film started a big outcry about her case, then suddenly there was a re-lease date and she got out.

JC: Also, Janise Gamble who was in for twenty-five years and was supposed to have a clemency trial after fifteen years, did in fact get clemency after the film was released. Holly was very instrumental in that.

HD: I was part of a group called Justice for Janise that formed as a result of the film. We started lobbying parliament, and received media attention and the volunteer help of lawyers.

JC: Even though it was some time before the prison closed [in 2001, twenty years after the film], some inmates thought that *P4W* had played a part in its termination.

Did you ever feel that you were at odds with those more conventional feminists who would have wanted you to focus on subjects other than these non-role models, these criminals?
HD: That question is more appropriate with *Hookers on Davie*. I think in *P4W*, a lot of the women inmates were revealed to be victims. They were in prison because they killed their abusive hus-bands, or because they were involved with some guy who got them in trouble. It was a very feminist statement in a very politically correct sense, not intentionally, but it jibed well with the feminist community. *Hookers on Davie*, on the other hand, initially received research money from Studio D [the National Film Board of Cana-da's women's studio unit, now defunct]. We had to part ways from

the organization because they didn't share the same views on what were feminist issues. We wanted to make a film about [Vancouver's] Davie Street, where the drag queens punched out the pimps for the real girls, and the real girls made the drag queens blend in like they were "real girls." At its core, *Hookers* truly was feminist, but according to Studio D it wasn't. While I feel Studio D did a lot of good things, they had a heavy-handed agenda.

The transsexual element was problematic for some feminists at the time because they felt like they were really men. The trannie sex trade worker Michelle really emerges as the star of the film.
JC: Critics had trouble with the transsexuals in the film. Some of them had a difficult time referring to Michelle as "she," for example. Michelle was she-identified, yet people would still call her "he."

Hookers on Davie **is an amazing documentary, showing the very real danger these sex trade workers faced while working the streets.**
JC: There were a number of things that happened that we didn't even show. One night we went with Jackie to Vicky's place [two of the sex trade workers in the film]. As it turned out, when the door to the apartment opened, there was a guy with his hand behind his back, and he had a gun. Vicky was standing there with her nose smashed over to one side of her face. He told us to get into the apartment, and Jackie made a move to go, but Holly and I said, "No, we're not going in there, you come out here." We all stood in the hallway until he finally let Vicky go and we all bolted.

That's interesting, because when I showed this film to my class, some of the students suggested the sex trade workers were being melodramatic.
HD: Their lives are melodramas from the moment that they get up until they go to bed. Whether it's the drama of getting into a car and not knowing what is going to happen, or the violence, or trying to score drugs, and the sickness and withdrawals. They live extremely dramatic lives, yet at the same time it is very mundane, day-in, day-out.

You talk about getting close to your subjects, but that is something that documentarian Frederick Wiseman says he never does.

He thinks it is wrong to lead your subjects to believe that you are their friend when you are just making a film about them.

JC: We didn't lead our subjects to believe that we were being friendly with them; we actually were friendly with them. We also made it very clear that we have never paid anybody to be a subject of our films.

HD: I also think that the type of background that Wiseman comes from—he was a lawyer before he became a documentary film-maker—means that the subjects of his films often aren't part of his world at all. I can see and understand the cinéma vérité approach where you stand back and try not to be part of it, where you try not to get to know your subjects, because then you are influencing them and thus influencing what they do [on camera]. But it is impossible not to have an influence on your subjects. In Alan King's *A Married Couple* [the landmark 1969 documentary about a couple suffering through marital troubles], I'm sure that the relationship [between husband and wife] and how they acted was probably very similar to how they were. But I'm also sure that at times certain parts of their personalities were altered by the camera. We always felt it was important to get to know our subjects and to give them trust and get their trust in return.

JC: It's not so much the filmmaker who will influence or change their subjects; I think it is the presence of a camera that changes how subjects react. I think even media-savvy people who get interviewed all the time can change when there is a camera around. It can be somewhat intimidating, or something that makes you more extroverted. It can cause any kind of reaction. But I think the camera is the object that changes things more than the filmmaker.

HD: That is the reason why I think that when you gain the trust of the people you are filming they are going to be more relaxed and more themselves when you bring the camera into the room.

JC: By gaining the trust of our subjects in *Hookers on Davie*, for example, they agreed to wear mics for us, and we were often filming from inside a van. They never knew when we were shooting, so we became part of the background of their lives.

In a sense, that is very similar to Wiseman. He shoots about 100

hours' worth of film on a project, then edits it down for the final cut.

JC: We would usually film on a 10:1 ratio rather than 100:1 because we didn't have much money. It cost about $30,000 to shoot *P4W* with 16mm film, while *Hookers* cost about $70,000, and we also took a crew to Vancouver. We had to be economical with our ratio. But by getting to know our subjects well, and having done as much research as possible beforehand, we had a solid framework and could be a lot leaner with our actual filming.

Your next film after *Hookers on Davie—Calling the Shots* [1998], about women filmmakers—was obviously close to home for you. Was it the relative dearth of women filmmakers working in the business that led you the subject?

JC: Making *Hookers on Davie* and being in Vancouver for that length of time was particularly hard and exhausting. We started thinking about our own profession, and the thing that interested us most was wondering if the lack of women filmmakers has in fact influenced the onscreen image of women. We interviewed as many women filmmakers as we could in New York, LA, Vancouver, Montreal, and Toronto. We filmed Margarethe von Trotta, Lee Grant, and several other women directors talking about their evolution as filmmakers in a male-dominated business. And the one big question that emerged from the interviews was, "Is the female perspective different from the male perspective?"

Was there one constant that you heard from the women filmmakers?

HD: A lot of that generation of women came from the world of documentaries, like ourselves, but not for the same reasons. We heard over and over that they were ghettoized into making only documentaries because they weren't able to get the big money to do dramas. Another issue was the challenge of being a woman in a male-dominated profession and how they survive in it. But now I find, having directed hundreds of dramatic hours since making that film, that there isn't the same kind of sexism [in the industry] as there was back then. It has really changed. Women are now respected and looked at as directors, which really used to be the man's job on the film set.

JC: Having said that, how many female directors are there in series television versus men?

HD: That's true. There are only a handful. I've been very fortunate to carve out a career. There are a lot more women in feature films than there are in television. Every TV series that I work on, I hear the same comment, "You are the first woman director we've had." I think it's very hard for women to get some traction in the business. People want to see that you've got experience, and that's hard to get. Meanwhile you've got male directors who get job after job. I was very fortunate to get on that wheel. I do about ten TV shows a year, and that is really rare.

You two were in a relationship when you first met, but you broke up and have remained friends and made all these films together.
JC: We are the best and most incredible of friends.

HD: We are like sisters. Both of us have lost our family members at the same time.

JC: I can tell what Holly thinks sometimes and she can tell what I think. In the old days when the media used to write about our documentaries, they would say that we finished each other's sentences, and that we were joined at the hip. We have an uncanny friendship.

Was the fact that you were lesbian brought up in the press?
HD: Sure, sometimes. We don't deny who we are. The idea of labeling ourselves would be in total contradiction to what we were doing with our films, though, and I guess labeling was kind of the attitude of the times. Everyone around us knows we are gay. We were on the first cover of *Xtra!* [the Toronto gay and lesbian newspaper] when it was just a pamphlet. We always fought labels, but we never denied who we were or what we were. The same goes for being feminists as well; we didn't call ourselves feminists. We didn't want to label ourselves when we were trying to take other people out of the margins, out of being labeled by their life circumstances.

FILMOGRAPHIES

Janis Cole:

Bliss (TV series, one episode) (writer), 2004

Exhibit A: Secrets of Forensic Science (TV series, one episode) (writer), 2003

Bowie: One in a Million (short documentary) (director), 2000

Dangerous Offender: The Marlene Moore Story (TV feature) (writer), 1996

Heritage Series: Agnes Macphail (TV series, one episode) (writer), 1994

Shaggie: Letters from Prison (short documentary) (director), 1990

Calling the Shots (feature documentary) (co-director with Holly Dale), 1988

Quiet on the Set: Filming Agnes of God (short documentary) (co-director with Holly Dale), 1985

Hookers on Davie (feature documentary) (co-director with Holly Dale), 1984

P4W Prison for Women (feature documentary) (co-director with Holly Dale), 1981

Thin Line (short documentary) (co-director with Holly Dale), 1977

Minimum Charge No Cover (short documentary) (co-director with Holly Dale), 1976

Cream Soda (short documentary) (co-director with Holly Dale), 1975

Holly Dale is director of the following unless otherwise noted:

Durham County (TV series, various episodes), 2007

1-800-Missing (TV series, various episodes), 2006

Absolution (made-for-TV movie), 2006

Angela's Eyes (TV series, one episode), 2006

Kyle XY (TV series, one episode), 2006

Blood Ties (TV series, one episode), 2005

Sue Thomas: F.B.Eye (TV series, various episodes), 2003–05

Wildfire (TV series, various episodes), 2005

The Collector (TV series, various episodes), 2004

Doc (TV series, one episode), 2004
Stargate: Atlantis (TV series, one episode), 2004
Cold Case (TV series, various episodes), 2003
Bliss (TV series, various episodes), 2002
Jeremiah (TV series, one episode), 2002
Just Cause (TV series, various episodes), 2001
A Nero Wolfe Mystery (TV series, various episodes), 2001
Relic Hunter (TV series, one episode), 2001
Tracker (TV series, various episodes), 2001
Amazon (TV series, various episodes), 1999
The City (TV series, various episodes), 1999
Twice in a Lifetime (TV series, various episodes), 1999
First Wave (TV series, various episodes), 1998
Exhibit A: Secrets of Forensic Science (TV series, various episodes),
    1997
Dangerous Offender: The Marlene Moore Story (made-for-TV
    movie), 1996
Traders (TV series, one episode), 1996
Blood & Donuts (feature), 1995
Heritage Series: Agnes Macphail (TV series, one episode), 1994
Side Effects (TV series, one episode), 1994
Dead Meat (short film) 1989
Calling the Shots (feature documentary) (co-director with Janis
    Cole), 1988
Quiet on the Set: Filming Agnes of God (short documentary) (co-
    director with Janis Cole), 1985
Hookers on Davie (feature documentary) (co-director with Janis
    Cole), 1984
P4W Prison for Women (feature documentary) (co-director with
    Janis Cole), 1981
Thin Line (short documentary) (co-director with Janis Cole),
    1977
Minimum Charge No Cover (short documentary) (co-director
    with Janis Cole), 1976
Cream Soda (short documentary) (co-director with Janis Cole),
    1975

Bill Condon: Screen Dreams

Though his work has evolved tremendously, it is perhaps fitting that Bill Condon began his career making horror films. The horror genre has very specific demands and constraints that require a filmmaker to have a keen sense of when to stick to a formula and when to break it down.

Early in his career, Condon wrote and/or directed films such as *Strange Invaders* (1983), *Murder 101* (1991), *Dead in the Water* (1991), *The Man Who Wouldn't Die* (1994), and *Candyman: Farewell to the Flesh* (1995)—horror movies that gave him a particular sensibility that he later applied to other genres: the biopic and the musical.

In 1998, Condon wrote and directed *Gods and Monsters*, a speculative biopic about the final months in the life of gay horror auteur James Whale, who directed such classics as *Frankenstein* (1931), *The Invisible Man* (1933), and *Bride of Frankenstein* (1935). Ian McKellen plays Whale, suffering from the effects of a stroke and wallowing in remembrances of his life, some of them traumatic. Condon's treatment of the subject is moving without ever being maudlin, and the film garnered several Oscar nominations, with Condon winning for his screenplay. Condon then worked on the screenplay adaptation of the Broadway hit *Chicago*. From the outside, it seemed a strange fit, but not for Condon, who had long been a fan of the stage musical, attending performances religiously. His artful adaptation proved a massive hit, and the film, which was directed by Rob Marshall, won the Oscar for Best Picture of 2002.

Condon then returned to the biopic genre, writing and directing one of the most intelligent and fully realized depictions of an historical figure with *Kinsey* (2004). The film stars Liam Neeson as Alfred Kinsey, the famous sex researcher who first suggested that human sexuality was not necessarily gay or straight, but rather part of a broad spectrum. As with *Gods and Monsters*, Condon demonstrates his strong ability to breathe life into staid history. The film won wide critical praise; though strangely it was largely overlooked by the Academy, garnering only one Oscar nomination for Laura Linney in the Best Supporting Actress category.

With filmmaking credentials and an Oscar in hand, Condon then pursued a long-standing dream: he approached media mogul David Geffen, who owned the film rights to *Dreamgirls*, the hit 1980s stage musical that was inspired by the story of the '60s African-American girl group the Supremes. Suitably impressed with Condon's vision for

Director Bill Condon on the set of Gods and Monsters *(1998), Lions Gate Films/ Photofest*

the film, Geffen gave the green light to the big-screen project. Condon recalls that he saw himself as a natural for the task: he saw the Supremes perform live when he was a wee ten-year-old and attended the *Dreamgirls'* opening night on Broadway.

The results of Condon's directorial and screenwriting efforts are impressive. While remaining true to the spirit of the original stage musical, he enhanced elements of the story and picked a stunning cast: Beyoncé Knowles, Jennifer Hudson (who won a supporting actress Oscar), Jamie Foxx, and Eddie Murphy.

Condon and I spoke briefly as he toured to promote *Dreamgirls* in the winter of 2006.

You seem at home with the musical. I understand you were at the opening night of *Dreamgirls* on Broadway?

I think it was Michael Bennett [the director] who got me there, though I loved the Supremes too. I had seen Bennett grow from *Company* to *Follies* to *A Chorus Line* and this was his first show in three years. The anticipation of seeing the musical was more than met by the brilliance of his staging. It was the most fluid staging I'd ever seen—people accurately described it as cinematic. It took off at this speeding-train pace that never stopped.

People still see musicals as a thing of the past. You had success with your screenplay of *Chicago*, but were you worried that audiences might not accept characters breaking into song?

It did worry me because that [characters breaking into song] was something we didn't do in *Chicago*. All the musical numbers took place on "stage," so we had a device to help [the audience]. In [the film] *Dreamgirls* [2006], we had to have characters break into song, which I knew was a convention that some audiences resist. So I was nervous about it, and spent a lot of time thinking about how to do it right. Where possible, I tried to turn book songs [in which characters break into song] into performance songs [in which characters perform on stage]. And then we worked to delay it as [far along into the film] as we could. Then the audience is so used to the fact that these people were performers, it's not such a jolt. By the time Jennifer [Hudson] goes into song, you've gotten so used to her voice, there's a very small distance between her [talking] and her singing. So I think audiences go with it. Just as Bennett's production was very cinematic, I hope that people embrace how theatrical this movie is. I think the idea that these characters are all performers makes it seem much more believable that they might break into song.

Were there any models you thought of while making *Dreamgirls*?
Absolutely. The backstage musicals of the 1950s: *Singin' in the Rain*, *Love Me or Leave Me*, *A Star is Born*, and Vincente Minnelli's *The Band Wagon*. Minnelli would tell so much of the story simply through camera and color. There were also some more obscure films, like *Lovely to Look At* that has a number that we adapted for *Dreamgirls*.

When I interviewed Liza Minnelli last year she said there would always be room in the public's heart for musicals, as long as they are done right.
That's true. There's this weird but real resistance to musicals, but I think that an audience wants you to break through that because there's pleasure waiting on the other side.

What was it like to make a film musical after making so many horror movies?
Well, I made the horror movies a while ago. But there isn't any question that I wouldn't have been in the mix for directing *Dreamgirls* if I hadn't written *Chicago*. That's why I went after *Dreamgirls* so strongly. I felt as if I had a university education in musicals. By figuring out how they work from the inside, I've learned how they work in a way that you don't from the outside—even if you're the biggest fan of musicals, as I am.

Gay men obviously have a long-standing relationship to the musical. How much do you think your sexuality had to do with your connection to this film?
A lot. The original show was a creative collaboration between gay men [including director Bennett] and an African-American cast. I think that's why this show has meant a lot to both communities over the years. In a sense, it's about wanting to be embraced by the larger culture but wanting to make sure that you don't give up who you are, and that you're not presenting an image that's not true to who you are. That's a very basic gay predicament.

Peter Sarsgaard (as Clyde Martin) in Kinsey *(2004), Fox Searchlight/Photofest*

Anika Noni Rose (as Lorrell Robinson), Beyoncé Knowles (as Deena Jones), and Jennifer Hudson (as Effie White) in Dreamgirls *(2006), DreamWorks SKG/ Photofest*

And so you feel that connection with the African-American community?

In this show, certainly, but I have always felt strongly political that way. The gay and African-American communities have different movements, but they intersect.

Did you ever consider incorporating some original Supremes songs?

They are so great, but no, I think *Dreamgirls* had to be its own theatrical creation.

Some film critics said that you borrow Bob Fosse's directorial style in this film.

It's interesting that people have said that. He is the greatest director of musicals we've ever had, and certainly *Cabaret* is the greatest movie musical ever made. I love his work, but I am not as influenced by him as much as Vincente Minnelli or Stanley Donan.

Dreamgirls **is also a thematic switch from** *Kinsey* **[2004], which was also a fine film.**

For me, you get older and you just want to do something that you really connect with. If that's the impetus for doing something, then it's bound to work out better ultimately.

Do you ever feel at odds with the Hollywood studio system, like you're an outsider?

Always. I always feel like an outsider, but I don't think it's about my sexuality. Even with *Dreamgirls*, even though it's a big budget movie, and it needs to be ... but where I come from, my interest in it is very personal. I feel like an outsider in much of that studio culture because I don't know how to connect with the movies that they want to make and the audience they're intent on getting.

FILMOGRAPHY

Dreamgirls (feature) (director and writer), 2006
Kinsey (feature) (director and writer), 2004
Shortcut to Happiness (feature) (writer), 2003
Chicago (feature) (writer), 2002

The Others (TV series) (director), 2000
Gods and Monsters (feature) (director and writer), 1998
Candyman: Farewell to the Flesh (feature) (director), 1995
The Man Who Wouldn't Die (made-for-TV movie) (director), 1994
Deadly Relations (made-for-TV movie) (director), 1993
Dead in the Water (made-for-TV movie) (director), 1991
Murder 101 (made-for-TV movie) (director and writer), 1991
White Lie (made-for-TV movie) (director), 1991
Sister, Sister (feature) (director and writer), 1987
Strange Invaders (feature) (writer), 1983
Strange Behavior (feature) (writer), 1981

Arthur Dong, photographed by Amy Rachlin

Arthur Dong: Documenting Homophobia

Arthur Dong's methodical documentary examinations of homophobia should be required viewing for all film school students. Each film in his trilogy, which is available on DVD under the title *Stories from the War on Homosexuality*, is a crucial deconstruction of one facet of anti-gay sentiment in America.

For straight audiences, they are certainly illuminating. But for gay audience members—including myself—they are refreshing because for years, tabloid talk shows in America typically paraded out gay, lesbian, bisexual, and transgendered guests alongside serial killers, rapists, philanderers, and the like. Though this phenomenon undeniably introduced queers and their concerns to Mr and Mrs Middle America—and many make the point that questionable visibility is better than invisibility—to me, the programs portrayed them as essentially troubled, and often underlined the same notion: that homosexuality was a social problem. (For an intricate and intelligent analysis of these issues, see Joshua Gamson's 1998 book *Freaks Talk Back: Tabloid Talk Shows and Sexual Nonconformity*.)

In his films, Dong turns the tables, showing us—not through didacticism but through complex storytelling and profiling—how homophobia is the social problem, not the queers themselves. In 1994, he released *Coming Out Under Fire*, based on Allan Berube's book of the same name, in response to President Clinton's "Don't Ask, Don't Tell" policy for gays serving in the US military. (This flawed policy itself, it must be noted, was an attempt at compromise after the massive backlash Clinton experienced, from both Republicans and Democrats, when he tried to lift the ban on gays and lesbians in the military entirely.) This documentary illustrated how absurd the policy was by poignantly depicting the lives of gay and lesbian veterans from World War II. In 2002, Dong released *Family Fundamentals*, about several Christian fundamentalist families who disowned their gay or lesbian family members when they declared their homosexuality.

But I would argue that Dong's most phenomenal work is his 1997 feature documentary *Licensed to Kill* (not to be confused, of course, with the 1989 James Bond film *License to Kill*). Inspired by Dong's own brush with gay-bashers, this film is a harrowing, heartbreaking, and intensely fascinating portrait of convicts jailed for murdering gay men. Their stories are as varied as they are all-consuming—for some convicts, their homophobia appears to have been learned, while others (by their own admittance) were repressing their own homosexual desires.

Together, Dong's films make a powerful statement about prejudice and discrimination that continues to shape—and shake up—political and social life in America.

Arthur Dong was born in San Francisco to Chinese immigrant parents in 1953. He came out in 1969 while in high school, at the time when he was first getting into filmmaking. His next project is a film about racial representation in cinema. I spoke to him at his company office (he distributes all of his own films), DeepFocus Productions, based in Los Angeles.

Do you remember the first documentary film you ever saw?
There was an American network television miniseries called *The Homosexuals* in the 1960s. That's the first one I distinctly remember. I was a kid. I think I probably watched it alone at my parents' place—if not alone, definitely alone in my captivation. The documentary had dark, seedy, grainy, black-and-white images of homosexuals looking pretty creepy. That's the first documentary I remember.

How fascinating that the earliest documentary you remember seeing was about gay people.
There's a reason why it stayed in my memory—they were the first images of people identified as gay that I saw, even if they were tawdry. But I realized that gay people existed and there was a name for them. That was a revelation—and an exciting one, regardless of the negative portrayal. Before that, there were countless, boring documentary films that we saw in grammar school when the teachers didn't feel like teaching. They'd show them for an hour and you'd feel like falling asleep.

Did you know you were gay at that point?
I'm not sure. Probably that's why I was so fascinated with that film and why it still sticks. But that was a long time ago.

When did you become interested in film?
It started when I was a kid. I used to go to Chinese-language films in Chinatown. When I was growing up, there were four theaters in Chinatown that showed Chinese-language melodramas and low-budget martial arts films with really cheesy effects. These theaters

don't exist anymore. There wasn't a market for these kinds of films, unlike now, when there is a kung-fu craze fuelled by higher-end productions like *Crouching Tiger, Hidden Dragon*. My sister and I used to collect all the [theater] programs. Every year we'd tally up how many films we'd seen, which stars appeared in which movies. I was a little kid; I just loved it. And then, when I was in my early teens, I started watching older films on TV. Back then, they showed a lot of old films—and we only had three stations, not like today's cable. I remember watching the *Apu Trilogy* on ABC, which you wouldn't see today in prime time. Then I began to go to all the repertory theaters in town. Early on, in my teen years, I decided I wanted to become a film historian. I was fascinated by the notion that you could watch a Bette Davis movie like *Of Human Bondage* [1934], and then see her in *Whatever Happened to Baby Jane?* [1962]. I thought it was so incredible that we had this record of images from decades ago. It wasn't quite three-dimensional, but close. It was intriguing to me, from a historical perspective. It felt like you could travel back in time when watching an old film.

During high school, I still thought I'd be a film historian. I had an art teacher who taught a film class. By that point, Francis Ford Coppola and George Lucas were starting their companies, and the independent film scene was beginning to buzz in San Francisco. It was an exciting time. One day, our teacher announced that we students would make a film. A few of us were put together as a group and the teacher said, "Arthur, you'll direct." My reply was, "You mean I don't get to hold the camera? I want to hold the camera!" As a consolation, he gave me a Nikon F still camera, which was quite a big jump from the Instamatics that I was using, and told me I could do the production stills as well as direct.

So we did this group project that involved us going down to Chinatown during Chinese New Year's and filming the lion dance. Afterward, my teacher told me, "Okay, you've got the footage, now you have to put this all together." He set me up in his living room with a Super 8 editing machine. I was supposed to put the film together with tape—it was very clumsy. I started right after dinner, and soon thereafter he and his wife went to sleep because they'd just had a baby. He had this wonderful record that he used to play during art class. It was a very meditative hybrid jazz and Japanese album, *Music for Zen Meditation*, by Tony Scott. I had that album playing all night long. When he woke up in the morning, he said, "You're still here?" He was flabbergasted that I'd spent all night doing this. To this day, I love the editing process. When you're in the editing room, it's as though time doesn't exist; the only thing that does is the image and the sound, and putting together a story.

Then I made a short film for school based on a poem that I had written for an English class called "Public." It was an experimental, pixellated film about morals and the Vietnam War, about sex and violence, all in five minutes. I put it together in my bedroom. I showed it, and the class was like, "What is this?" But I submitted it to the California High School Film Festival contest in 1970 and it won the grand prize, which was $1,000, a lot of money back then. One of the judges was Jim Goldner, who at that time was a film professor at San Francisco State University. It was Jim that I went to when I wanted to go to film school, and he got me started. At the film festival, after they announced that I was the grand prize winner, they showed my film to the crowd. At that moment, I realized that film is a very powerful medium. It reaches a lot of people. And it taught me that whatever I put on film can have a huge impact. And I don't even have to be there; the film can go on without me.

As a documentary filmmaker, who would you say are some of your major influences?

As a filmmaker, Stanley Kubrick has been a huge influence. But I think my influences are more derived from films than specific people. I would think *Word Is Out* [the landmark 1978 documentary in which gays and lesbians simply told their life stories] had a big influence. The effect it had on me is that ordinary people's lives can show us a great deal. The people interviewed in that film stood for larger social issues. And that's what I've tried to do with my films: to personalize, to humanize social issues and historical developments and how these issues affect us as individuals. To me, ideological, didactic films are boring, are without shades of grey. But when issues are humanized, that touches me. That's what I try to do with my films.

Author Thomas Waugh has made the argument that documentary films often act like cultural shock troops, in that documentaries have portrayed issues that the major Hollywood studios

Still from Coming Out Under Fire *(1994), courtesy Arthur Dong*

Corey Burley in Licensed to Kill *(1997), courtesy Arthur Dong*

might be afraid to touch in their movies. How much do you think documentary film has pushed forward gay representations in fiction filmmaking?

I'm not sure. What I try to do is exactly what you're saying. Whether or not there are quantitative measures that can be made, I don't know. Documentaries are part of our popular culture. *Word Is Out* encouraged me as a young kid that coming out was all right, and that these folks are walking around my streets and in my neighborhood. Film can cause those kinds of spiritual, emotional shifts. I don't think it's too far off to suggest that film effects change.

You pick apart homophobia in your films. Do people ever suggest that you're giving too much of a voice to homophobes?

I've heard that. That's a valid critique. There needs to be diverse voices in films to talk about issues in different ways. Especially when you're talking about homosexuality, which is so complex. It's partially about religion, politics, education. It's about so many things, we need to look at it in different ways. People have varying opinions of homosexuals and homosexuality. Some are rabidly, violently against any gay people. Some are just not quite sure what to think. What I try to do with my films is to touch on different communities. With *Family Fundamentals* [2002], it was very important to me that it reach a staunchly religious, right-wing audience, and for that audience to relate to at least part of that film, if not all of it. Part of creating a relationship with an audience is to offer portrayals of people or ideas that viewers can recognize, in a language that they can grasp. When I say language, I don't just mean words. I also mean images and ideas that draw people in, so you can deliver a message they might not otherwise be open to. With *Family Fundamentals*, the reaction has really run the gamut. Some have said it was great and very illuminating, while others have said, "Why are you being so one-sided and letting the fundamentalists speak unchallenged?" I didn't really want to challenge them. I wanted them to find the challenge within themselves when they watched the film—to show people what can happen when these attitudes are taken to an extreme. Much of our media is so directed and pointed in terms of telling us what to think. Here, the audience is confronted with media that allows them to think, which leads to a lot of confusion—but that's okay, perhaps out of that confusion will come new ideas and beliefs. That was my strategy with *Family Fundamentals* and *Licensed to Kill* [1997].

With *Licensed to Kill*, I wanted to reach young men who, statistically speaking, are the prime perpetrators of anti-gay violent crime. My idea was to show them portraits of young men they could perhaps relate to, in terms of their background, the phrases they use, their gestures, so that they might be open to hearing their stories, rather than shutting down [to gay issues]. At the time that I was producing *Licensed to Kill*, there were a number of films made from the perspective of the victims. I think they were important, but I think we still need to delve deeply into this kind of behavior. Certainly, there needs to be films about victims of violent crimes, and we could learn from their stories, but I think that if you showed potential perpetrators a film about a victim of anti-gay violent crime, I don't know how they could relate to that. They may feel guilt, but I'm not sure if they would be able to understand why these crimes occurred in the first place; I don't know that they'd be able to question their own lives. So that was my strategy for *Licensed to Kill*. I wanted to make inroads into that audience—for them to see the predicament of gay people, but through their eyes.

What you're talking about is making effective propaganda, which means the film should reach out to people who might not think precisely as you do. It's been a big criticism of Michael Moore's films, that he tends to simply preach to the converted.

I think Michael Moore's films are creatively fascinating and wonderful to watch. I'm sure they do the trick for a certain audience, but are they going to reach that hardcore, bible-thumping, church-going group? Probably not. Different films are made for different audiences. Audiences and filmmakers vary. There needs to be room for the full spectrum of political beliefs because, for example, when we say we want to fight the religious right, there are many different kinds of people involved within that group and they don't always agree among themselves. People want to see black and white, good and evil. Life is just not like that; I don't want my films to be like that. And I think films that are geared toward progressive change shouldn't be like that. There must be shades of grey. If we just go for the easy change, the quick change, it may bring hope for now, but I'm looking at the long term. Especially now that I have a kid. [Dong and his partner recently adopted a child.] I want progress to be for the long term.

Brian Bennett and Bob Dornan at the 1984 Republican National Convention, from Family Fundamentals *(2002), courtesy Arthur Dong*

David Jester, Kathleen Bremner, and Susan Jester ca 1963, from Family Fundamentals *(2002), courtesy Arthur Dong*

One of the things I really appreciated about *Licensed to Kill* was that it came out of your own experience.

I have to set the stage for you. It was the late '70s, and San Francisco and the Castro was the gay Mecca of the world. I don't know if it is today, but it was back then. Harvey Milk was up for election. Violent acts against gay people weren't on our immediate radar. I lived in the Castro and that was a safe haven. One night, my boyfriend and I were eating ice cream. We weren't even holding hands, kind of carefree. Suddenly, a car stopped beside us, and four or five teenaged boys got out and started attacking and chasing us. Luckily, in the Castro, the hills are very steep, and we saw this VW Bus chugging up the hill. We jumped onto the front of it—I think the driver must have seen what was going on—and we held on until we could get off at a safe distance. The gay community used to have these rap sessions in a church downtown. We never went, but one time we did because we heard that an Episcopal priest had been attacked in the neighborhood and seriously hurt, just around the corner from where we'd been attacked. So the same group of boys had been frustrated that we'd escaped, and went down to get someone else. That was supposed to be us. People began to organize in the community against the violence. I saved the newspaper reports of violence in a file. It wasn't so much a question of why did this happen to me, but rather, why did this happen at all. I still have those questions today.

Do you ever feel frustrated by the narrow-mindedness that still seems to accompany discussions of gay issues? I'm shocked when I hear the level of discourse around gay issues in the media, after so many have spent so much time trying to raise awareness.

I can only speak on what I've learned based on the United States. This kind of resistance—and I'm not sure that's the right word for it—but this unbending stand, for many Americans, is based on their religious beliefs. What I've learned from working with religious conservatives and spending time with them is that they don't question their religious values. I ask them: What do you mean there aren't other choices? What do you mean there are no other options? What do you mean there's no other way to see things? And they're like, "Yeah, there is no other way." And they mean it, they believe it. There's only one way—and it's their way. And as much as you may try to convince them, why waste your breath?

They're very righteous. They feel they're only doing it for your own good. I'm not sure I want to use the word sincere, but they really believe it. Just as much as we want to believe in diversity, they believe the opposite. I think a big difference between the religious right and gay civil rights activists is that gay activists, outside of those who are specifically working within the faith community, aren't spiritually motivated to win the war. It's more, shall we say, earthly—it's more about political rights, human rights, gender rights. The religious right have what they feel to be an almighty force behind them. Or so they believe. It's not so much for them about the life here, as their spiritual afterlife and the life they want for their kids. But, we [the gay community] are starting to have kids. And we haven't had that as part of our fight for a long time, at least as openly gay people. The anti-gay forces have their kids to fight for. It's a very strong motivating factor that we didn't have until now, the combination of the spiritual with the kids and grandkids. After having done my trilogy, I really needed to get away from it. The film I'm working on now is about racism.

How do racism and homophobia differ as prejudicial attitudes?
The gay community often struggles to find the common points between the two of them. The difference I see is that anti-gay attitudes know no racial barriers—people are prejudiced against gay people regardless of race, even if they're from their own racial group. Except for those suffering from internalized homophobia—which is a whole other discussion—you don't find openly gay people actively working to oppress other gay people because of their sexual orientation. People say it must be harder to fight anti-gay attitudes in the Chinese community because there's such a strong family tradition. I hear people say, "It's cultural." I disagree. Caucasians don't have strong family traditions? You can talk about Latin families, German families—whatever—you hear harsh anti-gay experiences from those communities too. I question the notion of equating our struggle with racial struggles. From what I see, so much of it is based on misguided religious values and procreation. A good portion of the Korean community is very conservative here in Los Angeles and they are very much against gay rights, but that has nothing to do with race. Rather, I would stick my neck out and say it's due to the anti-gay Christian teachings that the Korean community has followed. Some segments of the black community

are also anti-gay, but that's coming from their churches. And what about Muslim teachings? As much as we'd like prejudices to have common factors so we can all join in the fight, in the end there's a stronger religious-based force that divides us more than unites us.

The battle for same-sex marriage, as it was fought in the courts in Canada, however, was predicated on comparisons of race and sexual orientation. In fact, Canada used the US Supreme Court decision that deemed "separate but equal" unconstitutional to make the argument that gays had to be allowed into the institution of marriage.

I think on a jurisprudence level, there are certain precedents we can use in the court battles, and that's vitally important on the legal front. But then there are the spiritual battles, and that's a harder one. I used to think we could win the spiritual battle, but I'm not so sure these days. I think that may have been wishful thinking. Maybe that can only happen with the evolution of generations, with time. Perhaps the legal front is where we're going to make the breakthroughs. If we win those, at least we would have protection. But then we know that the other side is reacting to every one of the victories we achieve. And we know that families are still being nurtured to oppress us.

It's funny how the backlash works. I often feel that Canada's ruling Conservative Party has struggled to form a majority because voters look at them and think of Bush, and recoil in horror. Alternately, perhaps some American conservatives look at what's going on in Canada with gay marriage and vote for Republicans.

My feeling is that Americans aren't smart enough to put those ideas together. If you look at the 2004 election, I can't believe that so many millions of people were so blindsided. But it's true. Even people I encounter every day—they never cease to surprise me.

Sometimes the politics are necessary, but I'm really encouraged when I hear that more gay people are raising kids because I think we need a systemic change, a cultural revolution. We need the generations that we nurture to become part of the system. It is change that will take time—I'm talking about years. We can put all the legislative changes in place that we want, but if we really want broad change, it has to come from the heart. Paperwork is important, but that only goes so far in terms of everyday living. My partner and I wanted a family, but part of me adopting a child is a political struggle as well.

FILMOGRAPHY

Arthur Dong is director and writer of the following which are feature documentaries unless otherwise noted:

Hollywood Chinese, 2007
Family Fundamentals, 2002
Licensed to Kill, 1997
The Question of Equality: Out Rage '69 (TV documentary series, one episode), 1995
Coming Out Under Fire (director and co-writer with Allan Berube), 1994
Claiming a Voice: The Visual Communications Story, 1990
Forbidden City, U.S.A., 1989
Lotus (short film) (director and co-writer with Rebecca Soladay), 1987
Sewing Woman (short documentary), 1982
Living Music for Golden Ears (short documentary), 1981
Public (short animation), 1970

Sandi Simcha DuBowski: Loving G-d, Being G-y

Sandi Simcha DuBowski has only one feature film under his belt, the documentary *Trembling Before G-d* (2001). But as any filmmaker will tell you, the path to make one feature is often very long and arduous, and DuBowski turned this film into his life mission for over a decade.

After working as a gay rights activist, the Jewish, Brooklyn-born DuBowski threw himself into the covert and often painful lives of his subjects: Orthodox and Hasidic Jews who were struggling to reconcile their faith with their homosexuality. The result is an astonishing emotional film, one which has touched people of all faiths who have struggled with religious-based intolerance to their sexual orientation.

Trembling Before G-d (spelled thusly because according to strict Jewish religious practice, you are not supposed to write the name of the Almighty) begins by outlining the basic dilemma facing those who wish to live honestly as gay while also remaining Orthodox or Hasidic: "A man who lies with a man as one lies with a woman," the Torah states in Leviticus 10:13, "they have both done an abomination, they shall be put to death." With devastating honesty, DuBowski's subjects, many of whom conceal their identities, open up to the camera, speaking of their terrible loss after breaking from family and community; some still remain in the religious fold, living under a heavy cloak of secrecy.

One man, identified as David, recalls the advice he received from a rabbi after confessing his homosexual feelings to him. David (whose last name is withheld to protect his identity) spent years in aversion therapy eating figs and saying prayers while flicking a rubber band on his wrist or biting his tongue. DuBowski facilitated the reunion of David with this rabbi some twenty years later, all of which is captured in the film. Another subject, Israel (last name withheld), is a gay man in his fifties who recalls the shock therapy administered to him as a young Orthodox man in an effort to cure him of his homosexuality. Long estranged from his father, the film includes a poignant phone call to his now ninety-eight-year-old father who tells his son he is simply too busy to see him; this scene is juxtaposed with an anniversary party for Israel and his boyfriend of twenty-five years. Another parallel scene depicts a lesbian couple who maintain entirely traditional Orthodox lives. On Erev Shabbat (the Friday afternoon before the onset of the Sabbath), one of the women calls her father to wish him a good Sabbath; the phone conversation is clearly strained, and after hanging

Sandi Simcha DuBowski, courtesy New Yorker Films

up, she breaks down and cries, expressing the guilt she still suffers for being a lesbian. The film also introduces Rabbi Steven Greenberg, the world's first openly gay Orthodox rabbi, who eloquently discusses in detail his own coming out.

Understanding his film's ability to change attitudes—and with them, lives—DuBowski insisted screenings of *Trembling Before G-d* included group discussions afterward. At the Sundance Film Festival, a screening was followed by the first-ever Jewish-Mormon gay interfaith discussion in Utah. "A young couple who appeared to be straight attended," DuBowski recalls. "Then, after the screening, the husband stood up and told us that he'd had a boyfriend before getting married. He said that the Mormon Church had told him that with time [his homosexuality] would go away. 'It's five years later,' he said, 'and it's not going away.' This made me realize that the film is not just for Jews." DuBowski describes numerous scenes like this one, moments of honesty inspired by the film's message of tolerance and acceptance.

DuBowski took his film on the road, throughout North America, South America, Europe, the Middle East, Africa, and Asia. In a number of countries, he faced opposition to the film being screened and, where he did find venues, there were often noisy protests outside. *Trembling Before G-d* is now regarded as a model of issue-driven documentary filmmaking, recognized both for its strong aesthetic qualities as well as the filmmaker's effort to get it screened in as many places as possible. The film garnered numerous awards, including the Teddy Award for Best Documentary at the Berlin Film Festival, the Mayor's Prize for the Jewish Experience at the Jerusalem Film Festival, the GLAAD [Gay and Lesbian Alliance Against Defamation] Media Award for Best Documentary, and the Grand Jury Prize for Best Documentary at Outfest Los Angeles.

DuBowski is now busy fundraising for and producing filmmaker Parvez Sharma's feature-length documentary on gay and lesbian Muslims, *In the Name of Allah*, which is slated for completion in 2007. We spoke in the summer of 2006.

Trembling Before G-d [2001] began as a video diary project, the short film *Tomboychik* [1993]. What prompted you to start it?
Years ago [soon after finishing college], I stole my father's toupee and I brought it to my grandmother's house. She and I took that and her wigs that she hadn't worn in five years and we played dress-up and filmed each other with my family's camcorder. She

started to tell me stories about how she thought she was a man and how she thought my father wasn't a man. Eventually, it became a gender-blending video across three generations of my family. I had a friend who was curating a program called Oy Gay at Frameline, the gay and lesbian film festival in San Francisco, and he said he'd love to show my short. So, I finished *Tomboychik* [the title plays on the Yiddish word for little boy], and it premiered at Oy Gay. From there, it screened at the Rotterdam Film Festival, the Whitney Museum, the Jewish Museum, and so on. The video was an oral history of my grandmother at a time when I had just come back to Brooklyn from college and moved in with my parents, and was a way for the first and third generations of our family to gang up on the middle one. My grandmother and I became co-conspirators in a little queer playground.

I understand your grandmother passed away before you completed the film.

Yes, she had died of a stroke right before I finished the film, so showing *Tomboychik* became a way to grieve. It became this living memorial to her ferocity of spirit. Then I started to look at another aspect of my life: I had returned to Brooklyn and was living in the all-Jewish neighborhood where I'd grown up. I had come out during this wave in the late '80s and early '90s of ACT UP protests and Queer Nation Kiss-Ins, a politicized, pro-sex reclamation of the body in the face of the AIDS crisis. I think when Bill Clinton got elected president, there was a shift in the way people thought. That heady, fiery feeling of the '80s morphed into something where people felt a sense of power institutionally, and the question became less about how to create a movement than how to gain access to the market. *Trembling Before G-d* came out of that shift. I was working at infiltrating the Christian Right and the anti-abortion movement, doing research and video production, and at the same time, starting to explore homosexuality in the orthodox Jewish world. Here I was criticizing fundamentalist Christianity while having very little knowledge of my own tradition. Also, coming back to Brooklyn and my family post-coming out was a way of exploring who I was before I was gay. Who was I growing up? Who was that three-year-old? Who was that Jewish child, that gay child? It was like I was doing an archaeology of the self. So I would say that that was the impetus for *Trembling*. It also had something to do with the body—orthodoxy being a place where one can hide one's body, a place where you just dress in black and white, set against the gay world, which focuses so much on sex and the body. Also, in Orthodox Judaism, learning was something that a man was valued for, to be a good Torah scholar. You didn't have to be hard and masculine. I was trying to work out what manhood meant and what masculinity meant.

We spoke extensively about *Trembling* when it first came out, and your observations about it seem different now.

Yes, these aren't necessarily observations I had a few years ago, but a more recent realization of what drew me to do *Trembling* personally, psychologically, and familially. It has shaped my life in profound ways. In 2004, I needed to stop and take a break to examine every aspect of my life. I went on a rollicking, roller-coaster journey both during and after the making of *Trembling*, and I didn't have the time to digest the enormity of it—what happened to me, to the people who were in it, the communities and the people that we touched. So I stopped and said, "I need to process this. This is overwhelming."

How did the experience affect your own faith?

Maybe this is just a place that I am in right now, but while I love and believe in the tradition and the meaning of Judaism, it's the social context of the Orthodox community that doesn't satisfy my whole being or allow me to live there 24/7. It's one of my spiritual homes, a place where I can visit occasionally and gain nourishment, but I've been doing a lot more mind/body/soul/erotic exploration in the past few years that has changed me a lot. While I was making the film, I had to be in an incredibly humble place. I had to let go of the certainty of gay affirmation. I had to be in a place where homosexuality was possibly a sin. I had to sit with rabbis and not condemn them and wrestle with whether I was desecrating God's name by making the film. I asked whether homosexuality was something that was chosen or whether it was biological. And I asked the foundational question: what does "commandment" mean in Judaism? I couldn't do such a film now, but somehow I was able to go to that place and luckily I was able to emerge from it.

Was part of the ability to gain the trust of your subjects being able to go to that place?

I think that Orthodox gay people like David were looking for some-one to say it was okay. But for this not to be a film that was just about oppressors and victims, I had to include the tradition and the rabbis. I was trying to be open and have as much compassion as possible. Then Rabbi Steve Greenberg wrote his book, *Wrestling with God and Men: Homosexuality in the Jewish Tradition*, where his main argument is that homosexuality is not a sin and [he] argues it from the basis of Halacha [Jewish law that draws no distinction between religious and non-religious life]. I think the complexity between sexuality and tradition emerges in the scene of David meeting with Rabbi Langer, which, I think, is one of the highlights of the film. When David turns to Rabbi Langer and says, "Would you send me back to [aversion] therapy?" and then Rabbi Langer stops, you can see the wheels turning in his head. And then when he says no and David asks why, Langer says, "Would I want to send you through that again? It was so damaging for you, it was so hurtful." Langer knew that he could not just give a pat answer. I felt that moment made both him and David incredibly sympathetic. They were navi-gating uncertain terrain and not about to give stock answers, they were even willing to say, "I don't know."

I simply wanted to tell the stories of human beings. I believe that the film avoided the grappling with Jewish law because it was the human element that was going to be the most devastating evi-dence. I wanted to break rabbis' hearts with the pain of the people who tried to go straight and failed, like Devorah, who could only keep her marriage going by taking anti-depressants.

I can see how emotionally charged the making of the film must have been.

You know, Israel, the older gentleman in the film, just died last week. I went to the shiva, the mourning at the house of the be-reaved, who was in this case his partner Carl. I'm really going to miss him. He and Carl were like gay great-uncles. There is so little inter-generational bonding in the gay world. *Trembling* was my link to a generation of people like him.

I started *Trembling* when I was in my early twenties and I finished it the day before I turned thirty, so it really defined my twenties. Now I'm thirty-five, and touring *Trembling* internationally has defined

Still from Trembling Before G-d *(2001), courtesy New Yorker Films*

Still from Trembling Before G-d *(2001), courtesy New Yorker Films*

my early thirties. I now have relationships that go back ten years which are so different from when I was younger.

A few years ago, you spoke about objectivity; you asked how filmmakers could make a documentary like this and *not* become attached to the people they are filming. Some documentarians, however, would disagree.

I'm still not of that school. I don't understand "objectivity," which I feel is a false construction in filmmaking. I'm still in touch with many of the people in the film.

You got so many different responses to the film. Were there any reactions in particular that surprised you?

I have had Orthodox people tell me, "Forget the homosexuality, I am seeing my spirituality on screen for the first time." In front of the cinema in Baltimore, Orthodox Jews and Evangelical Christians together protested the film, but a year later, the first Orthodox synagogue in Baltimore invited us to screen the film at the synagogue. Within one year, we witnessed a transformation from protests outside the cinema to a screening inside the synagogue; that is a typical arc of what the film has been able to achieve. South Africa, where I toured the film a year ago, has an Orthodox-controlled Jewish community, the Beit Din, whose rabbinical court tried to shut us down. They prevented us from advertising in any Jewish establishment, and from going into any school. They tried to kick us out of a Jewish community center in Johannesburg with Rabbi Steve Greenburg's book presentation. But South Africa is one of the only countries that protects sexual orientation in the constitution; when we reminded them of the law, they had to back down. It became a huge issue in the country, and that of course drove everyone to the cinema and helped to kickstart a new South African Jewish gay and lesbian group. It was amazing. We also did all kinds of interfaith dialogues. I find it interesting that with *Trembling* we went well beyond the Jewish world, building many bridges through many different communities and faiths and races, which led me to this whole other direction [producing *In the Name of Allah*]. When working with embattled and fearful communities, there really needs to be leadership. A film can be an incredible activist and educational tool. I think eight million people have seen *Trembling*, but what does it mean to empower those voices that are being represented for the first time in the movie? Orthodox gay leadership did grow out of the film. For example, after a screening, all these young yeshiva kids in their twenties formed JQY, Jewish Queer Youth. That shows how film can actually create change. Now I'm very aware of how we can nurture leadership from a community that has been largely hidden and private and voiceless. Now, even before *In the Name of Allah* is finished, we are developing leadership programs for the people within the film.

Rabbi Steve Greenburg is a brilliant, charismatic thinker and leader, and touring *Trembling* across the world gave him an unbelievable platform to speak from. I see the way the media changed things. There is nothing like a film coming to town, and whether that town is Prague or Tel Aviv or Sao Paolo or New York, the medium allows a religious message to be heard a lot easier. *Trembling* was able to break down barriers.

You have spoken about your own personal journey in terms of faith. Where are you with that now?
It's larger than faith. I would say after such an intense personal journey, I wanted to stop being a *Trembling* monster. In 2004, I wanted to become a human being again. I wanted to regenerate my body, my spirituality, my sexuality, my family, my friendships, and my relationship to work. I became a retreat addict. I hired an organizer/psychologist. I threw out over a hundred garbage bags full of stuff from my house. I put sixty boxes of *Trembling* into storage. I started therapy. It was a pivotal year. When you are a documentary filmmaker, you are always in a position of need. You always need funding, you need support, you need someone to forward your email announcement about the screenings, you need people to come to screenings. You are out there driving this whole movement around a movie, especially the way that I work. It was really amazing to have nine months where I didn't need anything from anyone. I stepped back and thought about what was really healthy for me. We put our life and soul into these projects and they can completely swamp and overwhelm us. But I don't regret it for a second. The wisdom, growth, challenge, intensity, and blessing of helping so many people was an extraordinary experience that has led to where I am today.

You must feel pretty phenomenal about the lives you've changed with the film.

Continually, Carl said that Israel told him, "Every day I am so grateful I was in this film, I will continually be able to touch people's lives." When Israel was diagnosed with pancreatic cancer, he received an email from a fourteen-year-old in Chicago who is half-Chinese and half-Jewish, a gay eighth-grader in junior high school, who said he wanted to convert to Orthodox Judaism! He wrote, "I want to come to New York and want to meet you and go on a Big Knish Tour that you lead in Brooklyn." Israel replied, "I have pancreatic cancer, I can't go on a big knish tour, but you are welcome to come over to my home for a meal." Then Israel's health deteriorated, and all of a sudden Carl gets a call that the boy and his mother are coming to New York from Chicago to have their meal. Carl told them Israel was in the hospital, but they insisted on seeing him. Carl picked them up from the hotel and brought them to the hospital, where they cried at Israel's bedside. And now Israel is gone, and I'm so sad. But there is that fourteen-year-old boy, and there are going to be many more—that is the utter blessing of being able to do this work. We managed to reach a great many people with the film. That was extraordinary, to take this subject and have it discussed in entirely new contexts. It really reached people, even teenagers, all struggling with their sexual identity. We opened up dialogues in nations and cities and communities. I feel that if my goal is to reach half the Jewish people with *Trembling* before I die, we are well on our way. The same way that *Tomboychik* is a living memorial to my grandmother's spirit, *Trembling* will be a living memorial to Israel's spirit. Here are these two older, non-conforming pioneers ... I never put them together until just now. Roland Barthes says that photography is like death because it freezes time. But film for me is life, it has a movement to it that represents the movement of life. And that will live on long after we're gone.

FILMOGRAPHY

Sandi Simcha DuBowski is director and writer of the following:

Trembling Before G-d (feature documentary), 2001
Tomboychik (short documentary), 1993

Robert Epstein, photographed by Stephen Higgens

Robert Epstein: Getting the Word Out

Though Robert Epstein is not the most prolific filmmaker in this book, the six feature documentaries he directed or co-directed have made a massive cultural and political impact. In the mid-1970s, Epstein joined a filmmaking collective led by filmmaker Peter Adair, co-creating the landmark documentary *Word Is Out* (1978) that represents a broad spectrum of gays and lesbians from across the United States. The film's simple message is powerful: gay and lesbians are your neighbors and co-workers; they are indeed everywhere. As interview subjects describe painful family situations, stories of discrimination, and their decisions to come out of the closet, a true portrait of gay and lesbian experience emerges. *Word is Out* reveals the raw power of documentary film to capture oral histories, and to this date has stood the test of time.

Epstein then embarked on *The Times of Harvey Milk* (1984), a film that would have a profound effect on a generation of gay men and lesbians and win an Oscar for best documentary feature. Epstein had been fascinated by Harvey Milk, the adept San Francisco city council-lor who managed to become the first openly gay American politician elected, the result of a clever grassroots campaign and his folksy appeal. The charismatic Milk challenged homophobia throughout California, leading the successful campaign against the Briggs Initiative, a bill that, had it become law, would have banned gays and lesbians from becoming teachers. In 1978, after clashing with both Milk and San Francisco Mayor George Moscone over a variety of issues, city councillor Dan White entered city hall and assassinated both Milk and Moscone. The murders left the city in shock, but the aftermath was perhaps even more horrifying: White's lawyers successfully defended their client using the now-infamous "Twinkie defence," arguing that White was not of sound mind because he had consumed too much junk food; he was ultimately convicted of voluntary manslaughter.

As the release of *The Times of Harvey Milk* was celebrated, the burgeoning AIDS crisis was creating an entirely new set of challenges for the gay community. One of the earliest artistic responses in San Francisco was a funny and poignant stage production entitled *The AIDS Show*. In 1986, Epstein again worked with Adair to capture this vital work on film, which aired on PBS that same year.

In 1987, Epstein formed the film company Telling Pictures with his life and filmmaking partner Jeffrey Friedman. Their first co-directed project, *Common Threads: Stories From the Quilt* (1989), again concerned

the AIDS crisis and won an Oscar, memorializing those commemorat-
ed in the mammoth AIDS quilt project. In *Common Threads*, as in *Word
Is Out* and *The Times of Harvey Milk*, Epstein and Friedman tell their
story by profiling several compelling subjects; in this case, a number of
people—gay, straight, white, black, Latino, male, female—all of whom
were affected in some way by HIV and AIDS. Among them is Vito
Russo, a close friend of the filmmakers and the author of the landmark book on gay and lesbian representations in cinema, *The Celluloid
Closet*. Produced for HBO, the documentary is a powerful testimony to
the humanity of those facing down the pandemic.

By the early 1990s, Epstein and Friedman embarked on what has arguably been their most ambitious project: a film adaptation of Russo's
book, *The Celluloid Closet*. Through film clips and first-person testi-
monials, the film illustrates how a litany of negative depictions of gay
and lesbian characters over the decades both inspired and fuelled homophobia in film audiences. By mixing politics and entertainment,
Epstein and Friedman pleased critics and audiences alike. The film was
released in 1995, at a crucial moment in the American cinema, when a
new group of gay and lesbian filmmakers was emerging, among them
Rose Troche, Todd Haynes, and Gus Van Sant, all of whom were depicting queer characters on film in new and exciting ways. *The Celluloid
Closet* is as much a celebration of a new chapter in cinema's evolution
as it is a look back at Russo's original thesis. That film was followed by
Paragraph 175 (2000), in which Epstein and Friedman interview gay
survivors of the Nazi internments, narrated by British actor Rupert
Everett.

Epstein's filmmaking style is ostensibly basic, but a closer look at
his oeuvre reveals a canny ability to empathetically convey human
emotion and tell stories often overlooked by traditional accounts of
history. I spoke with Epstein in the summer of 2006 from his San Francisco home.

How did you first get involved with documentary filmmaking?

It was through the film *Word Is Out* [1978], which involves some
back-story. I was nineteen years old and I had taken a leave of absence from college back on the East Coast, where I grew up. At the
time—this is 1974—I was dealing with coming out, and like most
people of my generation I was convinced I was the only one. I was
both running from and toward it, trying to figure out what it all
meant. For me, it meant leaving everything that I was familiar

with—college, family, and the East Coast—and getting on the Grey Rabbit, a hippy bus which you could ride from New York to San Francisco for sixty-five dollars. When I arrived in San Francisco, I didn't know anybody. My first job was cleaning empty apartments. After a few months, I answered a classified ad in *City Magazine* which said, "We're working on a documentary on gay lifestyle and we are looking for a volunteer production assistant, no experience necessary, just insane dedication and a cooperative spirit." It also said that they were looking for a "non-sexist gay male" to work on the project—very '70s. I applied for the job and met Peter [Adair] and his sister Nancy. They had just begun work on what would eventually become the film *Word Is Out*. They brought me onto the first shoots and I never left—it changed my life. *Word* was a three-year project and I went from being a volunteer production assistant to one of six filmmakers in the Mariposa Film Group—Peter Adair, Veronica Selver, Lucy Massie Phenix, Andrew Brown, Nancy Adair, and myself. The collective directed the film under Peter's guidance as producer.

That must have been an amazing experience, both as a filmmaker and as a gay man coming out.

Yeah, it was such a confluence. What drew me to that project was all very personal in nature. The whole experience of making *Word* was a search for community and self-identity. It opened up the world to me, and it set me on a professional path that led to *The Times of Harvey Milk* [1984].

When you were making *Word Is Out*, it obviously was an entirely different time compared to the current reality TV world where people are more familiar with cameras capturing their every move. How did you gain the subjects' trust? Were some people reluctant to appear on camera?

It's hard to articulate how different it was then—the pre-Internet world, pre-reality television world, pre-documentaries-in-the-theater world. We were on the threshold of coming out of the dark ages. The way we approached people about potentially being in the film was personal and very one-on-one. Each member of the group went to different parts of the country, often starting in familiar locations. For example, I actually ended up going back to my college town where I discovered a gay bar as well as one of the main subjects in the film. People were willing to appear on camera primarily because they trusted our intentions. But it wasn't always easy. One of the most difficult things was to find people in the corporate world, those who had a professional life while also attempting to have a gay-identified life

What then led you to the Harvey Milk project? Did you know Harvey?

I did know Harvey. I was in my late teens/early twenties living in the Castro while working on *Word Is Out*. Harvey owned a camera store in the neighborhood. I would take film to him for developing and prints. That's how I knew him. I wasn't following his campaigns or working for him at that point—my life was all about making *Word*. When it was released in 1977, it was also the start of the whole Anita Bryant campaign. [Bryant, a popular singer and orange juice promoter, led prominent anti-gay campaigns in the '70s and '80s.] That was the first wave of the fights we're still fighting. The Anita Bryant campaign begot the Briggs Initiative campaign in California—on the ballot as Proposition 6—which was intended to prevent gay people and their supporters from teaching in public schools. That was happening just as *Word* was released, and I became interested in doing my next film on the contemporary context of being gay. While *Word* is about coming to terms with our own identities and overcoming what we had been taught to think about ourselves, I was interested in the Briggs Initiative's response to both sides of the issue. So in the wake of *Word*, I started developing a film idea about the Briggs campaign, which I worked on with Peter Adair. However, over the ensuing months, I became more drawn to Harvey Milk's story. He was brave and articulate and emerged as our standard bearer, and he really caught my attention. It was at that point that Peter essentially said to me, "Go fly off, young one," in the most supportive way possible. And then everything happened from there. Harvey Milk's story embodied the impulse for what I wanted to do with the Briggs campaign.

So while you were making the film, the assassinations occurred?

Yes, although I can't say I was very far into the making of the film. I did whatever I could to track what was going on, but I couldn't pull together a crew every time I needed one. More often I was out there with a little cassette recorder, and my friend, photographer

Dolores Neuman, would take stills. One key sequence from the film is actually from that material—the night of the victory over Proposition 6. Harvey's victory speech that night was recorded with just me standing there with a funky-ass cassette recorder. In the film, a climactic sequence is constructed with this recording and still photographs. We didn't have the film footage, but we had enough material after the assassinations to put together a sample reel to pitch the project. Then I received some grant money and Richard Schmeichen joined me as the producer. Richard actually moved out from New York for a year to produce the film with me. There are eight interview subjects, but they weren't filmed until '83 [due to funding issues]; the assassinations happened in '78, so those people told their story several years after the fact. This frustrated me at the time because I felt like it should be a cinéma vérité film, capturing the events as they were unfolding. But in the end, I think we reconstructed the story well enough. And I came to see it as a blessing that the film took so many years to make—having those intervening years allowed for a distillation of themes.

Talking-head interviews often get a bad rap, but I think many of those in *The Times of Harvey Milk* are quite amazing.
Now when I see it, occasionally when I'm asked to attend something, I think about the fact that these people are telling what happened so many years after the fact, and yet it is still so present for them. I'm always taken by that. We did a lot of pre-interviews during those intervening years [between '78 and '83], around 100 people, in order to cast those eight who made it into the film. To me it made sense to tell this story with fewer characters rather than a lot.

When I first saw *The Times of Harvey Milk*, it had a profound impact on me—I can't really put it into words. When you were making the film, did you have any sense of how epic the story was, or how it would affect people?
I certainly couldn't have. Who could have predicted how the film would be received and the fact that it still resonates for people? I knew that the filmmaking challenge was to find a way to give the events the emotional depth that I had experienced. If we could tell the story dramatically in a way that made the audience care for Harvey, feel saddened by his murder, and be outraged at the

subsequent injustice, then we would succeed. To a large degree we were also guided by a sense of restraint, which I think serves the film and the subject well. There's a certain catharsis in this kind of documentary work. I was trying to figure out a way to present to an audience what I've experienced or discovered, so that they too might have that experience and make their own discoveries. Having lived here, having gone through all of those events in the '70s, specifically the loss of Harvey Milk, all I knew was that this was a story that hadn't yet been told in a way that made sense to me. Randy Shilts' book [*The Mayor of Castro Street: The Life and Times of Harvey Milk*] and other books about Dan White and the trial told the story, but it wasn't told in any other medium. I think for most of the world it was a passing current-event story, on page whatever of most newspapers, and that was the end of it.

It is one of those films that doesn't feel like one is watching a documentary anymore because one gets so wrapped up in the characters and in Harvey's life and spirit.
Harvey's alive in the film, which is great. There wasn't much footage of Harvey, but I think between the storytellers and what we were able to find and present, he does live in the film.

I understand you experimented with the fundraising for the film.
Yes, we tried everything imaginable, short of hustling. First, we did a direct-mail campaign—probably the first film to ever do that—and that actually got us enough to keep going for a while. It also helped to create a sense of community around the film. We had work-in-progress screenings for donors. One-third of our funding came from individuals, something like 900 people, and their contributions ranged from one dollar to $1,000, which really helped during the early years. All total, the film cost $300,000. A big chunk of money came from WNET, a public television entity in New York, and the rest came from grants.

There have been a number of attempts at a dramatic version of the film; I think Dustin Hoffman and Robin Williams both expressed interest in playing Milk, and Gus Van Sant was attached to it for a while, as was Oliver Stone. Do you know why the path to the dramatic version has been so torturous?
I don't. I can't speak for the decisions made by corporate Hollywood. For a while I tried to involve myself, feeling some kind of

proprietary interest and also knowing that the documentary was being used to introduce Hollywood executives to the story. More people were picking up the tape and sticking it into their VCR than picking up [Shilts'] book and reading it. But I was able to let go of that a long time ago and realize that it's going to be what it's going to be.

The film came out in 1984, just as the gay community was hit hard by the AIDS crisis. San Francisco seemed like the eye of the storm.

It was a devastating time. I remember walking into my doctor's office in the heart of the Castro district at around the time that *The Times of Harvey Milk* was coming out, and he told me that he was retiring. He said he couldn't face what was about to happen. "It's going to be like the lost city of Atlantis," he said. To a degree, he was right. The Castro during the '80s was a dark, dark place. Even if you didn't have friends who were sick and dying not very pretty deaths, you saw it on the street. You saw people walking around the street with Kaposi's sarcoma. It was a very evident disease and there was no escaping it. I think it's quite different now.

***The AIDS Show* [1986] captures this moment in history when the gay community was completely besieged by the virus.**

And we had no perspective on the enormity of the situation other than the immediate. It was 1986 and we had no idea where things were ultimately headed.

What was the impetus behind filming this stage production?

Peter Adair and I both felt compelled to do something on AIDS so we decided to pool our resources. Leland Moss, a respected theater director, had pulled together an ensemble of actors and writers to do a theater piece as kind of clarion call about the impending epidemic. [The stage play] *The AIDS Show* was an acronym for Artists Involved with Death and Survival. [The play] was the first creative endeavour Peter and I had seen on the subject, and it worked on several levels—as a harbinger and as entertainment. So it seemed like a valuable thing to document.

Then came *Common Threads* [1989]. It must have been very difficult documenting this disease when there was so little hope, no semi-miraculous drug cocktail.

The only hope was the hope that you found in community—as clichéd as that sounds. And that was one of the themes Jeffrey and I were hoping to express through the quilt. There was also a kind of hope in the bravery of these people individually. At that point I hadn't been touched by death that closely. If such a thing can be possible, I felt more prepared after doing that film to face the reality of dear friends and buddies dying, as well as my father's death.

Did the rest of America's reactions to what was going on in that community ever seem shocking?

America is always shocking. I'm shocked by how people other than those I know react to things. Man, I can't speak for the rest of America. But I guess in some way we were making *Common Threads* for the rest of America. It was produced for HBO, for a broad mainstream audience, so in that sense, we were aiming to get the rest of America to understand what was happening and to look at something they probably didn't want to look at. After the initial HBO broadcast, we received amazing mail from people. I think the film opened some eyes at that juncture.

The Celluloid Closet [1995] is a very interesting project because you were adapting a book. Can you talk a little bit about the complexities of adapting Vito Russo's book for the big screen?

The biggest complexity is that we didn't have Vito—we didn't really get into the making of the film in earnest until after his death in 1990. So that was a great void, not having his vision. But he did leave us with a guiding philosophy, which was that he felt the film should be, above all, entertaining. He cited the series *That's Entertainment!* [a 1974 documentary that looks at various MGM stars and the history of the studio] as a model. He thought the *Celluloid* movie version of the book should be fun to watch, and that was something that we kept in mind. Some people criticized the film for not being political enough, as did one movie star who appears in the film. We went by Vito's directive, though. His book was political because it was his polemic. It's really Vito's voice that drives the book, but in the film it's another voice. The other big challenge was how to end the film. We were ending at a point in time where both society and movies were changing in some ways, while in other ways things were status quo. So how do you conclude *Celluloid* when the story is ongoing? That was a challenge. It was also a

Still from The Times of Harvey Milk *(1984), courtesy Telling Pictures*

Vito Russo with the panel he made for his lover Jeff Sevcik, from Common Threads *(1989), courtesy Telling Pictures*

difficult decision to focus only on Hollywood films and not include independent or non-American films. In the first cut, we included independent films and interviews with independent filmmakers. This might have worked if we structured the film as a documentary for television, but we had to narrow the focus for a narrative feature.

So really, you are talking about the studios versus gays.
At certain points we reference European film, but yes, we kept the focus on studio film.

I like the way you end it with a montage in which there are a lot of independent films.
It was meant to say that there are other voices making films outside of the studio system.

The film is like a sequel to Vito's book just because it is different from it.
I agree. Vito's book was written in the 1970s and we were making the film in the 1990s. He actually wrote a lot of that book in my apartment in San Francisco. He would often leave New York during the winters and come out and stay with me. When he was in LA, he stayed with Lily Tomlin.

I'm wondering how Lily Tomlin's reluctance to come out impacted you at the time *Celluloid* was coming out.
It was difficult because Armistead [Maupin, who co-wrote the film's screenplay and then distanced himself from the project because Lily Tomlin would not state that she was a lesbian] had his point of view, Lily had her point of view, and I had my point of view, but now that feels like a long time ago.

Did you think that Armistead had a point? It did seem strange that this movie, which is predicated on a book that criticized people for not being open, would have Tomlin so involved—and still closeted.
From Lily's point of view, she felt she was out. But if somebody wanted her to make a statement, then she would back away. You know, people make their own decisions. I don't believe there was a double standard. I also knew that the film wouldn't have been made without Lily. What more could we ask from her? She was so

important in getting that film made with HBO and I'll be grateful
to her forever. And of course Armistead also made a great contribu-
tion by writing the narration.

**When the film was at the Toronto International Film Festival, I
asked Tomlin, "What led you to get involved in this?" But before
she could answer, a fire alarm went off.**
I remember, and I don't know if it was me or Jeffrey who said,
"Saved by the bell."

**You've been an out gay filmmaker since you were nineteen and
have made numerous films on gay issues and topics. You live in
California surrounded by a lot of those people whom Vito Russo
chastised in his book for not being more honest and for being
too conservative and duplicitous. Has that ever been awkward
for you?**
I don't live in Hollywood, I live in San Francisco, and the two are
worlds apart. Nor do I work in Hollywood, so my world is a pretty
independent one. I am connected to Hollywood as an Academy
[of Motion Picture Arts and Sciences] member and am involved in
projects with people who live and work in Hollywood. So maybe I
have a big toe in that other world, but not all of my anatomy. That
is not my world.

What led you to *Paragraph 175* [2000]?
Jeffrey [Friedman] and I were in Amsterdam promoting *The Celluloid Closet*. We came back to our hotel and received a letter from
a Dr Klaus Müller asking for a meeting. He mentioned that he
worked with the Holocaust museum and that he was doing research on homosexual survivors who were persecuted during the
Nazi Era. We met with Klaus, expecting some older professorial-
type with bushy eyebrows, but in fact he was this young, hip guy
in his thirties with cool eyewear. He was very articulate and passionate about the subject and he believed we were the filmmakers
to make the film for an international audience. We left the meeting convinced that there was a film that needed to be made—and
made quickly, as these men were old. Soon afterward, we had a
meeting with Jackie Lawrence of UK Channel 4, which helped to
fund *Celluloid*. Jackie immediately got the urgency and significance
of the project, and gave us a bit of development money, which
got us underway. Then we hooked up with Zero Films, a German

production company, as our co-producer, and eventually Sheila Nevins and HBO came on board in a bigger way. With Klaus's help, we met some of the survivors; there were seven, and five of them agreed to appear on camera. For most of them it was very difficult and painful to participate. On the day we were to film one survivor, he got nervous because he thought that his landlord was going to see a film crew and then start asking questions, so he reneged. These are men of a different generation who generally lived their lives with fear and shame. Heinz F.—he's probably the character that most people remember from the film—breaks down and cries at the end when he is asked, "Have you ever told anyone this story before?" and, "Would you have liked to?" And he says, "I would have liked to have been able to tell my father," and breaks down sobbing. At first, he had agreed to be filmed only in silhouette, but then when he looked at his image on the monitor he said, "It's too dark, you can't see me!" In the end, vanity won out and he agreed to have his image revealed—which we were thankful for because he is such a strong screen presence.

As a filmmaker, do you think your work contributes toward some sense of progress for gays and lesbians? There is still such homophobia and discrimination despite the work of filmmakers such as yourself.

It's frustrating. It feels like history just keeps repeating itself. On the other hand, I think that there are new generations growing up with a whole other worldview. They grow up with openly gay uncles, siblings, and parents. This is happening at the same time as other regressive things are happening. It feels like we're still arguing the same arguments and fighting the same fights. Like, didn't they see *Word Is Out* that was made back in 1977? In some way all that rhetoric out there has nothing to do with me, but then again it has everything to do with me. I have to keep making myself aware of what my work means for other people. But in terms of the responsibility that we take for our own lives, all that anti-gay rhetoric means nothing, and I think that's true for a lot of people. I think that is a great change. It doesn't mean that we can be complacent, not for a moment. On some level, you have to say about those people, the ones who refuse to educate themselves and insist on hating us, fuck 'em.

FILMOGRAPHY

Ten Days That Unexpectedly Changed America: Gold Rush (TV feature documentary) (co-director with Jeffrey Friedman), 2006

An Evening with Eddie Gomez (feature documentary) (director), 2005

Underground Zero ("Isaiah's Rap" segment, feature documentary) (co-director with Jeffrey Friedman), 2002

Crime & Punishment (TV series, various episodes) (director), 2002

Paragraph 175 (feature documentary) (co-director with Jeffrey Friedman), 2000

The Celluloid Closet (feature documentary) (co-director with Jeffrey Friedman), 1995

Where Are We? Our Trip Through America (feature documentary) (co-director with Jeffrey Friedman), 1993

Common Threads: Stories From the Quilt (feature documentary) (co-director with Jeffrey Friedman), 1989

The AIDS Show (TV short documentary) (co-director with Peter Adair), 1986

The Times of Harvey Milk (feature documentary) (director), 1984

Word Is Out (feature documentary) (co-director with several filmmakers), 1978

Aerlyn Weissman and Lynne Fernie, courtesy Lynne Fernie

Lynne Fernie and Aerlyn Weissman: Out of the Shadows

Lynne Fernie and Aerlyn Weissman have made only one feature documentary together, *Forbidden Love: The Unashamed Stories of Lesbian Lives* (1992), but the film is of such significance in terms of its formal strategies, innovative hybrid structure, and research methodologies that it merits a full chapter.

Fernie and Weissman come from different backgrounds: Fernie primarily from art activism and Weissman from technical film work on various documentaries (including many of the films of Janis Cole and Holly Dale). Their collaboration began with *Forbidden Love: The Unashamed Stories of Lesbian Lives*, in which older lesbians tell the stories of their secret lives in Toronto, Montreal, and Vancouver during the 1950s and '60s—a time when being queer meant police harassment, job loss, and the severing of family ties. The result is a testimony to Fernie and Weissman's talents; *Forbidden Love* is a true revelation, and watching it, one is overwhelmed by a sense of relief and gratitude at how far queers have come. Interwoven with the interviews is a series of dramatic vignettes inspired by lesbian pulp novels of the period, featuring two women who are secretly, passionately in love. The vignettes are at once playful and thoughtful, and the film itself is a unique hybrid of documentary and drama.

Forbidden Love was warmly received by critics, and won awards at the Durban (South Africa) International Film Festival and a Genie Award (Canada's version of the Oscars) for best documentary in 1993. Perhaps it was the overwhelming grief due to the AIDS crisis, or the ongoing disenchantment with the conservative regimes in the US, UK, and Canada, but *Forbidden Love* arrived at a time when queer audiences were eager to find hope and optimism on the big screen—and they got it. At the Montreal premiere of *Forbidden Love* at the Image+Nation International Gay and Lesbian Film Festival in 1992, there was a thunderous ovation for the filmmakers (who were in attendance) that lasted close to fifteen minutes. Still, despite the film's undeniable impact, it does appear that *Forbidden Love* has difficulty getting its due. In the 2002 anthology of writing on Canadian film, *North of Everything: English-Canadian Cinema Since 1980*, for example, *Forbidden Love* is mentioned only briefly (and disparagingly, at that).

Fernie and Weissman have continued to make films, notably their Genie-Award-winning 1995 short *Fiction and Other Truths: A Film About Jane Rule*, a profile of the celebrated lesbian author (whose book *Desert of the Heart* was adapted to the big screen as *Desert Hearts*, the 1985 cult lesbian movie).

Fernie now teaches and co-curates the documentary film festival Hot Docs in Toronto, while Weissman directed *Little Sister's vs. Big Brother*, a 2002 feature documentary about the legal battles over the Canadian government's censorship of queer-themed books being imported by Little Sister's, a gay and lesbian bookstore in Vancouver. This film painstakingly details the alarming censorship one of Canada's best-known queer bookstores, Little Sister's, has faced. Weissman's documentary clearly illustrates that even in a country like Canada—one renowned for human rights advances and very progressive policies toward gays and lesbians—repressive policies are still being carried out by police and border officials. (Sadly, the film's postscript is a depressing one; in January 2007, Canada's Supreme Court ruled that Little Sister's was not eligible for any federal funding to help fight seizures by border officials.)

We spoke in the winter of 2006.

Aerlyn, you worked on Janis Cole and Holly Dale's films *P4W* [1981] and *Hookers on Davie* [1984] as a sound technician. Like those films, *Forbidden Love* [1992] is also about people who have been marginalized or forgotten, and about unearthing their history by letting them tell their own stories. They are obviously different films, but to me there is a connection.

AERLYN WEISSMAN: I certainly learned a lot from [Janis and Holly], more than I realized at the time—their work [habits], their commitment, how they made decisions. They are amazing filmmakers and amazing people too—an inspiration to me. It's true that I tend to think of [*Forbidden Love*] as—and I learned this from Lynne—about people who are underrepresented or misrepresented, and [by telling their] stories, you can open people's eyes. I think what is interesting about that is during the process, you also open the eyes of the subjects. They start seeing their own stories in a different way. I don't know if I expected that to happen with *Forbidden Love*—and it happened.

LYNNE FERNIE: Absolutely! That happened with almost every single person we interviewed. While researching the film, the women would say, almost without fail, "I don't have a history. I was just living my life." Making the film became an appreciation of their life, their courage, and their survival. That was an extraordinary feeling for us.

It's also a feel good movie, if you'll excuse the expression.
LF: It's not so much a feel good film as it is an empowerment film, which makes you feel good. It wasn't, "Let's hide the bad parts and everybody will feel good about it." But we also wanted to avoid politics of victimization. We wanted to have an empowering portrait of these women, not one of those horrible victim narratives.

AW: And I do recall we had some differences of approach with the NFB [National Film Board of Canada, the film's producing studio] at the time. There was a bit of pressure to not include some details that might be seen as dirty laundry. We both felt very strongly that it would be a betrayal of our subjects and the community to once again silence aspects of stories that were truthful about that experience. People have a hunger for truthfulness, especially people who have been stereotyped or demonized.

LF: Their stories showed us and the audience, whether straight or gay, that when we're in situations where we're being marginalized or harassed, there can be moments of resistance that empower us. I think that every single one of us have been in situations where we have been disempowered. Also, the women in the film showed us that they had developed great senses of humor to confront prejudice, and that humor was their first step of resistance. And about the issue of truthfulness that Aerlyn was talking about regarding storytelling: I think Holly [Dale] and Janis [Cole] encountered the same issue because they were dealing with people from the working class, and they found a way to avoid having their subjects—who had been treated badly or unfairly—look pitiful. We were not looking for anyone to pity these women. The worst documentaries show people only as victims as a way to make the mainstream feel guilty. That was never our agenda because we were already mad at [the mainstream]. Powerful social justice films involve different political strategies rather than just making people feel bad, and so I think that is also why this film is empowering.

AW: When you're making a film, you've got to think about where the focus is. The victimization? The resistance? I personally always took issue with the idea that I was marginal. I wasn't marginal, I was in the middle of things. I remember years ago at a workshop in Montreal, Michelle Parkerson [Storme], a wonderful black filmmaker who was based in Washington, was asked a question that was prefaced by, "as a minority filmmaker." She said, "First of all,

I'm not a minority filmmaker. Look at the whole world. I am not
a minority." So I think a part of the resistance is to refuse to put
yourself in that place. I never personally understood or framed
my participation in the industry or the things I was doing as being marginal, quite the contrary. There are those choices too, right
down to what you focus on and what empowers you. For many of
the people in the queer community and many of the women in
Forbidden Love for example, their resistance is characterized by a
remarkable sense of humor and irony, that sense of the disjunction
between the way things our institutions say life should be and the
reality on the ground, which they know in their own lives is so
different than the hetero norm. I think that's something that John
Waters understands very clearly with his work—that resistance
is not mean-spirited, it is not stupid, it is smart and it is funny.
Laughter in some sense is the revenge.

How did the idea for *Forbidden Love* come about?
LF: I had been doing in-depth research for a film by Margaret
Wescott [entitled *Stolen Moments*]. Also, I had worked in the art-
ist-run center world and had curated lesbian art exhibitions that
touched on history. When I met Aerlyn in 1988 on a shoot at a
Michigan women's music festival, we got to talking about films
and about lesbians, and how we didn't know anything about the
history of lesbians in Canada, and how great it would be to have a
film specifically about that. Months later, a producer from the NFB
suggested that we send in a proposal to Studio D [an NFB studio
that was dedicated to films by, for, and about women]. Rina Frati-
celli, the head of the Studio, was very active in Toronto as both a
cultural activist and a feminist activist. She wanted to bring the
kinds of issues that we were all dealing with at the time—race, gender, sexuality, feminist issues—into films produced by the NFB, so
she supported the proposal for *Forbidden Love*.

**Why did you incorporate pulp novels into the aesthetic and nar-
rative of the film?**
AW: I remember a bookstore on Queen Street [in Toronto] that
had these great pulp novels in the window. We always found them
pretty fascinating, that sort of *Reefer Madness* version of sexuality
and those crazy pictures for books with titles like "Women in the
Shadows." Our first proposal [to the NFB] included those [book

cover] images. That idea that, "Here's how [female homosexuality] is constructed in popular media, and then here are the real stories." I know I had issues with the way Margaret [Wescott] was approaching lesbian history [in her film]. There was a bit of joking about lesbians on horses galloping in front of volcanoes.

LF: The working title of *Forbidden Love* was B Movie, because Margaret's was kind of the "A" movie. She was making an international history [of lesbian culture] film that spanned centuries and she actually had money [to make it]; we were going to do the opposite, [make a film about] the local, Canadian underbelly [of lesbian culture] in the beer parlors.

You clearly did a lot of research to find the marvelous subjects in
Forbidden Love.
LF: I don't know if this is true at the Film Board now, but Rina was wonderful, she supported research for *Forbidden Love* very generously. We could not have found those women otherwise.

AW: The research took a year.

So how did you find these women?
LF: Aerlyn had a friend in Montreal named Alaine Blais, who connected us with a number of women in Montreal, which was really fabulous. I had a friend in Vancouver, video artist Cornelia Wyngaarden, who introduced us to Keely and Ruth and a number of other people. Maureen Fitzgerald and Amy Gotlieb in Toronto were doing a lesbian oral history project and introduced us to Lois and Jeanne. We also went to an OWL [Older Wiser Women] meeting at a club on Church Street [in Toronto] and we met Carole and her lover Betty. And then, people said, "Oh, you have to meet this person or that person." However, there were women whom we contacted who just didn't want to have anything to do with us.

AW: They were like, "Do not come here. We run the general store and we don't want to be involved with lesbian anything." We were dealing with a demographic of older women who cannot be asked, "I hear you are queer, do you want to be in a movie?" They had fear, issues of trust. Some people would actually phone their friends and say, "They are such sweet girls, we are going to send them over to talk to you."

LF: Documentary films of this nature are always about the relationship between the filmmaker and the subjects. Aerlyn really taught me this. The longer that I have been involved in film, the more that stands out. We did forty-five interviews across the country. Some people said we could only use their first names, or would disguise the names of people they were talking about. That is how sensitive they were. They were coming out of what was once a shameful thing.

AW: And a dangerous thing. Our research was certainly the opposite of the under-the-microscope approach that the mainstream media usually takes [on the subject of gays and lesbians]. We researched reports from the late 1950s and '60s, such as the Wolfenden Report [the report of the Departmental Committee on Homosexual Offences and Prostitution, published by the British government in 1957 that described homosexuality and prostitution as "victimless crimes" and urged their decriminalization] and [Canadian Prime Minister] Trudeau finally decriminalizing consensual homosexuality [in 1967].

LF: One Canadian politician in particular was known for saying, "These people aren't criminals. They are sick and should be sent to institutions," and he was considered progressive at the time. That is why we needed to do so many interviews, because we really needed to understand the context at that time from those who lived it.

AW: We were also very careful about how the material would be accessed at the NFB [archives], because of course we shot way more than ended up in the film [so unused material would be stored at the archives]. We had the NFB agree that archival material couldn't be taken out [by other parties] and used in such a way that the women would be portrayed [negatively]. Their stories are precious and cannot simply be pulled out [of the archives] for any reason. So we got the NFB to agree that the other footage from their vaults would not be used in other contexts.

It's interesting that you made that stipulation to the NFB.
LF: We had promised the women that they would not find a little clip of their interview in some whacked-out film or on the news; we had to have that relationship with them.

Poster for Forbidden Love *(1992), produced by Margaret Pettigrew, Ginny Stikeman, © 1992 National Film Board of Canada. Used with permission.*

Lynne Adams (as Mitch) and Stephanie Morgenstern (as Laura) in Forbidden Love *(1992), © 1992 National Film Board of Canada. Used with permission.*

I love your story about your experience conducting the historical research on the film: at one point, rather than look for the words "gay" or "lesbian," you searched for the word "police" to find relevant stories?

LF: The NFB stock shot library didn't have the category "gay" or "lesbian" or "homosexual." You had to look under "crime" and "police," because it was only covered under deviance or criminal activity.

AW: We spent weeks and weeks looking at every foot of every film that was categorized under "police." This was 1989, not that long ago. I think we did challenge the consciousness at the NFB about those issues [of gay and lesbian visibility]. We were so out and in your face about it. This is something that we learned from Jane Rule: you have to put "lesbian" in the title or it will be buried. That is why our film is subtitled *Unashamed Stories of Lesbian Lives*. You have to choose deliberately not to be erased or hidden.

It's incredible how the mainstream will not see things—especially if those things make them uncomfortable.

LF: There was a split between gay artists who were public and those who were not at that time. In the 1980s, famous artists like General Idea [a collective of three Canadian artists] were known to be gay in the arts community, but they were not publicly out until the AIDS crisis. Even Philip Monk, when he wrote a very significant curatorial essay on their work, didn't mention that they were gay. I mean, they had poodles on the cover of their art publication *File* magazine, and the three of them would be [depicted] in bed together, but the word "gay" was not mentioned.

[Gay historian] Thomas Waugh has a similar complaint about Andy Warhol, and with people who would talk about him and somehow manage to not mention that he was queer.

LF: Many artists did not speak publicly about their homosexuality because it would have harmed their career at that time. It is important to know there was a reason why they wouldn't own up to [their homosexuality], even when they had a certain profile within the culture; they didn't want their work to be marginalized.

AW: Another thing that I took great joy in—I think we both did—is that we used many historical, archival, and family photographs in *Forbidden Love*. We always hoped that audiences would go home and flip through their own photo albums and go, "Maybe this isn't quite what it seems. Maybe there was something going on between Aunt Mimi and that woman she lived with for forty years." I love the classic shot of V-E Day in 1945 right in front of Toronto City Hall—and down in the corner of the picture there is Bowles Cafe, where the men would meet for lunch and get a blowjob. There it is in this historic photograph, this public chronicle of world events commemorating that moment, and there in the corner is our history too. I love the way we use [archival] material to get people to think back and reconsider their assumptions about [the past]—to look for those subtexts that would inform those images in a different way. That was really fun, and I think for us it was also a form of resistance.

LF: As much as the film might be empowering for a community group, it also inserts a missing component of Canadian history, and it shows in the fact that it had a crossover success, playing at the Toronto International Film Festival and other mainstream festivals, and being broadcast on CBC, PBS, and other mainstream broadcasters.

Tell me more about the inspiration for the dramatic story that runs throughout the film, the interludes during which two fictional lesbians meet up and have a romance.
LF: We kept the storyline out of our first proposal, but we always planned for it because we wanted to include the sexuality of the women when they were younger. Aerlyn loved those pulp novels, and I had been reading a lot on the lesbian imaginary, and somehow these two elements came together.

AW: We wanted to present a reinterpretation of the traditional pulp-novel ending because most of them end with the lesbian killing herself and her temporarily-swept-away beautiful young lover going back to the husband, who had suddenly turned into a nice guy. We wanted to present the kind of happy ending that you didn't get to see in the 1950s, where it all turned out well. I remember shooting the bedroom scene and getting caught by [an NFB] security guard as Lynne and I were trying to choreograph it; I think I was on the bed writhing around or something.

Was there ever any serious resistance to what you wanted to do as filmmakers?

LF: Everybody was a little afraid to criticize us openly because we were the lesbians. So people would say they would "kind of" want us to get rid of something. But the worst thing that someone wanted us to get rid of in the fine cut was Lois saying, "I think post-menopausal women should run the world."

That's one of the most memorable lines in the entire film!

LF: They thought people would laugh at her.

Well, they did, but they loved it.

LF: They laughed with her.

AW: And the NFB wasn't so keen on Steph's story of being in an abusive relationship.

I remember when I saw the film at the Montreal gay and lesbian film festival, some of the women in the audience booed when Steph started to speak about her abusive relationship.

LF: There were so few lesbian films around, so creating a positive image was really important to audiences. They wanted to have a group hagiography, we wanted to have a complex history. We could have covered a lot more tough issues in the film, but it was about finding a balance. Steph really told that story well; she was such a survivor. People are always [dealing with issues] at different places in their lives, and artists just have to make those decisions that are accurate, honorable, and necessary.

AW: [The straight reviewers] were fascinated by the whole butch/femme thing. "What's all that about? What are they doing?" And I would say, "Go home and look at your relationship. You have a butch/femme relationship." It was as though it was some exotic thing that they could not possibly relate to.

LF: Ninety-nine percent of the time, the interviews with media were very comfortable. But there was one radio interview in Alberta [that went badly]. I was speaking to them by remote from a little studio in Toronto all by myself. I came away [from the interview] feeling I had been beaten up, so I went to the nearest bar and drank multiple glasses of scotch.

When you were making the film, did you think about the kind of impact it would have on the subjects' lives as well?
LF: Having spent so much of their lives living in the shadows—even if they resisted being marginalized, they were nonetheless subject to the law and to social punishment—and then years later, having eight or nine hundred people stand up and cheer them for their courage, was very moving. They really loved it. It is so lucky that we managed to do the film, and lucky that we didn't try to construct a history from people who had already died.

AW: Living memory was an issue for us.

LF: I heard that when the film played at the Durban International Film Festival in apartheid-era South Africa, it caused quite a stir. A lot of lesbians heard about the film and went to see it, and afterwards they took over all the men's bars because there weren't really any women's bars, and it was also highly illegal to be gay or lesbian in Durban. The spirit of the film just inspired them to take over the bars. It's so wonderful as filmmakers to hear those kinds of stories and to know that it is from your energy and hard work. We were a great team. With Aerlyn having the experience of working on many documentary film crews, we were confident that we would have a great balance of strengths [during the filmmaking]. We really wanted to celebrate resistance, to unearth this invisible history, but we wanted to do it in an entirely engaging and entertaining way. Why should it be dour? What really gives people energy in the resistance is not being dour, it's being rebellious.

FILMOGRAPHIES

Lynne Fernie is director and writer of the following which are short documentaries unless otherwise noted:

Apples and Oranges, 2003
School's Out, 1996
Fiction and Other Truths: A Film About Jane Rule (co-director and
  co-writer Aerlyn Weissman), 1995
Forbidden Love: The Unashamed Stories of Lesbian Lives (feature
  documentary) (co-director and co-writer Aerlyn Weissman),
  1992

Aerlyn Weissman:

Lost Secrets of Ancient Medicine: The Journey of the Blue Buddha (short documentary) (co-director with Tetsuya Itano and co-writer with Gary Marcuse), 2006

Little Sister's vs. Big Brother (feature documentary) (director and writer), 2002

Kink (TV series, various episodes) (director), 2001

Scams, Schemes, and Scoundrels (short documentary) (director), 1996

Fiction and Other Truths: A Film About Jane Rule (short documentary) (co-director and co-writer with Lynne Fernie), 1995

Without Fear (short documentary) (director), 1993

Forbidden Love: The Unashamed Stories of Lesbian Lives (feature documentary) (co-director and co-writer with Lynne Fernie), 1992

A Winter Tan (feature) (co-director with several directors), 1989

Eytan Fox and Gal Uchovsky: Israeli Idols

Filmmaking team Eytan Fox and Gal Uchovsky have created some of the most thought-provoking and controversial films in Israeli cinema, which have in turn greatly influenced the nation's attitudes toward its gay and lesbian citizens. Fox and Uchovsky consistently reflect the contradictions and complex dilemmas facing the Israeli psyche, exposing the scars of war and suggesting that Israeli-Palestinian peace will only be realized when Israelis accept their responsibility in the ongoing conflict.

Eytan Fox was born in New York and emigrated to Israel with his family when he was two years old. In 1990, his first short film, *After* (a.k.a. *Time Off*), examines issues of sexual identity for members of the Israeli military. Although Fox has revealed that he wanted to explore his own sexuality thematically in the film but remained closeted and rather timid in his treatment of the subject, the film succeeded by winning Fox instant recognition with a bevy of awards, including a Movie of the Year accolade from the Israeli Film Institute.

Later, Fox met Gal Uchovsky. They began a romantic relationship, and in 1997, collaborated professionally to create the landmark Israeli television series *Florentine*, which featured a gaggle of characters living in Tel Aviv facing various personal dilemmas; Uchovsky was one of the program's writers, while Fox directed several episodes. The show played much like a *Tel Aviv, 90210*, with numerous critics citing the show's Aaron Spelling-like aura. Notably, *Florentine* included gay characters, and was considered a watershed moment in Israeli popular culture—here, finally, gay characters were depicted on the same emotional plane as their heterosexual counterparts.

In 2002, Uchovsky produced and Fox directed *Yossi & Jagger*, a film about two Israeli soldiers who fall in love, and the private mourning that one is forced to deal with after the other is killed in battle. In what was perhaps a compliment, the Israeli military did not approve of *Yossi & Jagger*. The film did extremely well in Israel and titillated the international film festival circuit.

Uchovsky and Fox then followed up with *Walk on Water* (2004), an intriguing film about an Israeli soldier who is assigned the task of befriending the adult grandchild of a former Nazi now in his final years of life. As it turns out, the grandchild is a gay man, and the Israeli soldier finds himself forging an unusual friendship with him, despite his own barely-veiled homophobia. In *Walk on Water*, Uchovsky and Fox

Gal Uchovsky and Eytan Fox, courtesy Gal Uchovsky

create a nuanced meditation on Israeli identity, touching on sexuality, the Holocaust, and attitudes towards the Palestinians. Equally as fascinating as the film was press surrounding its release; Lior Ashkenazi, the star of the film who has been described as an Israeli Brad Pitt, acknowledged on Israeli television that he'd had an affair with a man in the past. As well, Ashkenazi and Fox posed together on the cover of *Time Out Tel Aviv* as part of the film's promotional campaign—Ashkenazi was entirely in the buff, his body wrapped around Fox.

In their latest film, *Ha-Buah* (*The Bubble*) (2006), Fox and Uchovsky depict a gay love affair amid the Israeli-Palestinian conflict. *Ha-Buah* opened a mere two weeks before the 2006 warfare between Israel and Lebanon broke out, making the film even more controversial. Critics accused Fox and Uchovsky of treachery for depicting Israel in such an unflattering light, but the filmmaking team countered that they were merely attempting to open up debate in their country, suggesting that the political right in Israel may well be part of the problems to which they claim to have the answers.

I spoke with Fox and Uchovsky the day after the North American premiere of *Ha-Buah* at the Toronto International Film Festival in September 2006.

In your opening remarks before *Ha-Buah* [2006] was screened [at the Toronto International Film Festival], you spoke out against the boycotts of Israeli films at some international festivals.

EYTAN FOX: I can understand and even identify with people's emotion that leads to decisions [to boycott things], but stopping films from playing at festivals or blocking cultural exchanges is not the way to do it. The way to take action is to give the filmmakers who are critical of Israeli policies the opportunity to speak.

GAL UCHOVSKY: There is a ridiculous side to this censorship. Last month, there was a festival in England that was supposed to screen *Walk on Water* [2004]. They sent us a message saying that they were having trouble deciding whether they should show the movie. They asked if Eytan would send them a statement that he opposes the actions of the Israeli government in Gaza and Lebanon. I wanted Eytan to reply with a letter condemning the deeds of the British government in Iraq and demanding an apology to the world for the Falklands War, which was one of the most unnecessary wars of the last century. If you start comparing sizes, as they say, everyone has their own little bag on their shoulders. It's funny, because we are so much against this war in Lebanon. We are doing everything within our power to oppose it; I wrote an article in the middle of the war saying, "Let Tzahal lose [the war]." [The Tzahal is the name for the Israeli military forces.]

EF: One good thing about being a Jew in Israel is that there is a state and [I can count on] the security of my own nation, my own country—a democratic country where I can talk and raise issues. When you are a Jew in the Diaspora, then you feel disconnected, you feel the Holocaust can come again. People in exile tend to be more patriotic than the people actually living in the country.

GU: Expatriates don't feel like they can be critical because they don't live in Israel.

You have been both partners and collaborators for eighteen years. How did you meet?
GU: We met through a mutual friend, a woman who was working with Eytan. She told me about him, and how wonderful he was. I said, "Are you sleeping with him?" And she said that he was gay. So she introduced us. At the time I was a journalist in Israel writing about culture and music. I was the editor of the Tel Aviv equivalent of the *Village Voice*. I had a good job, but then the journalism business in Israel started to weaken [financially], and having a career in journalism became very difficult. I needed a new direction and Eytan encouraged me to work with him, and with every movie my role became bigger.

EF: I loved Gal's writing. We had this system where I created the stories and the treatment and then he would write dialogue, turning it into a full-blown screenplay.

GU: It's a different kind of collaboration because we can't work side by side or we'll kill each other. He's the moviemaker and I work for him.

EF: That's not true. You've become a very successful producer.

There is a perception that Israel is the most liberal place in terms of homosexuality in the Middle East, but have you faced barriers as a gay filmmaking team?

EF: When I started making films, I was in the closet. I was making short films that had hints and innuendos about homosexuality, and then I made *Time Off* [a.k.a. *After*, 1990], about a gay love affair between an officer and a soldier in the Israeli army—it wasn't as explicit as *Yossi & Jagger* [2002], it was very nuanced. Then I moved on to the television show *Florentine*, which introduced the first real gay couple on Israeli TV. It was 1997 and two men kissed in it, which was as far as the mainstream film and television world had gone with gay content before [the television series] *Queer as Folk*.

GU: There has been a very sharp change in attitudes toward gays in Israel. Today, Israel is one of the most liberal places in the world for gays. Sometimes I think that one of the reasons for this is that so many people die young in Israel. Parents know their children can die in a war, or die just by getting on a bus, so the fact that knowing people are gay is not the end of the world. It brings a certain perspective to life.

EF: The gay youth movement in Israel is amazingly progressive.

GU: On *Israeli Idol*, our version of the international *Idol* television show phenomenon, I am on the panel of judges. It's a hugely popular show. The fact that I am gay is very obvious. There are jokes about it, but nice jokes.

EF: Things have changed. When I began filmmaking, I tried to tell the story with any gay aspect kept to a minimum. I was apologetic about it. But as years went by, Israel became more progressive— partly thanks to the success of *Florentine* and its gay characters who were loved by everyone.

GU: I think another aspect is the fact Israel is very small—there has never been space for a gay ghetto. So we could take over the entire city of Tel Aviv.

EF: He means to say, everything in Tel Aviv is very mixed. I would say it like this: in America, gays are more progressive. In Israel, our straight people are more progressive.

What was the inspiration for *Yossi & Jagger*?
EF: It was a real story about [a gay] officer who went through the Lebanese war in 1984 whose lover died in his arms while they were

[in combat]. Of course, he couldn't tell anybody. No one knew about this secret love affair. When the officer met the parents of his dead lover, all he did was shake their hands and say, "Your son was a superb soldier." He couldn't mourn. We have a tradition that when a man dies, the whole community embraces his wife or his daughters and sons, and they mourn together. But [the officer] couldn't do it and he was still carrying these scars.

GU: *Yossi & Jagger* was such a big hit in Israel. People were touched by the way that it described the soldiers' lives in such an accurate way. People also identified with these two characters. In fact, six months ago, during the withdrawal from the Gaza Strip, an army commander and a police commander who were in charge of the withdrawal made the sweetest reference to *Yossi & Jagger*. They gave an interview to one of the major dailies and were asked, "What was your most touching moment during all of this?" The policeman, who was very tough and macho, said, "There was this one day, it was sundown and we were standing on the wrecks of this synagogue in this little settlement and it was just the two of us, all the press was gone, all the soldiers were gone, all the protestors were gone, and it was just me and him standing on the ruins. It was sad and I felt a little bit like we were Yossi and Jagger." Yossi and Jagger are such icons in mainstream Israeli society that when this man considered real male friendship, they were the first to come to his mind. I think that's the most optimistic story you can get, and an indication of the extent of the film's impact.

During the recent conflict between Israel and Lebanon, you were both accused of treachery for your film *Ha-Buah*.

EF: Yes, we were. But on the other hand, [we had the support of] the new Israel, the younger people who are really sick and tired of all those old attitudes about who's a traitor and who's not. They want to talk about problems, put things on the table, and expose the mistakes that we've made, as a way [to move forward as a country]. So young people were rushing to see *Ha-Buah*, talking about it, and engaging with it. Perhaps some of their parents said, "What is this bullshit? It's war now, we all have to be together. We have to create one façade, one united front." But the younger generation replied, "No, this whole war—living with war and talking about war as the only way to solve problems and deal with things—this is

Poster for Ha-Buah (The Bubble) *(2006), courtesy Gal Uchovsky*

Yehuda Levi (as Jagger) and Ohad Knoller (as Yossi) from Yossi & Jagger *(2002), courtesy Gal Uchovsky*

bullshit. We want to live differently and we'll go see this film because it will make us talk and it will make us feel better about how
we really feel about life."

GU: Another thing we'd like to make a point about is that we're
Israelis, we love Israel, we are as patriotic as everybody else, but
we are not right wing. You can be patriotic and not be right wing.
When we made *Yossi & Jagger*, the [Israeli] army didn't want to
support the movie. Once the film was released, people around the
world asked, "What did the army say? What did the army think?"
We had to explain that the army did not help, but that the soldiers
liked it; or state the fact that our army is very progressive about out
soldiers. So before we made *Ha-Buah*, I called a spokesman for the
army and said, "Listen, I need five minutes of your time. I know
if you read this script you'll say that you won't support the film.
But let me tell you something, we are Israelis, we pay our taxes,
we are good citizens, and we are Israel's mainstream. I think that
you should rethink your stance. This is not an anti-Israeli movie.
This is the way we feel about our country and we are not blaming
anybody for anything. We are just telling a story and I think that
the army should be brave enough to help us because we are going
to do it anyway. People will ask about what the army thought of
the movie." So, the army spokesperson thought about it for two
days and then said yes to supporting *Ha-Buah*. I think this is a real
achievement for us.

**Walk on Water is a fascinating film. In particular, it suggests that
Israelis should move beyond the Holocaust.**
EF: It was difficult for the audiences that were still very much connected to the Holocaust. But then again, the [major demographic of
the] audience for *Walk on Water* was older people in Israel and they
loved it. Somehow, our films manage to bring people to a place
where they can deal with issues that are difficult for them. Part of
the manipulation that we used for *Ha-Buah* was that we marketed
it as a fun story about young people in Tel Aviv. Once you get them
into the movie house they will have to deal with the issues that the
movie brings up: a Palestinian and an Israeli in love, and a Palestinian who ultimately becomes a suicide bomber.

GU: We thought that first of all, people have to know that it is a
love story set in Tel Aviv. It is a movie that is positive and about

love. In order to get this, though, you have to get to know a Palestinian gay man and an Israeli lover and a suicide bombing and everything else.

EF: Once people watched the movie, they liked it. We live next to Rabin Square [named after the assassinated Israeli Prime Minister Yitzhak Rabin], and *Ha-Buah* played in a major theater in that square. One night I passed by and saw people coming out of the movie, and [a lot of] young people were sitting there talking about the film. I returned half an hour later and they were still talking about it quite passionately.

GU: In Israel, you need more than a movie to steer political debate, or it has to be extreme because life itself and political talk shows on TV are very violent and outrageous. A subtle movie that suggests Israel needs to stop acting as a victim and admit it is strong and should be more tolerant towards Palestinians could at best become a conversation piece for late night talk shows.

Ha-Buah opened on June 29, two weeks before the war [with Lebanon] started. All of the movie theaters in the north of Israel closed down. As well, everyone was against Tel Aviv [because it was in the South, away from the war] at that point. Tel Aviv became like a scapegoat. People were saying, "You are in Tel Aviv, you couldn't care less, but we are dying. Bombs are falling in the North." There were articles in the media suggesting that everyone in Tel Aviv was going out to their nightclubs and restaurants while people in the North were in bomb shelters.

But *Ha-Buah* did well.
EF: Yes, it did very well before the war, and then [during the war] a lot of young people said that they would not accept this new criticism. Ohad [Knoller], our lead actor, was conscripted to serve in the war. He called me and he said, "Eytan, you said you would go buy clothes with me for my wedding. But I am going to the war tomorrow and they are going to give me twenty-four hours off to get married next week. So if you want to buy clothes with me, it is today." He's kind of macho, and wanted to contribute to his country and thought that the thing to do as an Israeli male was to go into the army.

Israelis have an intense relationship with the military. Lior Ashkenazi, the lead actor from *Walk on Water*, certainly took a stance when he posed nude with you on the cover of *Time Out Tel Aviv* and talked about his gay experience [Ashkenazi is heterosexual but had some gay relationships].

EF: In Israel, people never talk about these things, so he was dragging a few skeletons out of the closet. People [in Israel] feel very defensive, as though the entire world is against them. I grew up in a world where it was unheard of not to go into the army. If you were a man from a good family, you joined a commando or fighting unit, otherwise the whole neighborhood would talk about you. Now, Israel's biggest pop idol did not go into the army—that would be unheard of when I was young. Israel is changing in so many ways.

GU: Here is proof that everything is really opening up. Ashkenazi's interviews and the *Time Out* cover did not hurt him, it just made him more popular. And we didn't even mention Ivri Lider, Israel's biggest rock star who became more famous after coming out, and after singing a man-to-man love song in *Yossi & Jagger*. He did the soundtrack for our last three movies, and in *Ha-Buah* he sings "The Man I Love," which all the teenagers download to their cell phones. They think it's an awesome new love song.

FILMOGRAPHIES

Eytan Fox is director of the following unless otherwise noted:

Ha-Buah (*The Bubble*) (feature) (director and co-writer with Gal Uchovsky), 2006
Walk on Water (feature), 2004
Yossi & Jagger (short film), 2002
Ba'al Ba'al Lev (*Gotta Have Heart*) (short film), 1997
Florentine (TV miniseries, various episodes), 1997
Shirat Ha'Sirena (*Song of the Siren*) (feature), 1994
After (*Time Off*) (short film), 1990

Gal Uchovsky:

Ha-Buah (*The Bubble*) (feature) (co-writer with Eytan Fox), 2006
Walk on Water (feature) (writer), 2004
Florentine (TV miniseries, various episodes) (co-writer), 1997
Ba'al Ba'al Lev (*Gotta Have Heart*) (short film) (writer), 1997

Wash Westmoreland and Richard Glatzer

Richard Glatzer and Wash Westmoreland: When Worlds Collide

Collaborators Richard Glatzer and Wash Westmoreland come from very different areas of the entertainment industry, yet their diverse talents have proven extremely complementary. In 1993, Glatzer made the independent queer film *Grief*, the autobiographical story of an LA-based trash TV writer who grapples with office politics and new romantic opportunities while marking the one-year anniversary of his boyfriend's AIDS-related death. Glatzer, who grew up in Queens, New York, wrote and directed the film, which adeptly balances humor and pathos in a story that accurately reflects the lives of many gay men at that time.

In 1995, the British-born Westmoreland worked on the film crew of Bruce LaBruce's scandalous porn hit *Hustler White*, then went on to make several memorable porn flicks of his own (using the abbreviated name Wash West)—*Toolbox* (1996), *Naked Highway* (1997), and *Dr. Jerkoff & Mr. Hard* (1997). He received critical praise for creating distinctive and unusual work in an arena that had become staid and dreary; indeed, according to Westmoreland, porn had become so predictable and decidedly unsexy that there was room for someone with a vision of its potential to come along and reinvent the genre.

It was during this time in the late 1990s that Glatzer and Westmoreland met at a party in Los Angeles. Their romantic relationship began immediately, with professional collaboration soon to follow. In 2001, the two co-directed Westmoreland's screenplay *The Fluffer*. Using his insider knowledge of the porn industry, Westmoreland explored the business's hilarious absurdities while examining the more universal theme of power dynamics within relationships. After this project, which drew attention on the film-fest circuit and had a limited theatrical run, Glatzer worked on various reality TV programs (including MTV's *The Osbournes* [2002–05]) while Westmoreland delved into documentary filmmaking, touching on such issues as gay consumerism (*Totally Gay!*, 2003) and gays on the political right (*Gay Republicans*, 2004).

But their 2006 film brought them their greatest attention to date, whether as individuals or a team. *Quinceañera*, which won both the Audience Award and the Grand Jury Prize at the Sundance Film Festival, depicts two young Latinos struggling to find their bearings after being tossed out of their homes by their families. Emily Rios plays

Magdalena, a teenage girl who is shocked to learn that she's pregnant. She seeks refuge with her great grand-uncle (Chalo González), where she finds herself under the same roof as her cousin Carlos (Jesse Garcia), who's also been kicked out by his parents, but because he's gay. Notably, Glatzer and Westmoreland wrote a controversial white gay couple into the screenplay who seem self-interested and use the young gay Latino character as little more than a sexual plaything. Critics speculated that Glatzer and Westmoreland were trying to represent themselves through these characters in the film. It is to their credit, however, that Glatzer and Westmoreland felt confident enough to represent a gay couple as being multi-dimensional and imperfect—two of many inhabitants of an urban neighborhood that is rapidly being gentrified. As such, the film is a powerfully realistic look at the complex intersection of race, class, and sexuality in America.

Glatzer and Westmoreland spoke with me in late 2006 from their Los Angeles home.

I saw *Grief* [1993] at a gay film festival many years ago and it had a big impact on me. The title was just so singularly descriptive of that period for gay men. That simple word said it all.
RICHARD GLATZER: I think a lot of people kept away from the movie because of the word. [But when] I thought of the title of the movie it just seemed so appropriate, there was no backing away. *Grief* is very autobiographical. In 1988, I lost my lover to AIDS and was working on the crappy TV courtroom show *Divorce Court*; the incongruity of the situation was so striking. My colleague, producer Ruth Charny, suggested that I should make a comedy film about working on that TV show. But I knew I could only do it if I included all the other stuff I was dealing with in my life that went along with it, otherwise it would have been so fluffy that it wouldn't have been very interesting.

I had never directed a film before and had been frustrated in the past because I had sold a couple of scripts to studios that never got made. How are you supposed to assess yourself as a writer if you never get to see anything on screen? [As for the story,] that period in my life was very difficult, but I thought it was appropriate for a film. Although I didn't want to get into all the pathos of dealing with somebody's death and wanted to keep all that stuff private, I thought it would be more interesting to see somebody trying to keep a stiff upper lip in public. There was something about this indirect, skewed approach to dealing with AIDS and mourning that appealed to me, in the way that a dead-on approach wouldn't have.

Once I decided to go ahead with the film, it all fell into place very quickly. It was October 1991 when I thought of making the film; the following June we were shooting. Yoram Mandel came on board—he was the producer of *Parting Glances* [1986]—so I felt like I was in good hands as a first-time filmmaker. We shot it in ten days and I was lucky enough to get a really fantastic cast.

In the film, you managed to convey of lot of the contradictions of that period in the history of AIDS, because there wasn't a lot of hope. It was a time of real grief and despair, when we were losing so many people.
RG: So much of the New Queer cinema was inspired by what we were going through during the onslaught of AIDS. Look at *Poison* [1991] and *Parting Glances* and *Grief*; there was clearly a need for expression.

Have you watched *Grief* recently?
RG: About two or three years ago I did a director's commentary for the DVD release. I did two commentaries, one with Craig [Chester] that was kind of serious and one with Jacki [Beat] and Illeana [Douglas] that was really, really funny and irreverent about the whole thing. That was the last time I saw it. I'm very proud of it. It was made for only $40,000, and the cast was amazing.

You've since been involved with reality television.
RG: I really enjoy it. I guess I gravitate towards "grade-Z" TV in between films. Much of reality TV is just so bottom drawer, yet I guess I've been very lucky that I've always had a show that I can engage with. I've worked on *The Osbournes* [2002–05] and been with *America's Next Top Model* since the beginning [in 2003]. Sometimes I get involved in the shows *too* much. I find it interesting when you are given [real-life people] and you have to tell their story, as opposed to originating the material, because it makes you focus purely on the storytelling aspect. It raises questions: if you include this scene earlier, does it make this person more sympathetic? Or if you move it here, does it make this person unsympathetic? It's about manipulating the elements. I feel like I've learned a lot doing it.

Meanwhile, Wash Westmoreland comes from the wonderful world of pornography. How did you two meet?
WASH WESTMORELAND: We met nearly eleven years ago, after I had just moved to Los Angeles. We met at a party and we clicked. We started talking about movies, and kept talking. I think we spent the whole weekend together and soon after that I moved in.

Were you working in pornography at the time?
WW: I had just started. I came to LA to work on *Hustler White* [released in 1996], the Bruce LaBruce movie. I began making films in 1994 when I had lived in New Orleans. I made an experimental film called *Squishy Does Porno* [1995]. At the time, there was a growing interest in porn, and people were starting to look at it in a different way. I met Bruce when he was in New Orleans to show *Super 8½*, and he invited me to come and work on *Hustler White* in LA. I was the entire technical crew: the assistant camera, grip, and gaffer. I worked really hard for two-and-a-half weeks—and that was my introduction to Los Angeles. It was also how I got my first job as a director in the porn industry. I had met the porn star Kevin Kramer, who gave me the phone number for an adult video company on a little receipt. After *Hustler White* finished filming, I had basically no money, nowhere to live, no job, no car, couldn't drive—disaster looming. But I did have this phone number on this little piece of paper and I rang it up. I said, "I make films and I'm really interested in doing porn really differently 'cause porn is so boring and it can be done in a much more creative and interesting way. I want to create a revolution in porn." For some reason they took me on, and literally three days later I was directing my first movie.

What did you want to do differently with porn?
WW: I never really got turned on by porn, so I approached it from an it's-not-working point of view. Generally, porn boils sex down into formulas, rather than portraying what goes on between two people. It's very mechanical and often has little to do with creativity or sexual chemistry. I started looking at different ways that porn could be shot, different ways it could be lit, different ways that the actors could respond to each other. Instead of just casting two random actors and telling them to have sex, I would find two people who actually wanted to have sex with each other, then film it in an experimental, guerrilla sort of way, and edit it very fast to

music. This resulted in this charged-up, very youthful spontaneous take on porn. People in the industry called it MTV porn, which I didn't like because I thought it trivialized what I was doing. But in the industry at the time, in the middle of the '90s, no one was doing anything very interesting. So a little bit of creativity went a long way.

Video seemed to have flattened a lot of the cinematic aspects of porn.

WW: And the Internet has flattened them even further. If you look back at the early days, in the 1970s during the "golden era" of porn, people were really interested in making "films." For example, *Kansas City Trucking Company* [1976] and *LA Plays Itself* [1972] were the work of real filmmakers—well-constructed, beautifully shot, visually experimental, and sexy. In some ways they were my biggest influences. I wanted to return to elements of '70s filmmaking and bring that up to date.

So your experiences making pornography were pretty positive?

WW: Yeah, good and bad, but on the whole, positive. I liked the creative freedom. I don't think I would have got the same thing if I was making music videos or commercials. A lot of my porn work was a riff on pornography itself as a genre. Lots of times in my movies, the characters watch a porno, like a movie-within-a-movie. Doing this let me explore issues around voyeurism, exhibitionism, power relations, and narcissism. In 1997, I made *Naked Highway*, my breakout hit that won a lot of porno awards and received a lot of acclaim. From then on, I could work selectively, making a movie just once or twice a year in order to pay the rent. The rest of the time, I could work on our independent film projects. By 1997, I became almost entirely focused on *The Fluffer* [released in 2001].

Tell me about how *The Fluffer* came about.

WW: Back when I was living in New Orleans, I picked up Linda Lovelace's autobiography, *Ordeal*. I read a comment about a fluffer on the set of *Deep Throat* and I just thought, Oh my God, what a ludicrous job description. The idea of fluffing interested me because it is an exaggerated version of a common power relationship—someone gives everything and the other receives everything. I thought: What would happen if a fluffer fell in love with a porn star? So when I got into the porn industry in LA, I started gathering material to make a feature film about the industry itself, but from the inside.

Were some people in the porn industry uncomfortable with this film?
WW: I've never gotten anything but positive support for *The Fluffer* from the porn industry. I think I show the industry as it is. Other films [that have depicted the porn industry] usually rely on second-hand stereotypes or sleazed-up versions of what they think the porn industry is. *The Fluffer* shows that there is a variety of interesting people working behind the scenes. It also shows the downside—the crystal meth, for example—and people [appreciate its honesty].

It seemed like in the 1990s, there was a large mainstream fascination with pornography.
WW: Porno chic. During the late '90s, especially. A lot of fashion ads were riffing on porn. Calvin Klein was running campaigns that were based on porn, academics were writing about "the semiotics of Chi Chi LaRue." Just the word itself got this kind of frisson.

John Cameron Mitchell's 2006 film *Shortbus* was basically a romantic comedy but with explicit sex scenes. Many reviews were sexphobic or homophobic, underlining the division between what is mainstream film and what is pornography.
WW: I don't think *Shortbus* was porn. It's an independent film that experiments with sex. But even the existence of *Shortbus* is a milestone [for the mainstream film industry].

I feel the world is gradually opening up, except for the religious right, which has its pornography confession groups who burn their DVDs in prayer. Urban society's tolerance for pornography is growing, and the 1970s feminist stance of being anti-porn is now being recast. The previous argument was that all porn is rape, but now porn is being seen as a medium that can be used in different and progressive ways. Women can get in there and make progressive porn—and they're doing just that.

In *The Fluffer*, you use this relationship between the fluffer and the porn star as a parable for human sexual relations generally.

RG: It is about the appeal of the unavailable, I think.

WW: The mechanisms of desire. Porn is ultimately inaccessible to the viewer. There is always a glass screen in between the viewers and the object of their desire. That distance is part of the appeal, but never fully satisfies them. It is like an obsessive relationship; it gives you a little bit, enough to keep you in a needy state, but never enough to completely fulfill you. In the movie, we parallel the fluffer's position with that of the porn star's girlfriend. The audience expects the characters to be very different, but in a way she is going through the same thing as the fluffer, showing two different levels of fluffing and shining a light on constructs of masculinity.

I think you handled the three-way dynamic very well in the film. It feels very real.
WW: The "gay-for-pay" thing does throw a new twist in the romantic triangle. Two people are fuelling this incredibly narcissistic character [the porn star], who needs increasing amounts of drugs and attention to support his huge ego. [The porn star character] is a composite of several gay-for-pay porn stars, and is an archetype. He was also inspired by a Johnny Rebel character in Tennessee Williams plays, that inaccessible straight guy who invites gay attention.

What was the impetus for *Quinceañera* [2006]?
RG: It came from our neighborhood. We moved to Echo Park five years ago and were invited to be the photographers for our next-door neighbors' Quinceañera [a celebration for a girl's fifteenth birthday]. It was very much like the Quinceañera at the beginning of the movie—with the same church and the same dress. We were amazed at the mix of tradition and modernity. There were all these tough-looking kids waltzing together very seriously, then going wild in the limo; the mixture of teen hormones and ancient ritual was fascinating.

Over the couple of months following that event, we were thinking about how remarkable it is that when a neighborhood is gentrifying, you get such a mix of cultures. At that point, the Quinceañera became our focal point. We thought it would be interesting to show the coming-of-age of two teenagers, Magdalena and her cousin Carlos, while showing a neighborhood in transition. At first, we thought, Oh God, this isn't our turf and it's not our tradition, how do we make a movie about this? Then we just knew we had to rely on our Latino friends and neighbors and we went ahead with it.

The Latino community is often stereotyped as homophobic.
RG: Personally, on this block [where we live], we ourselves have never experienced any homophobia from the Latino community— quite the opposite, in fact. But some of our gay Latino friends talk about how difficult it was for them to come out.

WW: Let's face it, most communities are homophobic. I come from the north of England and it was very difficult for me to come out—the culture of machismo can be very strong there, just as it is in Latin culture. It's the concept of homosexuality that frightens people. When people can deal with it on an individual basis, it's usually much less intimidating. And that's where you can make progress.

RG: The most autobiographical aspect of the movie for us was the teenagers dealing with their families. When we came out, both of us were rejected by our families and we felt a strong connection with both Magdalena and Carlos.

WW: We wanted all the characters to be three-dimensional, but not too likeable. They're certainly not positive images. In the story line, there is a kind of coded racism that is definitely present in the white gay male community. We didn't think that had been talked about before in a movie.

RG: You also see the machinery of the economics of the neighbor-hood at work. They can't really afford the place [they're living in] and it is kind of inevitable that they are going to boot Tomas out in order to spruce that apartment up and get top dollar for the rental. It is not like they have scads of money and are able to do whatever they please. There is a crunch, an economic imbalance in their re-lationships.

WW: In early Fassbinder films like *Fox and His Friends* [1974], there is an interesting situation involving the dynamic between gays with money and gays without money. We wanted to address this issue with Carlos. We were also really interested in class differences

Still from Grief *(1998), courtesy TLA Releasing*

Still from The Fluffer *(2001), courtesy TLA Releasing*

within the Latino community. Magdalena's family is in a very different economic bracket than her cousin's family, and this leads to a lot of tension.

It's done very well, and you also get into issues of white liberal guilt.

RG: We wanted to comment on these very issues that twitch the nerves of NPR listeners. The funny thing was, a lot of idiot journalists thought it was our own liberal guilt and that the gay couple in the film were a projection of ourselves. We always found it kind of weird, although we knew when we cast Dave Ross [as Gary, the manipulative gay man] that people might make some assumptions, because he's British and Wash is British. But he was the best actor for the part, that's why we went with him. As a writer, you put yourself in all the characters. I wouldn't say that there is absolutely nothing of us in those characters, but less so than in Magdalena and Carlos or any number of other characters in the movie.

WW: There's a lot of Richard in Aunt Silvia!

RG: Yeah. At the same time, we wanted to point out something we haven't experienced—which is what it feels like to be fetishized by the white gay community when you're a minority. We talked about the movie with a Latino gay men's group and a lot of them were like, "That was my life up there on the screen. Sometimes being objectified as the hot Latin guy can be fun, but it can also be dehumanizing—you need a bit of support."

WW: Carlos is a new type [of coming-out story]. He'd come out on the Internet, so he'd already formed his identity before coming into physical contact with gay people. This is something that has really only been happening in the last ten or twelve years. The way he is found out for being gay is his dad finds the websites that he has been visiting. He is thrown out of the house, literally, for a cyber crime, for going somewhere on the Internet that his parents didn't approve of. When he meets James and Gary and is invited to their party, he sees the whole mainstream gay scene for the first time and he doesn't identify with it. I think a lot of gay people still have problems identifying with mainstream gay culture. We don't all like the same things or want to look the same or listen to the same music.

The New Queer Cinema of the mid-1980s and early '90s, with films like *Parting Glances*, was important but also set up this aesthetic ideal where all gay men were white and lived in an urban center.

RG: The whole thing about the New Queer Cinema was this freedom, where we could vilify ourselves and talk about dark desires. It was a climate where you could experience a range of emotions about what gay meant in society. Since the mid-'90s, I feel there is this emphasis on rainbow-colored consumerism. All the big corporations started to advertise in gay newspapers, influencing the gay community to live this lavish yuppie lifestyle. We wanted to do something as a counterpoint to that.

We've been *Will and Grace*d.

WW: I did a documentary on that subject called *Totally Gay!* in 2003, looking at gay history from 1990 to the present. It talked about the fact that gay liberation has been co-opted because the corporate world found out that "gay equals money." If they put gay images on TV, more people watch. If there is a gay image in a music video, then more people buy the CD or download the track. The pink triangle of the early '90s has turned into the green triangle at the top of the pyramid with the eye in it.

RG: It is such a double-edged sword, because you want to see yourself in mainstream media, but the moment you do you go, "Ah, I want to go back."

WW: Leave civil rights to market forces and that is what you end up with.

Wash, I understand that the inspiration for the kindly relative who takes in the young outcasts in *Quinceañera* was your own uncle.

WW: My great-uncle Tom was my grandmother's twin who never got married but helped bring up my mum's generation during the Second World War. He also helped bring me and my brother up. When I was eleven, my parents split up and he moved in as a third parent. He would cook and clean and look after us and was just this beautiful person who didn't judge us. He was my emotional bedrock to get through my teenage years. I always wanted to write a character in a movie that would be based on Tom.

Quinceañera also has its roots in British Kitchen Sink drama. It is based on *A Taste of Honey*, a 1961 film where a pregnant teenage girl gets booted out of her home and moves in with a gay guy she meets in a shoe shop. The gay guy is very unapologetic, and they just form this little family together. It is a very touching and beautiful movie. We'd seen that about a year before and had that scenario in the back of our minds as a very interesting [plot] to transplant to East LA.

Todd Haynes executive-produced your film.
RG: He's been a friend for a long time and we always read each other's scripts and exchange feedback. When he read this script, he was really excited about it. We included some of his notes in a rewrite and sent him the first cut. It gave us a huge boost when he agreed to come on as executive producer. He is, let's face it, one of the greatest filmmakers working today.

How does it feel knowing that the Latino community has embraced the film?
RG: It was a huge relief to have people we trusted tell us that we got the details right—people like Miguel Arteta [director of *Star Maps* and *Chuck & Buck*]. We assumed that he might be critical of it because of us being non-Latinos, but instead he was like, "You just got it—you got the Chicano seal of approval." He made a speech at Sundance, saying that this movie made him feel great about being an outsider. And Latino audiences have been amazing, every one from Mexican grannies to Pasadena teenagers coming up to tell us how the movie touched them.

What about the reaction in Los Angeles, where you live and where the film is set?
RG: It is such a segregated city. We had a screening once on the West Side and a woman said, "Thank you for showing me a culture that is right at my doorstep that I never knew existed." A lot of people in LA don't know about Echo Park culture.

WW: It's the amazing thing about Los Angeles: it's a Spanish name, a Spanish-speaking city, and is the most filmed city in the world, and yet very few films have been made about the Latino community. It's a gross disparity that really needs addressing. There have been a lot of Latino television shows coming up in the last few years, but there hasn't yet been a corresponding rise in cinema: a strong, indigenous Latino cinema.

FILMOGRAPHIES

Richard Glatzer:

Quinceañera (feature) (co-director and co-writer with Wash Westmoreland), 2006

The Fluffer (feature) (co-director with Wash Westmoreland), 2001

Grief (feature) (director and writer), 1993

Maxie's World (TV series) (writer), 1987

Wash Westmoreland:

Quinceañera (feature) (co-director and co-writer with Richard Glatzer), 2006

Gay Republicans (short documentary) (director and writer), 2004

Totally Gay! (short documentary) (director and writer), 2003

The Porno Picture of Dorian Gray (feature) (director and writer), 2002

The Fluffer (feature) (co-director with Richard Glatzer), 2001

Animus (feature) (director and writer), 1999

Dr. Jerkoff & Mr. Hard (feature) (director and writer), 1997

Naked Highway (feature) (director and writer), 1997

Toolbox (feature) (director and writer), 1996

Squishy Does Porno! (short film) (director and writer), 1995

John Greyson: Activist with a Movie Camera

Though John Greyson is arguably best known for his 1996 stage-to-screen adaptation of *Lilies*, a gorgeous, elegiac work about young gay desire in prison that garnered the Genie Award (Canada's version of the Oscar) for best picture, his cinematic career had an underground, low-budget beginning.

As a young man, Greyson moved from London, Ontario to Toronto with the determination that he would join the city's burgeoning artistic community as well as its increasingly politicized queer community. His early video work, which challenged traditional documentary filmmaking practices, dealt with contemporary social issues, with a particular focus on gay and AIDS-related subject matter. In *The World is Sick (Sic)* (1989), Greyson creates his own reportage on the World AIDS Conference, held that year in Montreal, with a drag queen playing a mainstream news reporter whose ambivalence and disdain for the subjects of gays and AIDS is all too apparent. *The World is Sick (Sic)* relentlessly, and justifiably, prods and skewers the media for its poor handling of the AIDS epidemic. Greyson manages, on a shoestring budget, to remind audiences that sanity lurks elsewhere, all the while never taking himself too seriously.

His feature debut, *Urinal* (1988), depicts celebrated queers throughout history, Langston Hughes, Frida Kahlo, and Michel Foucault among them, who gather to discuss police interrogation and bathroom sex. Five years later, Greyson again fused his activism and intellect with a playful formalism in *Zero Patience* (1993), a musical about the AIDS epidemic and the medical/industrial complex. The film challenges the so-called Patient Zero theory that gay journalist Randy Shilts put forward in his 1987 book, *And the Band Played On*, which blamed the arrival of AIDS in North America on one promiscuous flight attendant from Quebec. Greyson gleefully deconstructs the blame game, using dance and song (and comedy) to underscore the absurdity of such scapegoating. After *Zero Patience*, Greyson set about to adapt another writer's work, taking the play *Les feluettes* by Quebec playwright Michel Marc Bouchard and adapting it for the screen as *Lilies*, which remains his most acclaimed film to date. Greyson followed this with *Uncut* (1997), his hilarious documentary/drama hybrid that riffs on circumcision, censorship, and various rumours about former Canadian Prime Minister Pierre Trudeau. Greyson then made the feature *The*

Law of Enclosures (2000), a sombre tale of tortured relationships based on the novel by Dale Peck and starring Sarah Polley and Diane Ladd. After directing some episodic television, including episodes of *Queer as Folk* in 2001–02, Greyson co-directed and co-wrote with Jack Lewis *Proteus* (2003), a moving period film about two prisoners in a South African prison who are executed for sodomy in 1735.

Throughout his cinematic career, Greyson has always leapt head first into thorny political and sexual issues, never afraid to traverse territory some might consider taboo. His dense, politically challenging work tends to galvanize audiences, often polarizing both critics and moviegoers alike, but represents a crucial reflection of the times from which they came. Greyson's oeuvre recalls Fassbinder's famous quote about making movies rather than throwing bombs.

The following interview is drawn from two conversations Greyson and I had over the past five years.

Has being gay directly shaped your work?

Looking at my work over two decades, it has been very directly informed by gay and AIDS activism, in all its permutations; I just hope the sense of humor has also accompanied that. [Being gay and an artist has] been in lockstep since the beginning. I decided to come out and be an artist and move to Toronto in the same year, 1978. At times I've dealt with other subject matter [in my work], but the [idea for a film] often rises out of my personal stake in sexuality, and my involvement with activists' work around these issues.

Looking back on some of your early video work, it seems very time-specific, reacting to certain crises in the gay community at that time. As well, video technology has changed dramatically over the years. What strikes you when you look at your previous video work today?

It's interesting, the first gut reaction is to the time and the people involved. Watching *The Jungle Boy* [1985] is all about watching the people in it who are now gone. Colin [Campbell] died from cancer, Renee Highway from AIDS. There's that reverie of memory, and the videos become a form of diary, a photo album in some respects. How do they speak to audiences today? [My early] films were being made in the context of a real conflict between the artistic community and the Canadian censor board. Showing those films to students today [is different because the mainstream idea of sexual] imagery is different. Pride Day [Toronto's annual gay and lesbian celebration] has become Toronto's biggest cash cow; there's also the mainstreaming of gay content.

You directed some episodes of the Showtime television series *Queer as Folk* **[between 2001–02]. Some of those risqué scenes were quite amazing to see on television, even if it was cable.**
That's water cooler fodder for girls at the office the next day. Just as *Sex and the City* had its own particular gauntlet within popular culture, so did *Queer as Folk*, though in a much less interesting way. I think *Queer as Folk* will be forgotten almost immediately, while obviously a greater claim can be made for *Sex and the City* in terms of its impact [on mainstream culture's perception of sexuality]. I think the most interesting thing about *Queer as Folk* will be what comes after it. I directed four episodes and had the best time. I couldn't believe I was being paid for it. But like all episodic TV, the director has no say in the script and can't change a word. I knew a lot of the other *Queer as Folk* directors and much of the cast and crew and we shared the same frustration: we were living in an age when *Six Feet Under* was showing us what good screenwriting can be, even within the context of mainstream television, and we were stuck with [the character] Brian's unrelenting whining. I like watching *Queer as Folk* with the volume down; it works better. And that's ironic because the show had very talented writers like Brad Fraser and Michael MacLennan, who were consistently handcuffed by the plot outlines they were handed—and then their drafts would be completely rewritten by the producers, which, of course, is the norm in television.

You took a unique approach to the political issues surrounding bathroom sex in *Urinal* **[1988] by having six queer historical figures talk about them.**
That grew out of my work with the Right to Privacy Committee of Toronto, which was organizing against the bathhouse raids of Toronto in 1981. I watched the public go to the police barricades to support the bathhouses, but at the same time ignore those who were getting arrested in public washrooms. Why were these guys not worthy of our concern? Because the public washrooms were

seen as outside of the realm of our consideration. Bathhouses were a part of the community, they were seen as a place where gay men went to congregate. Many of the guys caught in public washrooms were identified as straight, so they did not receive the similar sisterly support. The film is a response to emerging theories of sexuality from the 1970s. The shadow of Foucault hangs heavily over that piece, his expansive notion of social history being vital to understanding the social construction of a particular phenomenon. Thus, we dug up these six very unwilling, not openly gay, activist figures from our past—like Sergei Eisenstein and Yukio Mishima—to deliver various forms of discourse on the phenomenon of sexuality and public toilets. By casting the net broadly, we were trying to say that our political interventions should be informed by this larger project of social history. The wonderful thing about *Urinal* was that I didn't have a clue what I was doing. I just went in and did it, going where angels fear to tread. If I'd known what I was getting myself into, I'm not sure I would have run with it.

I was intrigued to learn that you created *The Making of Monsters* [1991] in large part as a reaction to the Canadian Film Centre's rejection of your *Uncut* script [to be accepted into its comprehensive film development program for up-and-coming filmmakers].
Yes, they rejected the script, an epic twenty-minute piece about [Canadian prime minister] Pierre Trudeau and circumcision. If truth be told, it wasn't all that good, but still. [*Laughs.*] There weren't any copyright issues involved at that time, but they still said, "No can do. You can't say those sorts of things about Trudeau." To their credit, they were completely upfront about it. I thought that I could either have my hissy fit, take my toys and go home, or I could see this as a unique opportunity. *The Making of Monsters* [a musical short about homophobia released in 1991] was the fastest script I'd ever written. [The Canadian Film Centre] gave me approval almost immediately; I think they were just so relieved that I was off the Trudeau thing. If that rejection hadn't happened, I never would have made *The Making of Monsters*, so it was okay in the end. That film was also very much a product of that moment—I had been reading Brecht and various Frankfurt School theorists at the time, and as well, I was struggling with this feel-good liberal realism that Norman Jewison [Canadian film director, producer, and actor who founded the Canadian Film Centre] embodies. I

wanted to explore all of those things and do so critically, and the Centre seemed like the place to do it.

With *Zero Patience* [1993], you took a daring movie musical approach to the issue of AIDS.

[It was seen as daring by] the larger mainstream public. But within the ACT UP activist community, *Zero Patience* was just paying tribute in a larger form to what so many video artists, activists, performance artists, and filmmakers were already doing—taking the feistiness of ACT UP and throwing it in the face of the Reagan administration, the pharmaceutical companies, and the homophobic public. *Zero Patience* was inspired by my involvement in AIDS Action Now in Toronto in the late '80s, and was really about taking those activist techniques of humor and irreverence and applying them to the scapegoating that was going on. The film was meant to play very much like the anti-*And the Band Played On*. Sure, the book remains an important documentation of Republican indifference to the epidemic, but author Randy Shilts constructed the narrative around a very sexy sub-plot—the demonization of Air Canada flight attendant Gaetan Dugas as a queer vampire—in the interests of making it a bestseller. And of course that was what got the book sold. Probably Shilts was thrilled because it was more money for him, but it meant that readers didn't remember Reagan's criminal indifference, but rather, the contagious promiscuity of a single gay man. Right up to the end of his life, Shilts remained a very anti-activist, mainstream, anti-sex figure within the gay movement.

Lilies [1996] represents a shift from your previous films, as it was an adaptation of another writer's work.

That remains one of the nicest collaborations I'd ever had. Working with Michel Marc Bouchard [who wrote the original stage play, *Les feluettes*, and its screen adaptation] was really incredible. Whatever problems I had, they were more to do with the distributors and the producers. There were a lot of cooks in the kitchen, shall we say! I'd been formed and socialized not by the film industry, but by an art community, where authorship is everything. The film industry is the opposite; it seems that anyone with bucks is able to buy their way into an opinion. Bouchard was great, though, because coming from theater, he had a wealth of experience knowing how to collaborate with directors, and he had never done film before, so there was a great collaborative process between us. It was fun to take this very theatrical work and keep it theatrical but with a cinematic language. It didn't end up like a play on film; we managed to make it very cinematic. We pulled together an amazing cast. Of all my work, that one seems to be the crowd pleaser, for sure.

How did *The Law of Enclosures* [2000] come about?
I'd been trying to develop a dramatic version of a kiddie porn scandal that happened in 1995 in London, Ontario, but the funders were just not having it. The working title was *Chicken*, and sadly, that script became a turkey and got put back in the deep freeze. Telefilm [a Canadian government agency that subsidizes the film and television industry] was not going to touch it. So I looked around at other projects that were out there. I had just read Dale Peck's novel *The Law of Enclosures* and was interested in adapting it to film. In the process of adaptation, things got convoluted, shall we say. The novel was set in Long Island, and we moved the story to Sarnia, Ontario, partially due to funding considerations, but also due to the fact that I thought if we were going to shoot [in Canada] then we may as well set the film here. Then for money reasons, we ended up shooting it in Winnipeg. Winnipeg as Sarnia [as Long Island].

You've said when *The Law of Enclosures* came out, you spent a week in bed trying to get over the reviews.
If I'd had an utter conviction that what we'd done was right, then I wouldn't have had such a problem with [the response]. I did end up feeling like the film I'd wanted to make was not the film I'd made. It was the cooks in the kitchen thing again. Cineplex Odeon, the distributor, was very hands on, and even told us at one time that the film had to have a happy ending. Thank God we resisted that! That working relationship [with the distributor] is probably the worst I've had in the industry. There was a lot of fighting with them in the editing room. But to be fair, no one was holding a gun to my head. We fought some things and went along with others. I regretted the whole process; not just certain conditions, but the whole process. I learned that I never wanted to work that way again.

Your next project was *Proteus* [2003], though, which was far more positive.
Yes. Learning our lesson from *Law of Enclosures*, we went into pro-

duction with no distributor, which gave us a lot more freedom. The budget was far less—about $500,000, as opposed to $2 million—but it gave co-director Jack Lewis and I far greater freedom.

Your work tends to polarize audiences. An article in *The Advocate* from 1997 said that *Lilies* was one of the best films of the year, but noted that everyone seemed to either love it or hate it.

It's tough to talk about my work overall, but *Lilies* really stands out because for the first time it was someone else's script. I also think *Lilies* divided critics less than my other work. I certainly know there have been detractors, [*Village Voice* critic] Jim Hoberman being one. His review really hurt because he's one of my favorite critics. In all my work, I try to occupy that no-man's land between a pomo avant-garde practice and mainstream storytelling, using humor as a bridge. So sometimes I please no one. There are people who don't like the form, who react against it because it's against the cinematic grain of character-driven storytelling. Whether using the musical form [in *The Making of Monsters* or *Zero Patience*] as a way to subvert classic realist narrative, or mixing documentary and narrative elements into an impossible story [in *Uncut*], such hybridity divides the troops. In different ways over the years, my aim has been to take the formal, aesthetic, and political strategies of what we used to call an avant-garde to move a project into user-friendly territory using devices like music and humor; to also make it come from a gay context, and then see who would watch. The results have been mixed, but the great thing has been the permission [economic and cultural] to try these things—being able to go to the Canada Council [for the Arts, an arts funder] and say, I want to make buttholes sing, and them saying, Okay.

You once said, "All my films make arguments," while some gay directors and writers talk about "maturing" and getting away from cinematic didacticism—moving beyond the political messages in their movies.

I think there's a difference between engaging in debate and standing on a soapbox. In some ways, a better word for me is dialogue, because these are debates I have real stakes in, like the representations of AIDS in the first decade of the epidemic, or policing the gay community, or circumcision [*laughs*]. And often, I don't necessarily have answers. I really envy people like Svend Robinson [the

David Gale, Charles Azulay, and Howard Rosenstein from Zero Patience *(1993), courtesy Toronto Film Reference Library*

Danny Gilmore (as Vallier) and Jason Cadieux (as Simon) in Lilies *(1996), courtesy Toronto Film Reference Library*

first openly gay Member of Parliament in Canada], whose job description was to stand on a soapbox and have answers, to proceed from a position of rhetorical certainty. I think part of why he was such an effective politician is because he was able to go to an ethical and political place and make a decision, take a stand. I often find with the issues I choose, my mind's never quite as made up. *Urinal* is about this sort of complexity: trying to say that this subject of the policing of public and private sexuality can't be reduced to simple slogans. Maybe that would be the through-line of the work I've tried to do, trying not to reduce things to simple slogans.

A lot of us gay filmmakers invoke 1991, the year when [Derek] Jarman's *Edward II*, [Todd] Haynes's *Poison*, [Gus] Van Sant's *My Own Private Idaho*, and [Sally] Potter's *Orlando* were released. Experimentation was back in vogue, and our stories could be told in complex, innovative ways. And then—bam—the pendulum swung back, and we were watching *Philadelphia* [1993], having queer and AIDS issues explained to us like we were five years old, to parrot Denzel Washington's catch phrase from the film. But it'll probably swing back again. These things never go away; they come back to haunt us. There's this incredible nostalgia for the late 1960s and early '70s independent cinema right now. Which would be a relief, after something like *Good Will Hunting*: sadly, there was a lack of gratuitous nudity to make up for the stupidity of that script. I think they should have had a really long skinny-dipping scene for about half an hour.

Something that intrigues me right now are the positive image arguments that we're having all over again. In the past ten years or so, I've heard you and numerous other queer directors say you were sick of positive images of gays and lesbians and didn't want to see any more. But still, when I look at the debates surrounding a film like the romantic comedy *The Object of My Affection* [1998], which I didn't think was such a terrible film ...
Well, no, because you wanted to ask him [actor Paul Rudd] out on a date.

[*laughs*] ... but in doing press for the film, [director] Nicholas Hytner was saying, "No limp wrists, no slashed wrists, I wanted to show gay men in a positive light." It was like reading Vito Russo's afterword in *The Celluloid Closet*.

Part of that is that we really do live in two different worlds: there's indie art cinema, and then there's Hollywood. What Hytner knows is the negative Hollywood stereotypes of the '60s and '70s and to some degree the '80s—he's still reacting to that. I think one of the interesting things is that sometimes our arguments gallop way ahead of our practise. An example of that is our debates around AIDS representation in films [in the early 1990s]. People, myself included, were saying that we didn't want any more AIDS melodramas that are based around grief; we wanted activist, fight-back films, representing the anger and power of our community. But of course, we were talking in a vacuum, because there had been at least two actual AIDS melodramas by that point—*An Early Frost* [1985] and *Longtime Companion* [1990]. American activists who beat up on those early efforts, weak as they might be, missed the point that Hollywood had abdicated complete responsibility until *Philadelphia*.

How many positive images of homosexuals have we seen in the history of Hollywood?

I think the vast majority of audiences have no choice [of what films they really want to see], they don't get to see European cinema, they certainly don't get to see independent cinema. They get to see television. And to its credit, TV—or at least, [the Canadian cable channel] Showcase—and video stores have been a big source of my queer cinema education. That's really important to discuss: the difference that TV and home video have made to a new generation.

Most people working in film buy into the dominant narrative of [building] a career: make the calling-card short [film], which leads to a feature, which leads to the Sundance premiere, which leads to the next film which goes to Cannes.... Of course, it never works that way, but it doesn't undermine the power of the narrative to make a new generation of filmmakers conform.

Do you feel your personal experiences have an impact on your films?

The work that I do tends to come from debates that touch me, that move my life. *Zero Patience* came from what I saw my friends going through. I was living in New York in 1981 when the first diagnosis happened, so I remember very well the growing awareness of the gay cancer or plague, and the way the media was so eager to scape-

goat. That left a very raw scare [in the community] that I was eager
to speak to. [With film,] I figured out a way to do so [many years
later]. The stories tend to come from a personal place, but they
don't necessarily have any of the trappings of autobiography. The
personal is buried quite deeply in the work, but it's certainly there.
[Toronto video artist] Richard Fung and I have had an ongoing talk
about audience: the emerging model of what a gay activist/artist
could be grew out of the '70s, and the model was very much about
speaking for the community, "For my people," but what happens
when so-called community spokespersons like Randy Shilts are
on the opposite side of the barricade? Richard's formulation is really apt: he talks of speaking from a place not of agreement, but
from a point of debate, so instead of speaking *for* the community,
he's speaking *from* it. Maybe it's idealistic, but I like the idea of
cinema as a dialogue, where the viewer is considered a partner in
a thoughtful exchange. Of course, some audiences don't want to
think—when there's a choice between the latest [experimental
documentary by] Harun Farocki and *Buffy the Vampire Slayer*, sometimes you just need Buffy.

FILMOGRAPHY

Fig Trees (short film) (director), 2003
Proteus (feature) (co-writer and co-director with Jack Lewis),
   2003
Made in Canada (TV series, various episodes) (director), 2001–
   03
Queer as Folk (TV series, various episodes) (director), 2001–02
Paradise Falls (TV series, various episodes) (director), 2001
Packin' (short film) (director and writer), 2001
The Law of Enclosures (feature) (director), 2000
Uncut (feature) (director and writer), 1997
Lilies (feature) (director), 1996
After the Bath (short documentary) (director and writer), 1995
You Taste American (short film) (director and writer), 1994
Zero Patience (feature) (director and writer), 1993
The Making of Monsters (short film) (director and writer), 1991
No Way Charlie Brown (short film) (director and writer), 1990

The Pink Pimpernel (short film) (director and writer), 1989

The World is Sick (Sic) (short film) (director and writer), 1989

Urinal (feature) (director and writer), 1988

Angry Initiatives, Defiant Strategies (short film) (director and writer), 1988

The ADS Epidemic (short film) (director and writer), 1987

You Taste American (short film) (director and writer), 1986

A Moffie Called Simon (short film) (director and writer), 1986

Moscow Does Not Believe in Queers (short film) (director and writer), 1986

To Pick is Not to Choose (short film) (director and writer), 1986

The Jungle Boy (short film) (director and writer), 1985

Kipling Meets the Cowboys (short film) (director and writer), 1985

The Perils of Pedagogy (short film) (director and writer), 1984

Changing the Current (short documentary) (director and writer), 1984

Manzana Por Manzana (short documentary) (co-director with Maryanne Yanulis and Eric Shultz), 1983

Breathing Through Opposing Nostrils (short film) (director and writer), 1982

Clockwise from left: John Schlesinger, Bryan Singer, John Waters, Randal Kleiser, Ian McKellen, David Hockney, Gus Van Sant, and Greg Gorman, photographed by Greg Gorman, courtesy Randal Kleiser

Randal Kleiser and legendary director George Cukor on the set of Grease *(1978), courtesy Randal Kleiser*

Randal Kleiser: Greasing the Wheels

As a filmmaker, Randal Kleiser is a man of apparent contradictions. He is at once at home within the Hollywood studio system, but has also managed to buck it. He is a competent director who has crafted sentimental family films that would please the most conservative lobby groups, as well as a few naughty, skin-baring flicks. Most of his films are entertainment-oriented and do not appear to challenge or confront the status quo, yet in 1996, Kleiser made *It's My Party*, a heartfelt feature about a man who decides to commit suicide rather than face the final stages of AIDS and holds a party to mark the impending occasion.

In the 1960s, Kleiser attended the University of Southern California's film program, meeting up with such future film directors as George Lucas. Kleiser financed his education by working as a model and actor (he appeared as an extra in *Camelot* in 1967 and *Hello, Dolly!* in 1969). In 1972, Kleiser made his directorial debut, *Peege*, a film based on his own family's story. His ability to tug at heartstrings was clear, earning Kleiser assignments such as the made-for-TV movies *The Gathering* (1977), about an estranged family reuniting one more time before the father dies, and *The Boy in the Plastic Bubble* (1976), in which John Travolta plays a teen grappling with an immune-deficiency disease. When the studios were searching for a suitable director to bring the massive stage hit *Grease* to the big screen, star Travolta suggested Kleiser, who landed the gig. The film adaptation of *Grease* became a cultural landmark—the last gasp of the once-hugely-profitable musical film genre and the second feature (after 1977's *Saturday Night Fever*) to confirm the emergence of Travolta as a bona fide movie star and major box-office draw.

Kleiser's filmography has since been eclectic, to say the least. He's helmed a number of mid-budget projects that can best be described as vanilla, while also slipping a few mainstream erotic films such as *The Blue Lagoon* (1980), about two teens (one of whom is a young Brooke Shields) stranded on a tropical island who discover their sexuality, and *Summer Lovers* (1982), about tourists who form a sexual threesome while on vacation in the Greek Islands. And more than a decade later, Kleiser's *It's My Party* is a grade-A tearjerker, referencing the period when men diagnosed with HIV were left with few options.

Though Kleiser has often stated that he doesn't feel he has a gay sensibility as a director, Raymond Murray notes in his book *Images in the*

Dark: An Encyclopedia of Gay and Lesbian Film and Video that Kleiser's oeuvre "shows a predilection for delving into the lives of individuals who are outsiders to society-at-large" while also addressing "elements of growth and personal discovery." Kleiser's work is eminently accessible, but when he is at his best as a filmmaker, it's no less thoughtful as a result. We spoke in the spring of 2006.

You were born in Philadelphia but ended up in Los Angeles. Why did you move there?
I was accepted to the University of Southern California Film School. I had researched which were the best film schools and USC was the one I wanted to go to because it was in the middle of Hollywood. It was a great program. I've actually taught there since.

In 1966, you had a role in a short film directed by George Lucas. What was that experience like?
It was called *Freiheit*, which means freedom in German. It was about a German student, played by me, escaping across the border into West Berlin and getting machine-gunned along the way.

Why did you want to become a film director?
I used to make 8mm films in high school, before there was Super 8. Ever since I was ten years old and saw the parting of the Red Sea in *The Ten Commandments*, I wanted to become a director. Then I went through the whole USC film program. My Master's thesis film was *Peege* [1972], a personal story about my grandmother in a nursing home. Film executives at Universal saw the film and they hired me to direct television.

By the mid-1970s you had become known in the industry as a capable director. Were you open about your sexuality during that period?
It didn't really seem to be an issue. I knew a lot of people in what you'd now call the "gay mafia." Some of them helped me, gave me jobs. I think Howard Rosenman was the first guy to give me a TV movie, but I never discussed with him anything about being gay. He just hired me because he was at the same parties and had seen my Master's thesis film. On the sets there was never any discussion of who was gay or who was straight or anything like that, you just did the work.

I watched *The Boy in the Plastic Bubble* [1976] a couple of months ago. That film is like a quintessential '70s movie of the week. How was it working with Travolta back then?

Up until then he'd only done supporting roles onstage and [the TV comedy series] *Welcome Back, Kotter*, which made him popular. He was thrilled to be the lead so he was pretty easy to work with at that time. He suffered from insomnia so he would call really late at night and ask which take I'd be using for a certain scene; like I was sitting up thinking about that.

You directed *Grease* [1978] shortly thereafter. How did you land that directing job?

Travolta requested me and I think that's how it all came about. I was originally supposed to do *Saturday Night Fever* and I met with some producers in New York and talked about directing that. Before I knew it they decided that I should do *Grease* instead. I'm glad they did that because I was much better suited to *Grease*.

We think of musicals as being quite gay. When I interviewed you earlier, you said that while you were directing *Grease* you weren't really thinking about a gay sensibility.

I didn't have to because [gay co-producer/co-screenwriter] Allan Carr was there putting his touch all over it. He and [co-screenwriter] Bronte Woodard put a lot of [gay] references in the screenplay. But I took a lot out and often went back to the original play so it ended up being [a combination of both]. If we'd gone with what they had done, it would have been very different from the play.

Before filming each scene, I would sit down with the actors and compare the screenplay with the play, then I'd cut and paste pieces of each scene together. When I was finished we'd read the edited script to Allan and Bronte and they would say, "It looks great."

I always read it as a coming out story, in that Olivia Newton-John's repressed sexuality is unleashed by the end of the film.

Well, that was kind of always in the play, but I think that in the costuming and the makeup we turned up the volume. We certainly enhanced that moment, yes.

And all those crotch shots of Travolta?

That wasn't on purpose. We were just shooting so quickly that it just happened to be there in front of the camera.

Yeah, right.

No, really. I had to survive through it. It was a very big crew and it was fifty days and the last thing I was thinking of focusing on was anyone's crotch.

That was one of the last mega-hit film musicals. There has been a bit of a revival in recent years with *Chicago* and *Dreamgirls*, but of course the genre is not what it once was. Do you see a time when film musicals could come back to where they were?

Music videos have filled a lot of that void. One of the reasons that I think *Grease* was number one at the box office was because people were hearing the *Grease* soundtrack on the radio all the time, and in order to see this music with images they had to see the movie again. They liked the idea of seeing picture and sound together and that sort of led to music videos. Now you have music videos all over the place—on your iPods, everywhere. So film musicals today require a fantastic story and great music coming together in a certain way [to attract audiences].

Your next two films, *The Blue Lagoon* [1980] and *Summer Lovers* [1982], became cult movies. They are both very sexual, libidinous films that flew into the mainstream under the radar. Was it difficult to make them?

The Blue Lagoon was a project that I wanted to do before *Grease*. It was a book written in the 1800s that I really loved. I didn't even know that there was already a movie made in the 1940s based on it. I took it to Allan Carr to see if he would finance it and he declined. I liked the story of the innocence and the sexuality emerging, so I kept trying and trying but [the studios] said, "No one wants to see a movie with just two people in it." Finally, Frank Price at Columbia agreed to do it. I asked Douglas Day Stewart, who wrote *The Boy in the Plastic Bubble*, to write the screenplay because I knew that he was very good at writing about adolescent sexuality. We went through the book and examined what it would be like for these kids to grow up together in seclusion and added details that weren't in the original, like masturbation and menstruation. I really didn't have any problems from the studio. They let me do whatever I wanted because I was in Fiji and they were in LA. At the time, restrictions were lighter on filmmakers. Today, one wouldn't be able to make that film. Here we had a fourteen-year-old Brooke

Olivia Newton-John, Randal Kleiser, and John Travolta on the set of Grease
(1978), Paramount/Photofest

Christopher Atkins in Blue Lagoon *(1980), Columbia Pictures Corporation/
Photofest*

Shields lying mostly naked under Chris Atkinson, who was nineteen, and they were doing love scenes. I would be arrested today if I filmed that.

When the movie came out, people were calling it kiddy porn, which shocked me—it seemed so totally innocent to me. [In response,] Frank Price took a big ad out in the *New York Times* quoting some psychologist or sociologist who had said the film was just natural love and all this innocent stuff.

Did you have a similar experience with *Summer Lovers?*
Summer Lovers was made for a company that was going through a change of hands. When that happens, whatever movies are being made by the outgoing regime are pretty much not supported by the incoming regime. There was supposed to be an $8 million ad campaign to get that movie out and into all the theaters, but the new studio owners dropped the promotional budget to $2 million, so it just died. It didn't really get a lot of attention because it was just not in many theaters. It was discovered later on VHS and DVD.

When the film came out, everyone who saw it wanted to go to Greece.
At the University of Arizona, we had about 500 college kids at a sneak preview. They were cheering over the nude beach scenes at the beginning of the film.

Speaking of cult movies, it's really interesting to look at your 1988 film, *Big Top Pee-Wee* [sequel to 1985's *Pee-Wee's Big Adventure*]. Many people regarded the first film as a gay cult film even though it was directed by Tim Burton, who's straight. In the sequel you directed, though, Pee-Wee is involved with all these women, making him seem really heterosexual.
Big Top was written by Paul [Reubens, a.k.a. Pee-Wee Herman] and he wrote and produced it, so I wasn't in control of it. I was pretty much there to help Paul get his vision on screen. He wanted to have the longest kiss in film history and the studio wanted him to cut it down. There was a lot more to that kiss that Paul wanted to keep in, but the studio wouldn't let him.

Paul's very clever, it all came from him. That was his movie. He saw himself more like a Harry Langdon or a Charlie Chaplin character.

Like, in the scene where the storm comes and the wind is blowing and he goes horizontal, that was right out of a silent movie. His makeup also made him look more like a silent movie kind of character.

Vito Russo's book *The Celluloid Closet* chastises those in Hollywood who are not more forthright about being gay, and not doing enough to fight negative gay stereotypes. What are your thoughts on this?

I was just focusing on my work and trying to keep my private life and my career separate. [However, sometimes] I do a little layering. I did a movie called *Getting It Right* in 1989, which had a gay subplot. It was about straight thirty-one-year-old virgin who loses his virginity to a couple of women. He has a gay friend, so everybody thinks he's gay. It wasn't until *It's My Party* [1996] that I dealt with [gay themes] straight on.

What led to *It's My Party*?

It was based on a real event. At the beginning of the AIDS crisis, being diagnosed with AIDS was a definite death sentence. At the time, there were no pills, no treatment—if you got it, you died. That movie is like a slice of history now, a time before there were [HIV drugs]. There were these parties where people with AIDS would say goodbye to everyone and then check out. I attended one of these parties. It was very life changing for everyone at the party because it was so intense. Everyone knew what was going to happen, but we were still trying to have a good time and cheer up the guest of honor. It was very bizarre and overwhelming and so I felt I had to make a movie about it.

What was it like to work with Roddy McDowall? He never really came out during his life, but everybody knew he was gay.

He had somehow gotten a hold of the script for *It's My Party* and saw that part and wanted to play it very badly. He campaigned for it. I was very happy to have him play this Catholic character who's against the suicide. At that time, he must have known that he had been diagnosed with whatever he died of [cancer]; it wasn't that long after the film that he died.

You've also directed a lot of family films. Do you find it difficult to change gears?

For family movies, I just shift my point of view a bit to that of a child. I made a film called *Red Riding Hood* [2004], which is for kids, but it has a lot of campy moments in it for adults. Henry Cavill plays the hunter, and he's a really great-looking actor. Red Riding Hood is smitten by him, so I photographed him well for all the gay guys in the audience. Another film, *Lovewrecked* [2005], is for teenage girls, and there is a lot of eye candy and references for guys too. The casting of it was pretty cool; Chris Carmack from *The O.C.* and Jonathan Bennett from *Mean Girls* are running around in bathing suits.

How do you find the climate for gays in Hollywood now?
I don't think it is a big deal. Just look at the Oscars [in 2006]: *Brokeback Mountain, Capote*. I don't think that there are any stigmas right now. It seems like a non-issue. Now there are two or three gay cable TV channels and Bravo does all kinds of gay stuff, so it's like it has become more absorbed into the culture.

Why do you think Hollywood is so out of step with the rest of the country's homophobia?
The crossover is *Brokeback Mountain*. That's the way that middle America looks at homosexuality. [Being gay] is not [shown as] something that is a good choice or can work out, and that's probably why audiences liked it. They saw the film as their point of view rather than a happy movie where everyone ends up living these long lives and having great relationships. *Brokeback Mountain* is the beginning at least of middle America looking at the [gay experiences], even though it comes across as something that is not positive.

Do you plan to make another film like *It's My Party*, that deals with gay characters?
I don't have any plans, but if one came my way that was well-written, I would consider it. I just want to do movies that have great scripts. I'm totally open to that. It would have to be something that I would feel I would do a good job with and would also have some commercial appeal. I've done quite a few movies just because I wanted to, but they didn't get out there. I had to alternate between commercial films and ones that I was passionate to make.

Are there any gay directors that you looked up to when you were young?

I got to meet George Cukor and hang out with him. John Schlesinger is another one who I became friends with. Both of them visited the set of *Grease* the same day. John Waters is a good friend. I've met Gus Van Sant, and he was terrific. But when I was growing up, *Cabaret* [1972, directed by Bob Fosse] was a really influential movie on me because I saw it during a period of my life when I wasn't really out, and the movie is kind of all about that. *Fellini Satyricon* [1969] was influential as well. Even though Fellini wasn't gay, that movie was very liberating for me.

FILMOGRAPHY

Randal Kleiser is director of the following which are features unless otherwise noted:

Lovewrecked, 2005
Red Riding Hood, 2004
Royal Standard (TV series), 1999
Shadow of Doubt (a.k.a. *Reasonable Doubt*), 1998
It's My Party (director and writer), 1996
New York News (TV series), 1995
Honey I Blew Up the Kids, 1992
White Fang, 1991
Getting It Right, 1989
Big Top Pee-Wee, 1988
North Shore (writer only), 1987
Flight of the Navigator, 1986
Grandview, U.S.A., 1984
Summer Lovers (director and writer), 1982
The Blue Lagoon, 1980
Grease, 1978
The Gathering (TV feature), 1977
Portrait of Grandpa Doc, 1977
The Boy in the Plastic Bubble (TV feature), 1976
Dawn: Portrait of a Teenage Runaway (TV series), 1976
Esecutori, Gli (a.k.a *Street People*) (co-writer only), 1976
Family (TV series, two episodes), 1976
The Rookies (TV series, one episode), 1976

All Together Now (TV series), 1975
Starsky and Hutch (TV series), 1975
Lucas Tanner (TV series, two episodes), 1974
Peege (director and writer), 1972
Marcus Welby M.D. (a.k.a *Robert Young, Family Doctor*) (TV
    series), 1969

Bruce LaBruce: Punk Art Porn

Toronto artist, writer, and filmmaker Bruce LaBruce has forged his own creative path, fusing the aesthetics of hardcore pornography with arthouse traditions, resulting in a varied and rich cinematic oeuvre that has remained largely low-budget and outside of the mainstream. His sensibility can be traced back to Toronto's 1980s underground punk scene; LaBruce was so appalled by its homophobia that he produced a series of zines in response to it.

LaBruce's first film, *No Skin Off My Ass* (1991), is an erotic punk fable, and an unusual ode to Sandy Dennis's performance in Robert Altman's 1969 oddity *That Cold Day in the Park*. He continues to write and direct sexually explicit films, including the semi-autobiographical *Super 8½* (1993) and *Hustler White* (1996). The latter was an international sensation with its often hilarious, unblinking portrayals of kinky sex and fringe characters. It also gained a great deal of press and notoriety due to LaBruce's clever casting: the film's leading man, Tony Ward, was a porn actor who had dated Madonna (and who appears in her infamous "Erotica" video).

With his two most recent films, LaBruce further pushes the envelope of his own art/porn or homocore subgenre: *Skin Flick* (1999, a.k.a. *Skin Gang*) involves race-related rape of gay men of color by neo-Nazis, and *The Raspberry Reich* (2004), deals with sexually experimenting German terrorists. Both films were released in two versions: an explicit one for hardcore porn distribution, and another, softcore version for the festival and repertory cinema circuits. In *Raspberry*, LaBruce makes numerous nods to Dusan Makavejev's subversive masterpiece *W.R.: Mysteries of the Organism* (1971) while taking on the left, concocting a merry band of sexual renegades who fashion themselves on the infamous Baader-Meinhof Gang, the most prominent left-wing radical group in post-World War II Germany. The film itself is alternately hilarious, erotic, and disturbing; creatively and stylistically speaking, it is as though Bertolt Brecht, Rainer Werner Fassbinder, and Radley Metzger are engaged in a threesome.

LaBruce has also worked extensively as a photographer, cofounded the Canadian film journal *Cineaction!*, and for many years wrote a weekly newspaper column in Toronto. What follows is a longer version of an interview that first appeared in the winter 2004 issue of *Cineaction!*

Bruce LaBruce, photographed by Candy Pauker,
courtesy Bruce LaBruce

Your films have always had a great deal of sexual content. But with _Skin Flick_ [1999], you moved into outright pornography. Was that liberating in a sense?

It was an experiment. It was liberating in that so many people have said my films are extreme because they have real sex in them, or they're not extreme enough because compared to hardcore porn they're actually rather mild. Therefore it was rather liberating to actually jump in and do something full-on like that. But you know, ultimately, it was rather disturbing for me: the "moral implications."

The neo-Nazi stuff?

Partly that. I personally think that ninety percent of current gay pornography is sort of fascist anyway. The very nature of it; it's so slick and single-minded. There's no multiplicity of meaning; it's just pumped out, and the way it's manufactured is very cynical, even though the company I did it for, Cazzo Film, is quite exceptional and was not sleazy, and none of the actors were on drugs, although they all took Viagra. Because Cazzo is based in Berlin, they have a very different attitude toward sex. There isn't that guilt around it the way there is in North America. They don't have the same kind of Puritanism. But for me, I felt a bit like I was still participating in this fascist industry. It was heavy too. The race issues I dealt with were very heavy.

Were you worried about the responses you were going to get with _Skin Flick_?

I wasn't worried. But I was concerned that it might not be a lot of fun.

I'm wondering what you think of the mainstream representations of the porn industry, like _Boogie Nights_ [1997].

I didn't like the movie. I thought it was very derivative. It was too much like [Quentin] Tarantino. I didn't think it was really about porn; it was about pop culture. It didn't have to be about porn at all. It could have been about anything. It's a very trendy, mainstream Hollywood view of porn—that it's hip to like it. But it didn't raise any of the meat-and-potatoes issues surrounding porn. One interesting angle they took, though, was the advent of video and how it has influenced porn. When video came in, it really did change things.

You can see a broad range of influences when looking at your work, everything from Sandy Dennis movies to porn. What would you say are your primary influences?

I've been very influenced by the Hollywood era of the late 1960s and early '70s. I was a teenager when I saw all of those films on TV. It was interesting because a lot of them are a deconstruction of Hollywood itself, an implication of Hollywood. It was an extremely bleak period—the dismantling of the '60s and of that idealism. Those films are also very sexually frank, like *Rosemary's Baby* or *Midnight Cowboy*. [Robert] Altman movies have been a big influence too, like *That Cold Day in the Park, Images,* and *3 Women*: mainstream movies dealing with extremely disturbing, psycho-sexual scenarios. I remember as a kid thinking that this must be what pornography is like. Trying to figure out exactly what these movies were all about was one of my favorite pastimes. I've always been a media creature. I was glued in front of the TV my entire childhood. Six hours a day, minimum.

I recall seeing you on television discussing your reading of the film *Making Love* [the mainstream 1982 film about homosexuality that some argue was groundbreaking]. I found your points interesting—it's such a widely discredited film.

I think it's really accurate. In many respects it was quite prescient. Harry Hamlin has this health crisis which seems like a foreshadowing of AIDS. He's represented as being relatively open about his homosexuality. The kissing scene is quite frank. People scoffed at it because it was about bourgeois characters, but much of the gay population is bourgeois. It's sort of like the flipside of *Cruising* [1980, about the serial murders of gay men in New York]. These two films represent the dual realities of the gay community. *Cruising* has been reclaimed; an article in *Sight & Sound* proclaimed it a lost masterpiece. There was an interview with its director William Friedkin in *Gay Times* in which he said he had to cut so much of the film that it almost became incoherent. That's why a lot of people find it so interesting, because it's so incoherent and strange.

In *Hustler White* [1996], there are a lot of wild images of gay life, which some find horrifying. Do you bristle when you hear arguments that depictions of gay life should always be positive images?

Well, *Skin Flick* makes *Hustler White* look like a walk in the park, so I had to get over it. It's such a non-argument for an artist or a film-maker. The idea of making ideological art is, I think, anathema to any serious artist. The idea of kowtowing to someone else's political agenda is just ridiculous. I felt very influenced by that ideological conformity for a while, like in *No Skin Off My Ass* [1991] when the sister says, "If you're a skinhead, you're stupid, and if you're queer, you're smart. It's a simple rule for kids to remember." It was an upbeat message that it's cool to be a fag, but it's also naïve and simplistic: we were trying to be provocative in other ways which undercut that straightforward message.

After that, some friends made me aware that I was still kind of brainwashed by my Marxist-feminist education at university. They slapped me out of it, which liberated me because at a certain point I was intimidated by feminism and afraid to represent women in certain ways. I got freed from that and got to be more intuitive about the ideas that I have and the narratives I wanted to write. I try not to think about [my work] in terms of having a gay agenda.

"Hell is Other Faggots" is the title of a chapter in your 1997 book *The Reluctant Pornographer*. Do you ever get accused of being self-hating?

Well, I don't think I've ever been called that to my face. Though I probably am. Comedian Scott Thompson always talks about em-bracing your self-hatred. My whole argument is that homophobia is almost genetically encoded into the human species because it's a safeguard to protect the procreation of the species. If you look at it on that level, philosophically, there's a certain truth to it. The whole thrust of life is to reproduce and procreate, and anything that goes against that will always be suspect. No matter how many advances that seem to be made by gay culture, I don't think it will ever go away entirely. After the lynching of Matthew Shepard, the gays were like, "Oh gee, maybe we haven't made as many advances as we thought." What shocked me was that people were surprised, and I can't believe it doesn't happen more often.

John Waters once said to me that in terms of filmmaking, gay is not enough.

Oh my God! That's brilliant!

Are you dismayed when gay people spend too much time focusing on their sexuality?

Well, I'm often dismayed, even by myself. One of my great paradoxes is that I spend a lot of time railing against gay culture as it exists. But then a lot of my work is still based around those kinds of issues, dealing with questions of identity and how I deal with my own homosexuality. It is something I would love to get away from, but I feel I haven't dealt with it completely myself. Maybe I never will. I resent being raised at a time when you felt you had to conform to the ways of being gay that are presented to you. The old school of homosexuality from the 1950s and '60s was about nonconformity and individualism. It was all about escaping from all of that. When the '80s happened, following the advent of activism, it became really conformist, an effort to get approval from parents and society. I think it has ruined everything.

Hustler White screened all over the world. Were there any international reactions that surprised you?

The French freaked out over _Hustler White_, in a good way. It was well reviewed by all of the major publications there. They tried to give it an X rating, but it was appealed in the press. A former minister of culture even publicly defended the film. Based on its popularity, my two previous films were also released in France. There was this kind of appreciation of the films as cinema. They were seen less as products of a gay sensibility and more as products of a cinematic sensibility, which was really great. In Great Britain and Japan, my films have a certain cult cachet, and they really push boundaries because in both countries you can't show penetration. I think that _No Skin Off My Ass_ was partially responsible for the fashionable new clone look in London—the shaved heads, the skinhead clothing. Certainly Canada is the country I'm least known in and least appreciated. I've had trouble getting distribution here over the years, but that's partly because it's such a small market.

It's fascinating that you have a considerable Japanese teen girl following.

There's a lot of speculation about why Japanese girls like western gay male products: movies, books, and comics. I just think that they find it a genre that they can relate to, partly because it's about damaged characters, or characters who are delicate or sensitive. I think they relate to the feminized male in different ways.

So why the hustler fixation?

Skinheads and hustlers are the two types I keep coming back to.
I don't know why. Of course there are personal reasons. I had a
hustler boyfriend years ago, and it [the relationship] was extremely
crazy and painful. I got to know the hustler mentality inside and
out. For the gay avant-garde, the hustler is a pretty important archetype. From Kenneth Anger to Warhol to Jack Smith, their films
were either about hustlers or incorporated them in some way. It's
also partly style-based, though; there's just something very cool
about the look. It's not always about politics. And in terms of
skinheads, I've always been interested in the fetishization of fascist imagery in gay art. I think there's been a lot of denial about
the implications of that. It might be why Tom of Finland is such
a touchstone. Uniforms are so revered and worshipped. I think
there's something very fascist that's built into the homosexual experience or homosexual drive. Its extreme elements are liberated
because we're freed from the idea of procreative sex. There's also
this potential for the extreme fixation on sex. In Freudian terms,
it's built into the sex drive. There's a certain aspect of our sexual
drive whose function is to defeat the object of love, or even to an-
nihilate it. And then you could talk about someone like Robert
Mapplethorpe, who fetishizes black men in extreme ways. That's
sort of what *Skin Flick* is doing by juxtaposing these two extreme
fetishes. The neo-Nazi, racist skinheads are watching black porn
while they have sex with each other, and they have an image on
their kitchen wall of a black man with a huge dick. I guess it's
about fetishizing the other.

**Some of the filmmakers I've interviewed who mainly work in
the mainstream film industry have discussed ways in which homophobia has affected them.**

I've been held back as much by homophobia within gay culture,
probably more so than by straights. Certain elements of the gay
press and politically correct elements of gay culture have not held
me back directly, but they've ignored me or tried to pretend that I
don't exist. I've also had a lot of people on the film festival circuit
be extremely supportive, however.

**Your most recent film *The Raspberry Reich* [2004] couldn't have
been more timely, what with George W. Bush's second-term victory. It seems we really are ready for a gay intifada.**

I think so too. I'm hawking the T-shirts now, which have slogans about joining the gay intifada on them.

You've said it's almost better that Bush got elected than John Kerry.
It probably would have been more disastrous for the Democratic Party for Kerry to be elected. Not that I really care about the Democratic Party, but they would have inherited this unwinnable war and a huge deficit and probably another terrorist attack. It's probably better that Bush be left to deal with it. His administration will mess it up and maybe that will usher in a Democratic regime. But you know, the Democrats are more conservative than Canada's Conservative Party, so it's not much of a choice. It seems like the whole system must be destroyed!

I find it ironic because they're saying that the issue of gay marriage pushed many into Bush's camp and yet the people who are pushing for gay marriage are often gay conservatives.
It was a total wedge issue, along with stem-cell research. It's typical of navel-gazing gays to think that their little struggle is more important than saving the world. I don't believe in gay marriage anyway. Obviously, I believe in civil unions and equal rights under the law, but to try to have it sanctified, it's totally unnecessary. I hate gay conservatives as much as I hate hip-hop corporate blacks who have loads of money and claim to represent the interests of disenfranchised, low-income blacks. Driving around in Bentleys and drinking champagne. Get rich or die tryin'. It's the oppressed becoming the oppressor, which is my favorite theme.

Why did you choose the Baader-Meinhof gang?
The Baader-Meinhof were the most glamorous terrorists from that era. They wore leather jackets and drove BMWs. They were very style-conscious and had a hip look. They came out of the anti-Vietnam war '60s movement and had that student protest energy behind them. They were intellectuals. Ulrike Meinhof was an academic before she became a terrorist. There were rumors that Andreas Baader was a male prostitute before he became a terrorist, and that Gudrun Ensslin had appeared in a porn movie. All these things combined to give them quite a mystique. When I was a punk in the '80s, they were very compelling. My friends and I read *Hitler's Children* by Jillian Becker, which was the first book to

present their whole history. I have a bit of German blood in me, and my producer happens to be from Berlin, which has given me a pretty strong connection to that city over the past fourteen years. I find it intriguing that the Germans went from being this Aryan überpower to being a kind of downtrodden nation. All the great shame they've suffered; perpetrating the Holocaust has created a certain humility in many of them. Yet they still have that German pride about them, an ego. It's an interesting psychology, this restrained ego.

I read your work as deeply ironic, especially *The Raspberry Reich*, and your last film, *Skin Flick*. Are you ever concerned about how certain audiences might interpret them?

I don't see it as ironic, exactly; I think of it as paradoxical. I always make the distinction. Irony or sarcasm involves saying one thing and meaning the exact opposite. Paradox is saying two things that seem contradictory but are nonetheless true. With all of my work, if I seem to be sarcastic, I'm probably not. There's usually some ambiguity there. I hope that comes through in these films. On one hand it seems to be critiquing and taking the piss out of the radical left, but on the other hand it's clear that I'm quite sympathetic to many of their views. So there's a bit of tension there and people don't know exactly where I'm positioning myself, which I think is a good way to make a movie. Sometimes I think I don't even know where I'm positioning myself. I had heard that *Team America: World Police* was a very right-wing film, that they had gone in a politically incorrect direction with it. But when I saw it, I just thought it was hilarious, the way they attacked sanctimonious, left-leaning Hollywood stars who probably hurt Kerry's campaign more than they helped it because of their pomposity and presumptions; that they really believe they have any idea what's going on when they live in that Hollywood dementia is ridiculous. When they were getting blown away at the end [of *Team America*], I was cheering along with my Muslim boyfriend.

Some film critics on the lib-left were quite uncomfortable with that.

I thought it was great. I mean, come on, we live in a world of *Celebrity Boxing* and *Celebrity Deathmatch*. I found it quite cathartic to see Helen Hunt being blown away, and I don't mean by a twister.

Still from Hustler White *(1996), courtesy Bruce LaBruce*

Still from The Raspberry Reich *(2004), courtesy Bruce LaBruce*

Some felt it was ultimately a right-wing film, but Team America itself in the movie was a group of ludicrously jingoistic soldiers, who had no idea that blowing up the Eiffel Tower was an overextension and misuse of their power.

I know. Their leader is basically a pervert who tricks one of his male followers into giving him a blowjob. It goes after everybody, which is what I like to do too. With *Skin Flick* I went after the extreme right-wing, and with *The Raspberry Reich* the extreme left-wing. Some were freaked out by *Skin Flick* because I presented the neo-Nazi skinheads more sympathetically than the bourgeois gay couple. But then the skinheads were also critiqued and ridiculed when Cameltoe, the female character, pointed out to them that they were essentially a bunch of faggots. She was pointing out their hypocrisy and contradictions.

You have made hardcore and softcore versions of your two most recent films, so you must think about your audience when you're making a film.

Honestly, I made the last two films for porn companies with the stipulation that I would also be able to make softcore, narrative-heavy versions of them, with the hardcore version marketed to a different audience. It's just a little experiment to do it this way. If I made a full-on hardcore version with interminably long sex scenes, which is what porn conventions dictate and how porn is consumed, the films wouldn't be shown on the festival circuit or in legitimate theaters.

The complications surrounding any shoot must be more difficult when the film is pornographic. I heard you got kicked out of a couple of places where you were shooting.

With *The Raspberry Reich*, there was a central location we had in east Berlin, an apartment belonging to some friends of my producer who were moving out and who let us use it before their lease was up. We went to the trouble of putting up those huge blowups of Che Guevara and Angela Davis and the Baader-Meinhof gang everywhere. We were shooting sex scenes in the elevator and had people running in and out of the building wearing ski masks and carrying guns. We didn't have any permits, so people in the building started to freak out a bit because, you know, if you see people running around in ski masks carrying guns in your apartment hallway, it tends to scare people these days. Otherwise, you can get away with stuff in Berlin that you could never get away with in New York, for example. When we were shooting the scene in which the four terrorists are doing the kidnapping, and they're wearing masks and carrying guns as they jump out of the car, a cop drove by and didn't even bother to stop.

It's an alternative lifestyle.
Exactly. Or a domestic dispute.

How do you find working with porn actors?
I really like it. I get irritated with people who harp on how bad the acting is in my movies. It's like, have you ever seen a Warhol movie, or a John Waters movie, or a Paul Morrissey movie? There's an actual appreciation for bad acting or for non-actors acting. So what if the actors don't stay within the lines of the coloring book when they're acting? There are these rules around suspension of disbelief that are absurd. It's a given that they're non-actors. Acting in porn is acting, but they're never really challenged beyond basic lines. I try to get them involved creatively in the process and make sure that they know what the movie is about. The challenge is to get them to give a performance. I'm not trying to turn them into professional actors, but their interpretation of their roles is important. But some people can't get past the "bad acting" because it's not in that overly emotive Hollywood style. I actually like the notion of bad acting.

It's very Brechtian because the performances draw attention to the filmmaking process.
Yes. I post-dubbed the entire movie, and four of the main characters were dubbed by professional actors. And the readings of the professional actors weren't that much different from those of the porn actors. Pretty much everyone in Germany speaks English, but their English isn't always perfect.

I think the post-dubbing was very intriguing because it gave a further sense of distance from the characters, of everyone being disembodied.
I knew I was going to have to dub it when we were making it because the sound recorder had no idea what he was doing, but I was fine with it. I was pretty sure I could make it work. With some of

the actors, because they were [from what used to be East Germany], their second language was Russian, not English, so I got the sense that they were simply saying the lines phonetically and didn't even understand what they were saying, sort of like ABBA used to do. It ended up working, surprisingly. I had hoped it would give the feeling of a 1970s exploitation movie, which it kind of did. In terms of casting, I think of myself as an "availablist," a term I borrowed from my friend the artist Kembra Pfahler: I work with whatever I'm presented with, with whatever is within my means.

You've said you think most pornography is innately fascistic.
The fact that so much of it is so univocal, so relentless, sure. But I actually think the porn world is this sort of collective unconscious where people work out their dark or politically incorrect fantasies. In that respect, it doesn't have the same kind of morality you'd expect in certain mainstream representations. Porn is based on sexual power and submission and domination, and those things are played out regardless of race or gender. It's rare to see that in the pop culture. Racially based fantasies are rare in mainstream culture, but you see them in porn all the time; all those things that are cleaned up in the public discourse are fair game in pornography. I guess that's not fascist, but amoral. It's about sexual power dynamics. In terms of gay porn, I think it's fascist in that it has that same iconography as the Third Reich: the idea of the perfect body. It's body fascism. They're often fucking like pistons, very mechanical. It's that kind of fascism, like Leni Riefenstahl's *The Olympiad* [1938].

I certainly thought about *W.R.: Mysteries of the Organism* as I watched *The Raspberry Reich*.
That was my primary influence. I literally stole entire scenes from *W.R.* That's how I make most of my films, by just taking bits and pieces of other films and putting them together in a different context. That scene of the two guys kissing in the street was an homage to the scene in *W.R.* with Jackie Curtis and her boyfriend eating ice-cream.

Like *Mysteries of the Organism*, you juxtapose shots that are erotic with images that are violent and disturbing. There's a photo you did that's on your website that I find very disturbing: two men, one giving the other a blow job, and they are both covered in

blood, or what appears to be blood…. You have told the story of getting beaten up by a punk years ago, but finding it hot later.
I used to get beaten up by punks. My hustler boyfriend was involved in the punk scene and we saw each other for a while and then broke up. I bumped into him a year later and he'd become a neo-Nazi skinhead. He needed a place to stay, and I didn't know how into Nazism he was, so I took him in. I kept ridiculing him for his views and beliefs and trying to talk him out of it. Then he got fed up with me one night and beat the crap out of me. So I kicked him out. But there was definitely a sexual dimension to it. On some level, I got turned on.

There seems to be a direct correlation between who was slamming our head against a locker in high school and who we find sexy now. It's like the Stockholm Syndrome or something.
Sure. So many gay black men have contacted me about the scene in *Skin Flick* where the black character gets raped by the white skinhead and say they found it incredibly hot. It really turns some people's crank. I go out with a Muslim now. The dynamic of going out with someone who's a devout Muslim from the east when you're born in the Christian west—there's a whole load of social and political signifiers that arrive in the bedroom. You can't divorce the sexual act from historical and political realities when you're dealing with people from two different cultures and races and backgrounds.

So who ties who up?
I'm openly bottom. Some people say that they're versatile, but I don't cushion it. I'm a bottom.

It's funny that you relate filmmaking to a terrorist act, which relates to Fassbinder's famous quote: "I don't throw bombs, I make movies."
When we were making *The Raspberry Reich*, I got the sense of what it might be like to be in the Baader-Meinhof gang. It was "guerrilla filmmaking." We had to make everything on the cheap, on the fly, without permits, running around the city with guns, trying to be secret, getting found out, and then getting kicked out of places. In one location where we shot, a bunch of kids found out that it was a porn set, so they climbed the trees to peer in the windows. It felt like we were under surveillance. Even on that level, the whole

thing felt like a terrorist act. Just to manage to make a porn film about terrorism and get it shown at major film festivals feels like a coup.

Three prominent filmmakers carefully timed the release of their films in an effort to sway the electorate in the 2004 US election: Michael Moore (*Fahrenheit 9/11*), John Sayles (*Silver City*), and Mike Leigh (*Vera Drake*). Do you ever consider making more mainstream films?

I may move in that direction. I have a script for another porn, called *LA Gangbangers*, about Latino gangs in LA. It's very much about racial and sexual identity, and would complete the porn trilogy [with *Skin Flick* and *The Raspberry Reich*]. There's a brown woman in the script who talks like a black woman but wants to be white because whites are the minority in the world and it's cool to be in a minority, so that's why she wants to be white. It's another low-budget art porn movie. I have a few other things in the works that are in development. For me, filmmaking is just a process that's very gradual. I would never force myself into something. I let things happen organically. As an artist, I wait for paths to present themselves. It's feasible that I could go in that direction. I think when you're ready to do something, you do it.

FILMOGRAPHY

Bruce LaBruce is director and writer of the following which are features unless otherwise noted:

The Raspberry Reich, 2004
Skin Flick, 1999
Hustler White, 1996
Super 8½, 1993
Slam! (short film), 1992
The Glennda Orgasm Show (TV, various episodes), 1992
No Skin Off My Ass, 1991
Home Movies (short film) (co-director with Candy Parker), 1988
Boy, Girl (short film), 1987
I Know What It's Like to Be Dead (short film), 1987

Robert Lepage: Art in the Danger Zone

Though Canadian Robert Lepage is known primarily for his work in theater, he is also an accomplished filmmaker. He burst onto the theater scene in 1985 with *The Dragons' Trilogy*, an aesthetically daring piece, which he directed and co-wrote, incorporating skating and dance in a history of Chinatowns in Montreal, Quebec City, and Vancouver. He then wrote, directed, and acted in *Vinci*, a one-man show, inspired by the life of Leonardo da Vinci, staged in both Canada and France in 1986. He also created the international phenomenon *Needles and Opium*, which had extended runs in New York, London, and Montreal; in it, Lepage performed an elaborate trapeze act while meditating on Miles Davis and addiction. His other theatrical work includes the epic, seven-hour play *Seven Streams of the River Ota* (1994) about the Holocaust, Hiroshima, and AIDS, and the internationally celebrated *Elsinore* (1995), a one-man version of *Hamlet* in which Lepage played all of the roles. In a word, the quality and consistency of Lepage's theatrical output is staggering.

It was in the early 1990s that Quebec film producer Denise Robert convinced Lepage to make the leap to film. (Robert went on to win a 2004 Oscar for Best Foreign Language Film for *Les Invasions barbares* [*The Barbarian Invasions*], directed by her husband Denys Arcand.) Lepage's first film, *Le Confessionnal* (1995), set in Quebec City, features a dual storyline that unfolds in both 1952 and 1989. In the early setting, a sixteen-year-old Catholic girl deals with the shame of being pregnant; thirty-seven years later, a man seeks the truth behind his identity as he grapples with the death of his adoptive father. Lepage's first filmmaking effort included references to the medium, including Alfred Hitchcock's 1953 film *I Confess*. When *Le Confessionnal* premiered at the Toronto International Film Festival in 1995, it won broad critical acclaim, and subsequently won several Genie Awards (Canada's version of the Oscars), including best picture and best director.

Lepage followed *Le Confessional* with *Le Polygraphe* (1997), based on his own stage play which was inspired by his personal experiences being interrogated by police after one of his closest friends was murdered. In 1998, Lepage made his most controversial film to date, *Nô*. Quebec critics in particular cried foul; here was a film set during the October Crisis of 1970, when Quebec nationalist terrorists took politicians hostage in order to promote their cause of an independent Quebec separate from Canada. But the film's tone was often comedic, and even though almost thirty years had passed, some Quebec critics felt that was not enough time to depict the subject in this kind of light. But after receiving a drubbing by French critics in Montreal, *Nô* won the Best Canadian Feature Film award at the Toronto International Film Festival. In 2000, Lepage made *Possible Worlds*, marking two more firsts for the director: his first film in English, and the first time he made a film based on someone else's material (John Mighton's play of the same name). *Possible Worlds*, which stars Tilda Swinton and Tom McCamus, depicts the parallel lives of one man who lives in several different dimensions.

The following year marked one of the strangest junctures in Lepage's career. He spent the month of August preparing his latest show, *Zulu Time*, to premiere in New York City. The play was an intricate reflection of the anxieties induced by new technologies; in particular, Lepage said he was drawing on his own hatred of airports. *Zulu Time* was to feature Islamic extremist terrorists and footage of planes flying into buildings. It was to debut less than one week after the Sept. 11, 2001 terrorist attacks. Alas, organizers cancelled the Manhattan premiere of *Zulu Time*, due to the show's eerie prescience.

In 2003, Lepage created *La face cachée de la lune (The Far Side of the Moon)*, what some consider his most autobiographical work, dealing with one man's struggle to reconcile with his brother (both roles played by Lepage), after years of a tortured relationship and the death of their mother.

Lepage's most recent filmmaking effort has been to bring his theatrical work *The Dragons' Trilogy* to the screen, but the Quebec government repeatedly declined his request for funding assistance, so Lepage was forced to shut down the production, much to his dimay.

Lepage and I spoke at the Toronto International Film Festival in September 2006.

What was your childhood like?

Well, I have alopecia. It's a strange disease, actually the contrary to AIDS. My immune system is too strong so in a sense I am defending myself against myself. [Its main symptom] is hair loss at a young age, like five or six years old. That is what happened when I started to go to school, which is the cruellest place to be when going through something like that. [I was losing hair when] the Beatles were popular, when hair was long. Hair was about liberation and so I was very counter to the fashion. I was the object of a lot of cruelty and conflict, so it made me a very secretive and uncomfortable child. It was a strange experience because I felt like I was handicapped, even though it wasn't a handicap. It was an interesting thing for me, because later on it made me see racism in a different way. I grew up in Quebec City, which was [made up of] all white Catholic Francophones. There was a little Anglophone community that was Catholic Irish, but I rarely saw black people, or people from other races. [After losing my hair,] I felt like I had an understanding of how immigrant communities felt and certainly I had a better understanding of civil rights debates that were going on in the United States. Even as a child, I could really relate to it.

How were your teen years?

I suffered from a very severe depression when I was fourteen. I had a bad experience with drugs—I had done some hashish that was laced with opium, and it was my first joint. That fucked me up for about two weeks straight. When I started to come out of it, I sort of flipped. I slipped into a sort of psychosis and entered a two-year period when I was very unsocial. I would rush to school in the morning and then rush home after school as soon as possible and watch [television shows like] *Maude*, and *All in the Family*. That's what I did for about two years.

Did being gay tie into your depression?

Eventually, but in a surprising way, because one would suppose that a gay community which has been rejected [by society] might see me as equal, or give me a chance; but the gay struggle is also accompanied by a desire for physical perfection and all of these things, and I felt chased into a corner. I felt rejected by the gay community because of that.

The gay scene can be awfully conformist.

You have to act straight, look good, look healthy. Since the AIDS crisis, gay men have to look healthy so they are not burdened by the fact that they are a minority or that they are different. So of course, I have never really felt part of that community. I rarely participate [in gay events]. Also, as a screenwriter or as a playwright, the gay characters in my shows just happen to be gay. [Including gay content] is not central to my work, it's just there. I was very surprised one day when I went to a DVD store for a copy of *Le Confessionnal* [1995] to give as a gift to somebody. When I asked the clerk, who didn't recognize me, where I could find it, she said, "Oh, that's Robert Lepage? That's in the gay section." They had put all of my films in the gay section. I just went, "Whoa, wait a minute, what's this?" I wasn't offended, but I was so surprised that they had put me in that category because it is only one of many types of subject matter in my films.

I remember seeing you at a press conference for *Le Confessionnal* at the Toronto International Film Festival, and you were a bit reluctant to participate in the discussion of gay identity. It seemed it was a label that you didn't want for yourself.

It was just that I didn't want to be known as a gay filmmaker, and I didn't see that as being a part of *Le Confessionnal*.

At the same press conference, I asked you, "Do you consider yourself a filmmaker who happens to be gay rather than a gay filmmaker?" You simply responded, "Yeah," and there was some laughter and a few people clapped. I was surprised because *Le Confessionnal* is a film that includes bathhouses and gay characters, but you didn't really want to talk about it. Around the same time, [fellow Canadian director] Patricia Rozema made the film *When Night is Falling*, which has lesbian sex in it, but she didn't want to talk to me about it either.

There's a cultural thing as well. I can't answer for Patricia, but in Quebec we're more in touch with French culture, and in France they never talk about such things. I know that when I go to London, it's always, "So, are you gay?" People want to know probably because in the cultural politics of London or English Canada, it's a hot issue—the closet is bigger or something like that. Of course, it is normal that it would be something that you would want to be discussed and advocated, but in Quebec or in France [being gay] is not a big deal. When [late French president François] Mitterrand died, his mistress and their daughter were present at the funeral. There was absolutely no gossiping about that, it was just there, a reality. [Former Quebec premier] René Lévesque lived with a woman who wasn't his wife and he had an affair with another; it was never an issue. Here [outside of Quebec], you would never have that. Sexuality, whether it is gay or straight, is a big thing here. A public figure needs to show his colors, keep it in the closet, or make a statement. Because I am bilingual, I play in both camps and I know that when you go to Europe it is very clear they are obsessed with where you are [in the closet], whether you are coming out or staying in. It's like when Ian McKellen was knighted by the Queen when he's gay and [British filmmaker] Derek Jarman questioned why he would want to accept such an honor when the House of Lords passed anti-gay legislation. I can't be interviewed without being asked, "So are you married? Do you have kids? Do you have a partner? Are you gay?"

I had an interesting interview a long, long time ago. It was one of the first interviews that I did and one of the first questions was, "Are you gay?" I said, "Well, things are not as definite as that." And the natural response was, "Oh, so you're bisexual?" It's a strange thing. You can't measure the honesty of somebody by exposing his sexual orientation.

I understand that people don't like to be defined by their sexuality, but I think that the more people in the public eye have come out—whether yourself or Ellen DeGeneres or Elton John—the better it is for younger people who struggle with their sexual identity.
It's not a mission anymore. Frankly, I've always been extremely fascinated by gender much more than by sexual orientation. There are many better writers [than me] who want to write about sexual orientation and rights. I was more interested in gender; somewhere in there gender is connected to sexuality and sexual practice, but gender is also connected to myth and other subjects I find that are more interesting to talk about. [Gender] details [in the French language] also interest me. To decide that a table is a female, but a heater is a male ... [objects are] connected to gender. Other languages have gender too. The German moon is male and the sun is female, but in the Latin languages it is exactly the opposite. These are not just linguistic curiosities; they tell a lot about culture. They tell how cultures perceive gender roles or social rank. Culture and language is intimately connected to sexuality. I'm interested in those kinds of issues.

Back to your beginnings: when you were growing up, what led you to a life in theater?
Well, I was very much interested in geography—that was my first love. When I was a teenager in high school, I was also interested in

Patrick Goyette (as Marc Lamontagne) and Lothaire Bluteau (as Pierre Lamontagne) in Le Confessional *(1995), courtesy Toronto Film Reference Library*

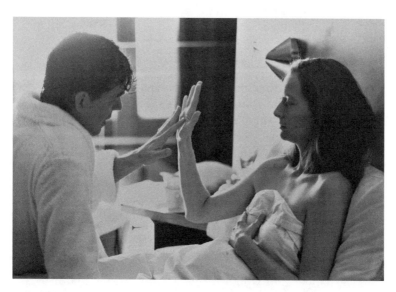

Tom McCamus (as George) and Tilda Swinton (as Joyce) in Possible Worlds *(2000), photographed by Philippe Bosse and courtesy the Toronto Film Reference Library*

music and art. In Quebec, art was compulsory in high school, and once a student completes two years of one art subject he or she has to choose another art subject. I chose music for the first two years, then I did visual art, then in my fourth year the only thing left was theater. I was a paranoid kid, and what was great about theater was that suddenly I could hide behind a gang. So as an artist, I didn't have to defend my bad guitar playing or my lack of drawing talent or my lack of self expression—it could be the director's fault or the writer's fault. [But as I got more involved in theater,] I started to distinguish myself as a director and I eventually moved on to the conservatory, which was another sort of weird accident. In those days, in order to go to the conservatory you had to have a high school certificate, but I was only seventeen [and still in high school] so I just lied ... well, I didn't lie I about my age, but I lied about my certificate. I said I was doing my exams and I was going to get it once the auditions were done. They accepted me anyway then discovered too late that I didn't have it. I have to admit that I went to theater school way too early. I should have gone a couple of years later because my lack of life experience made the conservatory more difficult. I didn't know about life or love or whatever. But I was really interested in the theater, mainly because, as I said, I could always hide behind other people and disguise myself. I could always try to be myself through a character.

You've said that acting meant that you had to confront fears, and that it was crucial in your development as a creative person.
Absolutely. I'm drawn to what I'm afraid of. I don't really like jumping off the cliff at all, and yet I've chosen a profession where I have to jump twice a week. So eventually I got over it. My life is full of fear at every level: there's always this thing that scares me to death. I don't know why but whenever there's something put in my path, I have to confront it, to dive into it, to solve it. The good moments in our lives are always connected with putting ourselves in the danger zone. Our priorities change when we're in a danger zone. Our ego vanishes in those situations.

So is the danger zone what led you from the theater to film?
Eventually all this led to film, but that also was an accident. [Quebec film producer] Denise Robert saw a stage show I did in London,

came backstage and said I had to do a film. I said, "I don't have training." She said, "You don't need training, you are already a filmmaker." Which wasn't true—I ended up training on the sets.

Le Confessionnal didn't look like a film made by a first-time director.

Yeah, but it wasn't the film I wanted to do. I had way too many coaches, way too many people saying, "That's not film, *this* is film." I listened to them for too long and there was a moment during shooting where I started to think, "I don't want to do that kind of film [that they want me to do]."

You must have been pretty overwhelmed by the critical praise for it.

Sure, but you have to put it in a context. Canadian film wasn't in the same place back then. There weren't as many people interested [in Canadian film] and it was a kind of a *naissance* [birth]. [The buzz about Canadian filmmakers, with] François Girard [*The Red Violin*] was just starting after *Le Confessionnal* was released. But film is not really my first love. I'd like to make films occasionally. I do opera, I do rock shows, all sorts of stuff.

I'd like to hear the story about the inspiration for *Le Polygraphe* [1997].

An actress, who was my best friend, was brutally murdered. I was working as an actor in a show with her and I was the one who walked her home the night she was murdered. Her boyfriend said that she was alone in her apartment when she was raped and killed. Four of us were suspects for months and months: her boyfriend, her ex-boyfriend who was also a producer we were working with at that time, myself, and another guy who was also a close friend; we were put through the mill. It was a strange time. Besides losing my best friend, which is a horrible thing, we were being mistreated by detectives. The only way to get us off the hook was to do this polygraph test.

But the crime was solved and you were all cleared?

About a year and a half later. A guy who just kind of showed up murdered her. He was a lunatic. The experience, and this use of [the polygraph to determine] what is the truth, and how the truth is unimportant in certain cases and totally manipulated in others, inspired the creation of the play and film. I never doubted my innocence, but there was this moment when they locked me up in a cell for hours and hours and they said, "Your polygraph test says that you are not telling the truth." And they let me go crazy and brought me to the edge where I thought, "Oh my God, what did I say that might have been wrongly interpreted? What have I done?" I started doubting so many things, and then after [the test] they said my test was inconclusive, but they didn't tell me why. The manipulation was really incredible. The play was my first attempt at trying to understand what went on. At the same time all of this mess was happening, Yves Simoneau was writing his first feature film. The script he was writing had similar things in it. And he wanted me to play the murderer! I said, "Are you *serious?*" It was very naïve on his part to do that, but I forgave him.

Didn't he write the character as having alopecia, as you do?
Yes. But he was just a young, ambitious filmmaker and I understand where he was at that point.

What inspires you when you sit down to write a piece, whether for the stage or the screen?
I try to make my subject matter as vague as possible. It's good to be in a danger zone; if you know exactly what you're going to write about, that's [too safe]. I try to invite other artists in who are also inspired by the danger zone. When I went to Japan and visited Hiroshima, I came out with a feeling that was overwhelming and indescribable. And that's [the kind of thing that] prompts me to do a show: things that trigger something inside me. [That visit to Hiroshima inspired Lepage's seven-hour epic play *The Seven Streams of the River Ota*.] So I go for that, I don't write a list of what it is I'm going to do and then do it. I think about something I'm unsure of and then I proceed to examine it. It takes time; it means taking a risk. It means falling on my face. It means having terrible opening nights, but wonderful closing nights.

FILMOGRAPHY

La face cachée de la lune (*The Far Side of the Moon*) (feature)
(director and writer), 2003

Possible Worlds (feature) (director and co-writer with John
Mighton), 2000

Nô (feature) (director and writer), 1998

Le Polygraphe (feature) (director and co-writer with several
screenwriters), 1997

Le Confessionnal (feature) (director and writer), 1995

Craig Lucas: The Secret Life of Screenwriters

Screenwriter and director Craig Lucas began his career as a stage actor, appearing in the chorus of Stephen Sondheim's 1979 musical *Sweeney Todd*. He had already begun writing at that point, and in 1980 Sondheim suggested to him that he would probably be much happier if he pursued writing full time. Lucas remains grateful for this advice, telling me that "Sondheim was right."

In 1990, Lucas penned his first feature screenplay, *Longtime Companion*. The film—which marked the first of three collaborations with director Norman René—joined the ranks of the first American feature-length responses to the AIDS crisis, among them Arthur J. Bressan Jr.'s *Buddies* (1985) and Bill Sherwood's *Parting Glances* (1986). *Longtime Companion* garnered a great deal of press for its frank depictions of gay men struggling to survive the epidemic.

Lucas's next two screenplays, *Prelude to a Kiss* (1992) and *Reckless* (1995), were more grounded in fantasy than reality. The film adaptation of the stage play *Prelude to a Kiss*, which brought Lucas a Tony nomination in 1990, was also directed by René. In the film, Meg Ryan and Alec Baldwin play a couple who fall in love and marry; things go awry when Ryan's spirit is exchanged with that of an old man (played by Sydney Walker). Through this unusual plot, Lucas explores the nature of romantic love while slipping in a same-sex kiss. *Reckless* was another collaboration between Lucas and René, in which Mia Farrow stars as a rather shallow housewife who learns, on Christmas Eve no less, that her husband plans to have her killed. She flees the house and sets off on a bizarre journey through every state in the American union, where she encounters a number of off-kilter characters. The style of the film is obtuse, but it is extremely funny, a scathing indictment of American mores. Farrow has cited this as one of her best films. Sadly, this turned out to be the last time Lucas worked with René, who succumbed to AIDS in 1996. Despite the mistaken impression that René and Lucas were personal as well as professional partners, Lucas says their relationship was strictly about filmmaking.

In 2002, Lucas wrote the screenplay adaptation of Jane Smiley's novel, *The Secret Lives of Dentists*. The film, directed by Alan Rudolph, has Campbell Scott as a dentist overcome by suspicion that his wife (Hope Davis) is having an affair. For this adaptation, Lucas won the New York Film Critics Award for best screenplay.

In 2005, Lucas made his directorial debut with *The Dying Gaul*, for which he also wrote the screenplay. In this caustic and often hilarious movie about Hollywood hypocrisy, Peter Sarsgaard plays a gay screenwriter clearly based on Lucas himself. In desperately trying to sell his work, he agrees to take a reasonable fee for a script, on the condition that it be heterosexualized—i.e., the gay couple it depicts will be turned into a male-female relationship. Sarsgaard soon befriends the producer (Scott) and his wife (Patricia Clarkson), and ends up having an affair with Scott, who, as it turns out, is bisexual. *The Dying Gaul* is a wickedly clever and astute film, in which Lucas once again delves into otherworldly fantasy. As a scathing attack on Hollywood and its foibles, it should be required viewing in film history classes. As well, the AIDS epidemic is never far behind, as Sarsgaard's character is recovering from the devastating loss of a lover to the disease.

In the fall of 2006, Lucas was in the midst of writing a script for the stage, and he kindly took time out to talk with me.

You began your career as a performer. How did you get into writing?

I was a writer even as a child of nine—creating puppet plays and magic shows that I performed at children's birthday parties and hospitals. As a college student, I studied to be a poet at Boston University under Anne Sexton and George Starbuck. Then throughout my performing years in New York, I wrote plays.

Critics saw *Longtime Companion* as a major breakthrough in 1990. How did the AIDS crisis become the impetus for this screenplay?

AIDS exploded right into my life in the summer of 1981; there was no corner of my existence that wasn't completely threatened and fractured and, in many cases, obliterated [by it]. Peace of mind, political naiveté, trust, hope, friendship, financial solidity—every single facet of my life was cast into a sudden and terrifying light. It would be remarkable if I had *not* written about it. My lovers, friends, colleagues were getting sick and dying all around me. I was terrified for my life, and it seemed I lived every day and night in a cold sweat of panic and rage. A lot of that remains.

What were your impressions of some of the other early artistic responses to the AIDS crisis, like the plays *The Normal Heart* [1985] or *As Is* [1985]?

Poster for The Dying Gaul *(2005), courtesy Craig Lucas*

Peter Sarsgaard, Patricia Clarkson, and Campbell Scott in The Dying Gaul *(2005), courtesy Craig Lucas*

The Normal Heart is one of the few works of art in recent memory
that changed the direction of public discourse on AIDS at that
time. I remember how many people read that play, before The Public [Theater] produced it, and dismissed it as agitprop.

**Are you dismayed that a younger generation of gay men seem out
of touch with the epidemic?**
Well, I see it as part of the larger picture of the Republican agenda
to make people ignorant about their agency and political issues, to
engender cynicism and indifference. We are swiftly moving into
pre-fascist conditions in this country, and ignorance about AIDS is
but one aspect of that movement or trend.

Longtime Companion **[1990] had its critics. Many felt it only focused on the plight of middle-class gay men.**
Well, it doesn't really amount to a criticism. It's a bit like saying
that *Hamlet* only focuses on the plight of royalty. Yes, *Longtime
Companion* is about well-off people, though one of them works in
a gym. Somehow, given the subject matter, there was an assump-
tion on the part of some that the movie should *not* have been
about those characters, it should have been about ... whatever the
person making the criticism decided the movie should have been
about. How does one respond to that? I wrote about what I wanted
to write about, and what I knew well.

**There was also a single black character in it, who was essentially
the maid. Did you feel that this criticism was justified?**
What was dramatized was true to that moment in that place for
those characters. There is also a female Indian doctor and a Latino
GMHC [Gay Men's Health Crisis, a non-profit AIDS organization]
client in the movie. And the scenes in the hospitals, at political
gatherings, and in the GMHC offices are brimming with African-
American characters and other people of color whose lives have
been ripped open by the disease and who possess agency to varying
degrees. The fact that the rich white male couple have a black maid
is neither out of keeping with reality nor would it have raised eyebrows or alarms from anyone living in New York City at that time,
black or white. Political correctness is of no more use to the movie
than it would have been to the characters and their dilemmas.

Were you annoyed when *Philadelphia* **[1993] was declared the**

first major AIDS feature to come out of Hollywood, when it was released three years after *Longtime Companion*?
No, because *Longtime Companion* did not come out of Hollywood, it was made on a shoestring budget by a publicly funded, independent movie producer in New York City—Lindsay Law at American Playhouse, now defunct—with low-profile actors, and an untrained writer and director. The script wasn't subjected to the kind of vapid gloss that is normally applied by Hollywood producers. *Philadelphia* was a Hollywood movie.

You wrote *Prelude to a Kiss* as a play, then as a film [released in 1992]. It prompts the question: how different do you find the cultures of Broadway and Hollywood?
I can't say that my experiences have been primarily about Hollywood or Broadway. My milieus are not-for-profit theater and independent movies. And in these worlds, the differences are not so marked, though it is true that in the American theater the playwright tends to retain copyright, and this has repercussions for the work: it can more readily be the expression of a single point of view, whereas in movies it is the producer who almost always holds the copyright, and therefore the content is subject to more interference, pressure, groupthink. I don't think it is controversial to say that movies often tend to pander, particularly once the budgets start to increase in the nether regions. Theater is one of the final outposts of uncensored expression in late-stage capitalism, although Broadway is not necessarily any less grotesque and venal than Hollywood. And while it is true that upon occasion a play on Broadway will surprise and challenge an audience, so will a Hollywood movie on rare occasion. When an audience buys tickets to see an independent feature or a play produced by a not-for-profit, however, there is a slightly higher chance they will see something that does not fit into a predictable mold of some other relatively recent, financially-successful prototype with sentimental and/or reactionary content. Most any play or film of any lasting [social, political, or artistic] value causes Broadway and Hollywood producers alike to shiver and run for cover.

How do their attitudes towards homosexuality differ?
Well, neither Hollywood nor Broadway, let us say, are monolithic; the field in each case is made up of individual producers

and artists, and these vary: some producers are more insightful and less cowardly when it comes to challenging an audience. A bloated-budget movie like *Alexander* [2004], where the protagonist repeatedly gazes passionately, tenderly into the eyes of his male lover standing four inches away from him, also glassy-eyed and pillowy-lipped, would have been unthinkable ten years ago. Each member of the audience is ideally changing his or her attitude and understanding of the real world, of identity politics, of every aspect of their lives [as they watch a film]. When *La cage aux folles* came out originally in the French version [1978], I was so tired of seeing screaming drag queens in plays, but I thought the movie was really moronic and irksome, a complete bone to the homophobes. My problem with it, however, had little to do with its achievement or lack thereof. Today, I can view it without a ruffle. Obviously, where someone like Mel Gibson or Tom Cruise is concerned, Hollywood still means homophobia. When the movie of *Prelude to a Kiss* came out, teenagers in the audience groaned and booed when Peter kissed the old man on the lips. Today, no one blinks when the same image flashes before them on their cable TV channel at ten p.m. That said, I still feel that political correctness is applied more pervasively in movies. A very famous movie producer who is gay came up to the producer of *The Dying Gaul* [2005] after our first screening at Sundance [Film Festival] and said he found the movie "hateful" and "very very bad for gay people in general." Gay people in general? What I imagine he meant was, "How dare you show a seemingly nice gay man kill a woman and her two children, that will be bad for us." Who's "us"? Will right-wing gay bashers take comfort in the movie? Do I care? Should I tailor my work to their stupidity? If a racist is going to see the black maid in *Longtime Companion* and feel all gooey-good because the character is right where he or she belongs, goddammit, does that mean what I've written isn't real or valuable? One must be cautious with generalities or abstract notions. Hollywood and Broadway are not coherent entities in all instances, and so the usefulness of speaking of them as such is perforce somewhat limited.

What was the inspiration for *Reckless* [1995]?
It is based on a play of the same name, which I wrote in 1983, early in the AIDS epidemic. It's a fable, in my mind, about the American propensity for running from reality and using "looking on the

bright side" to take no responsibility for one's own actions. To me [today] it is as much about the war in Iraq as suburban banality.

The Dying Gaul raises intriguing questions on Hollywood studios and their hypocrisy. It also marked your directorial debut. How much of this film was autobiographical?

Everything a writer does is autobiographical in the sense that it reflects an imaginative landscape born of experience, but not at all in the sense that it represents some attempt to report on past trauma. I never knew, or knew that I knew, a bisexual Hollywood producer, I was never asked to "de-gay" a script, I never got caught in a triangular relationship with a bisexual man, and I never killed a woman and her children—oh, wait a minute, I take back *one* of the above.

Your first three films were made as a partnership with Norman René. How was it for you to move into the director's chair, as you did with *The Dying Gaul*, after having been solely a screenwriter for so long?

I loved directing. I became a caregiver and someone capable of taking the reins and steering everything, including the script, into the strongest place possible. Norman taught me how to work with actors of all stripes; I sat in the cutting room with him on all our movies together, plus I learned a lot from Alan Rudolph, who directed my screenplay, *The Secret Lives of Dentists* [2002]. As a result, I'm fast, I'm nimble on my feet, reliable, and I come in under budget [as a director].

Do you feel people in the film industry have pigeonholed you because you've written about gay issues and are out?

No, I get all kinds of inquiries and offers. The only thing that has limited my viability in Hollywood is my past record of burning bridges, which I am slowly mending, and the tendency of my work to eschew easy solutions to complex narrative and content challenges.

How did you burn bridges in Hollywood?

My worst scraps with industry folk came from the two movies I wrote that involved gay content, and in both instances, the producers convinced me that those aspects of the movies made my work appear "substandard." But the bridge-burning really was all my doing—I was carrying around a lot of rage after the death of my lover of eleven years and also from the repeated assaults on my theatrical work from the *New York Times*, which completely governs the life of any serious play in America—the critic at the time of *The Dying Gaul*'s stage production referred to it as "a minor tantrum of a play." I was also drinking heavily. So I don't blame the studios, I hold myself responsible.

Vito Russo suggested that we gays are our own worst enemy in Hollywood.
I used to come across a lot of highly-placed gay producers and they were indeed resistant to engaging with gay-themed material. I don't think that is quite the case anymore. I adored Vito. He was immensely supportive of me at the beginning, and his work changed the entire film landscape for many of us.

FILMOGRAPHY

Craig Lucas is the writer of the following which are features unless otherwise noted:

The Dying Gaul (director and writer), 2005
The Secret Lives of Dentists, 2002
Reckless, 1995
Prelude to a Kiss, 1992
Longtime Companion, 1990

Don Mancini and friend, courtesy Don Mancini

Don Mancini: Gays and Dolls

I feel compelled to begin with a confession: I am a huge, massive, and total fan of Chucky, the serial-killing, wisecracking possessed doll who has slashed his way through five successful horror films. The series began in 1988 with *Child's Play*, in which Oscar-nominated actor Brad Dourif plays a serial killer who is finally cornered by police after a harried chase. By chance, he is shot in a toy store, and manages—through some magical spell only ever witnessed in crazy horror movies—to escape his dying body and transport his soul into the body of a talking toy, a "Good Guy" doll, who chirps irritating things on command, like "I'm your friend to the end!" And a franchise was thus born.

In *Child's Play*, Boston-born and Virginia-raised screenwriter Don Mancini managed to inject a hilarious running commentary on the marketing of toys to children, while at the same time creating some bona fide suspense. After possessing the doll, Chucky himself becomes the possession of Andy, the offspring of an overworked single mom. As babysitters get slaughtered and people go missing, Andy becomes Suspect No. 1, but, as Andy explains, it's Chucky who's doing the misdeeds. Mom only becomes a believer when she opens Chucky's back to discover that, despite his occasional chatter, *he has no batteries!* Indeed, the high camp quotient of the *Child's Play* movies was set right from the beginning.

Child's Play became a runaway success, setting the obvious stage for sequels: *Child's Play 2* in 1990, and *Child's Play 3: Look Who's Stalking* in 1991, both penned again by Mancini. The name of the serial killer possessing Chucky, Charles Lee Ray, was culled from the three real-life murderers that franchise producer David Kirschner most feared: Charles Manson, Lee Harvey Oswald, and James Earl Ray. Chucky didn't just kill, he killed with *style*, and in between his gruesome murders—in which victims would be both scared and shocked that they were being skewered by a two-foot-tall doll—Chucky would deliver various expletive-laden one-liners. As he explained to one victim in mid-slaughter, "Don't fuck with the Chuck!"

By the third film, however, as Mancini concedes, things became a bit stale. And this, as the out screenwriter recounts, is when he decided Chucky would go totally gay. For the fourth film, *Bride of Chucky* (1998), Mancini created a new character, a female groupie of Chucky's. Tiffany (played by the busty Jennifer Tilly) resurrects and reconstructs Chucky, who by this point in the franchise's narrative evolution has become an urban legend. Tiffany herself soon becomes locked in the body of another doll, and the two end up on the lam from authorities in a surreal horror doll version of *Bonnie and Clyde*.

Then came the inevitable mating of the two dolls in *Seed of Chucky* (2004), in which Chucky and Tiffany face off over their gender-confused offspring, Glen (or Glenda, depending on who you're talking to). Though there are some scary moments here, by this point the series had entered comedy-horror territory. The film is full of hilarious jabs at Hollywood—as well as playing the doll Tiffany, Tilly plays herself as a struggling, no-longer-ingenue actress—as well as a ludicrous subplot in which Chucky and Tiffany attempt to kick the serial-killing habit via a twelve-step program.

Some may be surprised to learn that both *Bride* and *Seed* made my top ten lists in their respective years of release. Though often dismissed by many critics, I would argue that the Chucky movies—in particular the last two—have all the nerve, gall, bravado, chutzpah, audacity, and brass that the vast majority of Hollywood studio films lack. I'm not alone in my admiration of the franchise; filmmaker John Waters has repeatedly expressed his fondness for the doll, so much so that Mancini rewarded Waters with a supporting role in *Seed of Chucky* (a film that also served as Mancini's directorial debut). Picking up on the film's camp quotient, as well as the heavy referencing of horror film history, film critic Matthew Wilder noted in the Minneapolis weekly *City Pages* that *"Seed of Chucky* has the drunkenly swaggering, who-gives-a-fuck tone of the old-broad horror flicks that followed *What Ever Happened to Baby Jane?"* I couldn't agree more. Mancini's penchant for pushing Chucky over the top with each successive film makes their appeal to someone like Waters make perfect sense. The innate absurdity of a plastic killer leaving a string of corpses in its wake is high camp; indeed, Mancini's Chucky films feel like a fusion of many of his formative influences: '70s horror movies involving children; epic, kitschy disaster movies; and John Waters' films. They are a brilliant collision of calamity, catastrophe, absurdity, and comedy.

Don Mancini lives in Los Angeles, where he spoke with me about his influences and the creation and evolution of Chucky.

When did you come out?
Come out of the closet or come out to California?

Closet first.
In my twenties, both.

Was it difficult growing up gay in Virginia?
Yeah, that wasn't a place you could say you were gay. I fooled
around with guys in high school, but it wasn't anything you ever
spoke about.

Tell me a bit about your beginnings.
I went to Columbia University in New York and studied English.
Then I did the Kerouac thing and hitchhiked across the country. I
worked on a soap opera in New York for a year, doing camera crew
stuff, working at the bottom of the totem pole; someone had to be
in charge of making sure the cables weren't tangled. That's how I
started in the business, literally. But I ended up with a union card
and could do camera work that paid okay, so it was worth it. When
I finished that, I transferred to UCLA.

And that's where you did your film degree?
I never actually finished it. It was during my second quarter at
UCLA that I wrote the first *Child's Play* [1988] and ended up selling it. Much to my parents' chagrin, I left school and never looked
back.

**Do you recall the first horror movie you ever saw and connected
with?**
The first horror stuff I was ever into was the TV show *Dark Shadows*. This was in the '60s and I was very little. I learned the word
"shadow" from that show. The first R-rated movie I ever saw was
The Omen [1976], which made a huge impression on me. I love that
movie, even prefer it to *The Exorcist*. *The Poseidon Adventure* [1972]
was the first movie I ever saw more than once; it was the one that
made me want to make films. That and *The Towering Inferno* [1974];
those Irwin Allen disaster movies made a huge impression on me.

**I love Irwin Allen movies too. Ken Feil wrote an excellent analysis
of those films in his book *Dying For a Laugh: Disaster Movies and
the Camp Imagination*. Were there any other standout influences?**
Jaws [1975] was one as well. It was a transition movie for me in a
way. That film was positioned and publicized as another disaster
movie, but it isn't, really. *Airport 1975* had just come out before
that. There was a smell of a certain kind of movie that was about
disaster at the time. But *Jaws* was impeccably made; it's more like a
horror thriller. From that day forward I was a huge Steven Spielberg
fan. And *Carrie* [1976] and *The Fury* [1978] made me a huge Brian

De Palma fan as well. I think I was drawn to that fantasy of being able to telekinetically punish my enemies. What those movies have in common are these epic, stylized depictions of mass destruction—death and destruction on a grand scale. Like any kid, I was fascinated by special effects. With *The Poseidon Adventure*, I became aware of a presence behind the camera. The special effects that were needed were very impressive. I wonder if there wasn't something a bit gay about those Irwin Allen movies, since they are very over-the-top. They lend themselves to a certain operatic style that's in tune with a gay sensibility; they are very campy. But as a kid, I took them seriously. It was only as an adult that I realized people don't actually act that way.

Can you tell me about the inspiration for *Child's Play*?
I was at UCLA film school in the mid-'80s when the Cabbage Patch dolls had become popular. I had already written one horror screenplay for a class and received an A, so I was rather emboldened and wanted to write another one. I wanted to write something that was darkly satirical about marketing and advertising. There's something very cynical and weird about the marketing world, and the Cabbage Patch craze seemed to sum it up pretty well. The movie *Gremlins* [1984] had also just come out, which had a comic horror sensibility that I enjoyed. What I saw in *Gremlins* was that the animatronic special effects had become so sophisticated that you could treat puppets as full-fledged characters. I had seen *Magic* [1978] and *Trilogy of Terror* [1975], films that had made use of the living doll concept, but I realized no one had ever given a puppet a full-fledged character. Also, the *Friday the 13th* and *A Nightmare on Elm Street* franchises made it clear that resilient killer characters had a place at the box office. What I think is really innovative about *Child's Play* is that previously, living dolls in films had been very rudimentary, and their characters were often on the sidelines. They weren't really capable of doing more than popping their eyes open. I realized you could do more now and give the puppet full dialogue scenes, and that they would be able to articulate things with more than just a Muppet-like floppy mouth. And I really wanted to get into how marketing affects children.

I think the marketing-to-children theme in *Child's Play* works very well—it's a bit of a social commentary that's funny and

creepy at once. **It turns the film into a cautionary tale about capi-talism and the rampant over-marketing to children.**

There was a lot more of that in the original script that didn't make it to the final. Chucky, instead of being possessed by the soul of a serial killer, was a manifestation of Andy's [the boy's] id. In my original concept, Chucky the toy was full of fake blood, so if he was cut he would actually bleed and then you'd have to go out and buy special toy band-aids. So it was about marketing synergy and about getting kids to buy more and more stuff. And because it was blood and band-aids, it was especially creepy. In the original script, the mom was a marketing executive who was behind the whole toy campaign. She gives him the doll so he wouldn't be lonely. I had Andy and Chucky doing the blood brotherhood thing where they cut their thumbs and mix their blood. And that's what brought the doll to life. I wanted to tease the audience for a lot longer, so it wouldn't be clear if it was Chucky doing the killings or if it was Andy. The scene where the mom finds out that Chucky has no bat-teries and is thus alive happened later in my original screenplay. I wanted there to be more of a question mark about whether or not Andy was a sociopath. They made it much more black and white in the end, much simpler. In the original script, the kid was more complicit in the murders. I wanted Chucky to be a manifestation of the kid's dark side, expressing the kind of nastiness that chil-dren are not allowed to express. Andy was also full of anger for his mother, who he felt was not paying enough attention to him.

That's interesting, because of course *The Omen*, *The Exorcist*, and *The Bad Seed* all rely on the notion that children aren't always so innocent.

I'm sure I was very influenced by those films, and the notion of kids being so awful. I think that teen culture in the 1970s was viewed as this unruly force, as something suspect. I'm sure that was running through me, but the '80s were the Reagan era and more *Leave it to Beaver*-ish, so I'm sure that's why the studio yanked that all out of the film.

What is it about scary dolls? There's the doll episode of *Night Gal-lery*, there's the clown doll in *Poltergeist* that goes under the bed.

I think that it's similar to why clowns are so creepy. Dolls are hu-manoid, but they're distortions of the human form. Hence there's something very creepy about that. I think they represent child-hood innocence, so I think that when you introduce the idea of them being evil, we have a very primal response to them.

Okay, so it must be asked: obviously, I think there's something very campy about the notion of a two-foot-tall, serial-killing, wisecracking doll. Do you make any connection between your sexuality and Chucky?

Definitely, in particular with the last two movies. They have a very apparent gay sensibility about them. In *Bride of Chucky* [1998], there was Jennifer Tilly and [out actor] Alexis Arquette, and there was also a specifically gay character. All of these films to an in-creasing degree have a certain visual stylization about them. The horror genre in general tends to attract a gay following, practitio-ners [the filmmakers] as well as audiences. There's Clive Barker, Kevin Williamson, and of course James Whale. I think the genre is often marked by a kind of operatic, over-the-top stylization that I think gay people really respond to. That's one of my interests in the genre. You're dealing with issues like love and death, the big-gest themes in the world. They can be writ large. The bottom line of *Seed of Chucky* [2004] is Chucky having to deal with a gay kid, or a gender-confused kid, who's very innocent and sweet, as opposed to Chucky's aggressive machismo. To use that situation as a meta-phor for any kind of family discourse made it universal, but would also resonate with gays, who often have strained relations with their fathers. Young people everywhere often feel this tension with their parents at some point. It's certainly my intention to inject a gay vibe into these movies. It's easy to condescend in this genre; it's very difficult to distinguish yourself in it too. I wanted to make something that was personal and eccentric. For better or worse, this is my voice.

You definitely take things up a notch with the last two films.

With *Bride of Chucky*, we made the conscious decision to embrace humor and make it an all-out comedy horror film. The first three were more straightforward horror. For my money, the second and third ones weren't very effective, in retrospect. When you do these sequels, the audience demands that you get to see more of the main character. But the problem with these iconic horror figures, whether it's Jason or Freddy or Chucky, is that the more you see

Still from Bride of Chucky *(1998), courtesy Toronto Film Reference Library*

Chucky with Jennifer Tilly (as Tiffany) in Bride of Chucky *(1998), phtographed by George Kraychyk, courtesy Toronto Film Reference Library*

them, the less frightening they are. It's a particular problem with Chucky, because he's two feet tall. He's already absurd to begin with. I felt that given that, in order to ensure the longevity of the series, and also as a writer-director, I don't want to repeat myself. I would like to give fans something different. Let's play up the comedy, let's bring these characters front and center, and start dealing with their psychology. I hesitate to use the word "complexity" because when people hear that in the context of Chucky, they're just going to roll their eyes. But I do think that the most recent two movies deal with issues subtextually that you don't see dealt with in your average slasher movies. I wanted to get into the psychology of the characters in a way that was really funny and interesting.

Chucky is possessed by such a sleazebag. I find him to be a parody of a stereotypically nasty hetero guy.
Totally. Starting with *Bride of Chucky*, I was doing that very consciously. Brad Dourif and I did the *Bride* commentary track and he disagrees with me about this. There's a scene where Chucky and Tiffany are in the van and watching the teen couple being lovey-dovey together and Chucky is making these very lewd remarks. And I said in the commentary, "Yeah, Chucky is really a pig." And Brad did this very actorly thing of wanting to identify with his character, and he defended Chucky and said he didn't think Chucky was such a pig. Which was surprising to me because it was so obvious that that's what we were doing with that movie. Chucky is very conservative and reactionary. He's undoubtedly a Republican. I mean, he can't vote, he's a puppet, but if he could he would have voted for George W. Bush for sure. He's very Archie Bunker-ish in the last movie.

That's funny because I was watching *All in the Family* on DVD recently and it struck me that Carroll O'Connor looks a lot like Chucky—or vice versa.
They both have this pugnacious look about them.

You've created a resilient horror icon in Chucky. Are you ever surprised by negative responses to the films?
I think it's a combination of things, Chucky is very silly and absurd to begin with, and there's a tendency for people to not take horror seriously, or to be embarrassed about going to see it. I think *Seed of*

Chucky is bound to do better on DVD than it did at the box office because people can view it in the privacy of their own home.

Years ago, Robin Wood wrote a piece in *Film Comment* called "The Return of the Repressed," in which he took critic Roger Ebert to task for using the term "guilty pleasure." Wood argued that if someone liked a movie they should just say so and not have to feel guilty about it. He also argued that horror movies could get away with all sorts of radical ideological commentary precisely because they were so often dismissed as trash. I think you were able to make some very subversive gender commentary with *Seed of Chucky*, something that would have been much harder to do in a more mainstream genre.

When you make films like these, you can be a bit more under the radar with it. The studio executives look down their noses at these kinds of movies. It's really just business to them. The upside of that is that they leave you alone. You can go a bit crazy.

How did you get John Waters to appear in *Seed of Chucky*?

I had heard for years that he was a huge fan, and he used to go out of his way in interviews to say that he liked the franchise. He said that *Bride of Chucky* was his favorite film of that year [1998], and that he really wanted to get killed by Chucky. So I wrote a role with him in mind and he agreed to do it. We were both doing DVD promotion at the same time—his was for *A Dirty Shame*—so we had dinner together. He's a lovely man.

You've worked extensively in Hollywood. Have you ever experienced any homophobia there?

No, not really. I once had a falling out with a major director, whose name I can't mention. He basically had me fired from my own project. That happens every day in Hollywood, but I couldn't really figure out why we got along so badly. I've often thought that perhaps it was homophobia, but I don't know for sure. There is a kind of boys' club here. Things have changed, though.

Wes Craven has said in interviews that he has had a hard time pitching a project that's any genre other than horror. He felt pigeonholed as a horror-only guy. Have you felt restricted by being the man behind Chucky?

It's funny because I did a call-in radio show a few months ago and an aspiring screenwriter phoned in who'd written a horror screenplay. He said that Craven had told him not to go ahead with it. I don't know Wes Craven, but I think it's very important to keep in mind that he's speaking from his own personal experience. People in Hollywood always want more from people who have had some success, so there is this tendency to pigeonhole people. I suspect that Craven has got everything he wants out of the horror genre and now he wants something that will get him an Oscar. Maybe it's just that I'm not ambitious enough, but I have this really philosophical view of it. I try not to torture myself with those kinds of thoughts. I love the horror genre. If I only ever made horror movies, or even only Chucky movies for that matter, you know what? It's okay. I'm leading a good life, I'm making a good living. I've written other screenplays that I've sold that never got made and that's frustrating, but it's the same thing for everybody. It's not something that keeps me up at night. I've created a horror character who has become an icon. I was a huge horror fan as a kid and if I'd known that one day I'd create a character who would become so iconic, that would be the biggest thing I'd ever want to do. Some may look at me as a one-trick pony, but I'm still working that trick and it's a good one.

FILMOGRAPHY

Don Mancini is writer of the following which are features unless otherwise noted:

Seed of Chucky (director and writer), 2004
Bride of Chucky, 1998
Child's Play 3: Look Who's Stalking, 1991
Child's Play 2, 1990
Tales from the Crypt (TV series, one episode), 1990
Cellar Dweller (under pseudonym Kit Du Bois), 1988
Child's Play, 1988

John Cameron Mitchell: Sexual Healing

John Cameron Mitchell has made two feature films, both of them brazenly unusual and decidedly iconoclastic. It's no surprise that they came from a writer-director who began his career as an actor. (Mitchell's acting CV includes the ludicrously cheesy 1987 made-for-TV sequel *The Stepford Children*—which might well explain where at least part of his irreverent sense of humor comes from.)

Mitchell's films are decidedly queer, full of reflections on camp and artifice. His directorial debut, *Hedwig and the Angry Inch* (2001), is based on Mitchell's own stage musical, which he adapted for the screen himself. Billed as "an anatomically incorrect rock odyssey," Hedwig tells the story of Hansel (played by Mitchell), a man born in East Berlin who falls in love with an American soldier and goes under the knife to become a woman, which, he determines, will mean he can marry the soldier and emigrate to America. However, the botched operation ends up leaving just a bit too much behind, thus the title of the movie. Hedwig has an astonishing energy and achieved instant cult status, many comparing it to the original cult grandmamma *The Rocky Horror Picture Show*.

In 2006, Mitchell released *Shortbus*, one of the splashiest sophomore features ever made. When the film premiered at Cannes and the Toronto International Film Festival, it was already endowed with intense advance buzz, the stuff of a publicist's dream. During the making of *Shortbus*—which is a very sexually explicit film—one of the actors, a real-life radio personality Sook-Yin Lee, got into trouble with her bosses at the Canadian Broadcasting Corporation (CBC), who were none-too-thrilled when they heard she was involved with what sounded like an experimental porn film. "They were strongly advising me not to do this," Lee told me. She then took the advice of her friend, gay author Douglas Coupland, and initiated a letter-writing campaign in protest, drawing on every luminary she and director Mitchell could muster. The letters arrived from a litany of the cultural A-list: Francis Ford Coppola, David Cronenberg, Atom Egoyan, Moby, Julianne Moore, Yoko Ono, Patricia Rozema, and Michael Stipe, among others. The CBC backed down; Lee kept her job and kept on filming.

It turned out to be a good call. Yes, *Shortbus* is as sexually explicit as the advance hype had suggested, but it's also a great movie and the carnal acts are but one of its aspects. Mitchell interweaves the stories of an ensemble of New Yorkers, all of whom are clearly still reeling from the psychological trauma of 9/11, and who are now searching to find meaning in their lives by way of marrying emotional intimacy with sexual contact. With *Shortbus*, Mitchell succeeds where many filmmakers have failed: to make a film in which explicit sex is a major component, but is executed in such way that it pushes the plot and character development forward. Yes, the sex in *Shortbus* makes the European cut of Kubrick's *Eyes Wide Shut* look like a Doris Day-Rock Hudson romp, but the rub (and tug) is that Mitchell transcends the gimmick, using sex to get at larger emotional truths. Mitchell and I sat down to talk at the Toronto International Film Festival in September of 2006.

Your first film was a musical. What led you to make your second film a very sexually explicit one like *Shortbus* [2006]?
Hedwig and the Angry Inch [2004] formally began as a rock and roll musical, and the origin of love and all these other things were added to it. In *Shortbus*, I wanted to use the language of sex in the film like I used the language of songs in Hedwig—just like the songs, sex services the plot. Because we show sex as sex, it can be an elaborate metaphor for something else about the characters' lives. There is a guy trying to suck his own dick, and he's trying really hard, and there are voice-overs saying, "I wish I could procreate alone in the dark like a worm. I want to be alone in my orgasm." It's like he's trying to truly be self-sufficient. The audience is thinking, "Who is this guy? He's in his thirties, he's going to break his neck!" And it ends in tears. It's an example of sex being used as a metaphor for a character and his emotional goal.

Over the course of developing *Shortbus*, I realized the actors needed to be co-creators—I knew I wanted the film to be sexually diverse, I wanted it to be in New York, I wanted it to be a salon, but that's all I knew. We had an open casting call before we had a script—interesting people, possible couples, diverse sexualities—and we asked the actors we chose to go into workshop for five weeks and start creating characters, learn improvisational vocabulary, watch relevant movies, get an aesthetic.

What were some of the specific films you and the actors watched?
They knew that we didn't have to follow the script verbatim, but the process could still be very structured. We looked at John Cassavetes and Robert Altman. I showed them a 1996 Iranian film

by Mohsen Makhmalbaf called *A Moment of Innocence*. I showed them *Nashville, A Woman Under the Influence, Opening Night, Faces, 3 Women, The Heartbreak Kid*—diverse films to stimulate them. I showed Woody Allen, specifically *Husbands and Wives, Annie Hall,* and *Hannah and Her Sisters,* his better films, to let them know that laughter and emotion could be part of the same scene. We were all absorbing and playing: we went bowling and played wiffle ball, did improv and trust exercises, and had a couple of sexual rehearsals.

How do you do sexual rehearsals?

Just doing an improv that might become sexual. Like any improv, actors are in a situation that is what they want. They might have a date, and if it becomes sexual, they let it go there as long as they continue toward their goal. Some improvs might become totally sexual, which was nerve-racking at first, but that is why we wanted to work on it for a long time so we could reduce our nerves and trust each other.

That was the five-week process before shooting?

No, five weeks was just the beginning. Then I would go away and work on the script, then come back six months later and do more workshopping. We did that for two-and-a-half years. But working on plays and musicals can take that long too. I like taking my time. That is an advantage of not using stars and agents, because they would have been terrified by the long process. Stars aren't the same as actors; stars are people who like to control their image and sell more than just their talent. Stars sell a package and it usually has to do with sex. But oddly, they wouldn't have real sex onscreen, because that might actually blow their cover. There are some talented stars out there, but I wouldn't have wanted them anyway because they couldn't have rehearsed for that long. In a way, the sex was a prophylactic against having to work with stars. Sex is the star of this film—it wouldn't have been made or distributed with the same cast and the same story if it hadn't had been explicit, which I realize in retrospect is very interesting. Sex wasn't the purpose of making *Shortbus* but that is one of the facts surrounding its creation. I'm happy with it; the actors had a blast with it. We've become great friends. Many of them are now collaborating on various projects, which is very exciting. The *Shortbus* aesthetic or ethic became very much about collaboration; a certain egalitarian situation with a benevolent dictator.

John Cameron Mitchell in Hedwig and the Angry Inch *(2001), New Line Cinema/Photofest*

Raphael Barker, Sook-Yin Lee, and John Cameron Mitchell on the set of Shortbus *(2006), courtesy THINKFilm*

There is an optimism to *Shortbus*, a sense that the New Yorkers are emerging from the post-9/11 anxiety.

I was thinking about making a film that used sex before 9/11, but certainly what happened on 9/11 changed things. The only thing that Bush was right about was that everything changed after 9/11. It was always in the shadow of what you did artistically, politically, or even economically. It was just there, in the air, in the animation. There's a definite reaction to 9/11 in the film. In New York, people were very kind to each other [during and after 9/11] and that's what I remember—how much I loved New York and its history as a land of outcasts, which the Statue of Liberty embodies and which *Shortbus* is the modern incarnation of.

How would you say that your sexuality and your filmmaking practice intersect?

I think there is a queer sensibility. There is a wide range to what that can mean, but to me queer sensibility just means that you are a sexual or gender outsider. Gay men are aware of code, aware of camp, an exaggeration of surface. It doesn't mean all gay men have good taste—all you have to do is walk through the gay village to see that taste is not necessarily linked to sexuality. But there is a sensibility, and I think it is a wonderful privilege that we can use in art. Certainly, the arts and media are flooded with queer people because media and arts are about surfaces and realities and codes and metaphor. Queer sensibility is in journalism too, in trying to find truths others may have overlooked.

The difference between my film and some other recent ones that have used a lot of explicit sex is that in my film it is pretty soft-hearted, there is a real optimism and mercy, and while there is certainly sadness, it's not harsh or cynical. A lot of people have connected sex to violence and despair, which certainly exists in the world, but that is not only aspect of sex. I wanted to have a broader palette with *Shortbus*.

You wanted to show the positive side of sex instead of the negative.

Obviously, there is negative in *Shortbus* too, but there is a sense of humor about it. Most of the sex is very bad. Only a couple of people are having a good time. In the sex room [where people let loose and have sex, like an orgy room] everyone is desperate, but it's funny. The audience laughs and cries all at once. Let's remember that sex is one of the funniest things around.

I got the sense that you were conscious of the differences between gay and straight sex. Gay men seem to be able to separate themselves from the intimacy of the sex act, which seems different from the representation of straight sex.
It's the fact that there are only guys involved in gay sex. With men, there is more of a compartmentalization of sex, separated from all the things it is connected to. The Internet makes this even more common. Sometimes just getting your rocks off is fine, but this weird, faceless, fast, casual sex—and the post-orgasm depression—is the more deeply embedded experience. Because of this compartmentalization and commercialization people separate themselves. "I'm into this, I'm a top, I'm a bottom, I'm into this and nothing else." It's like kids learning about sex from porn, like, "I must now do it in this order." I think it's really fucking sex up. To divorce sex from humanity, to reduce it to a body part, is easy for men and sometimes that's just fine. But when sex has become a marketing niche just like food, its nutritive value is gone. With *Shortbus*, we are trying to connect sex and intimacy again, but in a non-moralistic way.

What do you hope people will walk away with from *Shortbus*?
With a song in their heart—I don't know. Not necessarily a hard-on, because it is not actually that arousing. That wasn't a priority while making this film. I did want there to be a sense of hope at the end. In the US, there is a tendency to equate terrorism with illegal immigrants and sexual outlaws. They are seen as "other," as equally dangerous as the terrorists. People came to the US and Canada to escape persecution, to create something better as they saw fit. What happened to that? The scene when a character sings the national anthem into his lover's asshole was the most patriotic thing that I could think of. That made sense to me, though it is completely at odds with the powers-that-be. I want people to be reminded that they do have power. Maybe it's only in their own home, but we can try to spread it out through collaboration, creativity, and imagination. Since 9/11, people have been scared and stupid and they are waking up to it now. We just hope that *Shortbus* is a little beacon in the night to say, "It's all going to be okay."

FILMOGRAPHY

John Cameron Mitchell is director and writer of the following features:

Shortbus, 2006
Hedwig and the Angry Inch, 2001

Léa Pool on the set of Emporte-moi *(1998) courtesy Toronto Film Reference Library*

Léa Pool: Darkness into Light

In person, there's something comforting about director-screenwriter Léa Pool. Her sentences are wrapped in the warm lilt of her voice, and she appears Zen-like—if there is stress in her life, she doesn't show it. Her demeanor, however, starkly contrasts with her work.

Pool confirms that her screenplays often begin from a very autobiographical place, one that includes a stormy childhood in Switzerland and self-exile at the age of twenty-five to Montreal, Canada. "Indeed," she concedes, "my films are very much a reflection of myself: my body, my soul, my mind, my sexuality: it's all there."

Her films have been hits on the international film festival and arthouse circuit, and while she has been making features since 1979 with *Strass Café*, her first hit came with *Anne Trister* (1986), a bold and unapologetic film about lesbian love. Then came her unnerving portrait of a crumbling ménage a trois in *A corps perdu* (*Straight for the Heart*) in 1988, which further enhanced Pool's reputation as a big-screen sexual trailblazer: the film featured a shower scene in which two men and a woman made love, including full-on kissing between the men (which, at the time, if not now, constituted a big deal). Her 1993 film *Mouvements du désir* (*Desire in Motion*) about a tortured train-trek romance, was followed by *Emporte-moi* (*Set Me Free*) in 1998, an autobiographical take on a young girl's obsessions with the movies, and *Lost and Delirious* in 2001, her English-language breakthrough about tragic same-sex romantic obsession at an all-girls school. This is only a partial list of her cinematic work, but the themes, motifs, and overall style of Pool's films form an oeuvre that is both poetic and powerful. Her work is also full of intentional contradictions and contrasts, films that are clearly fictional but which constantly resonate with the truth of documentary filmmaking.

Pool, considered one of the most important filmmakers in Quebec's robust and burgeoning film scene, has long expressed a gratitude to Montreal, the multicultural, cosmopolitan hub that she calls home. Her attachment to the city makes perfect sense: Montreal is a city rife with contradictions itself, a bilingual place continually searching for its political and personal identity.

Pool's most recent work, *The Blue Butterfly* (2004), marks something of a departure for the director; it is a children's film that stars William Hurt as a butterfly hunter who helps a terminally ill boy go into the wilds to find a rare insect.

I have interviewed Pool on several occasions; we spoke again in the fall of 2006.

What is your earliest film memory?
I would say [the original 1961 version of] *101 Dalmatians*—I don't remember exactly what struck me about the film, but I loved it. In the cinema in Lauzon, Switzerland, you could stay through three or four showings, and so I stayed for all four. By seven p.m. I was still there, and my parents thought I'd disappeared so they called the police. I thought it was wonderful to be able to watch the same film over and over and over again. We didn't have home video back then, of course.

You had a Jewish father and a Gentile mother, and this bicultural background plays a strong role in much of your screenwriting.
It's funny, because I remember that it was never important for me to discuss this dual culture in Switzerland. But being here in Quebec and knowing that my father had no country, the issue became important to me. When I first started making films, they were very personal, and suddenly all of these things started to surface. My identity, and my search for identity, aren't necessarily things I think about in my daily life, but there they are in my films. They came up as a result of the creative process.

What about your move from Switzerland to Canada at the age of twenty-five?
[For many reasons,] I was going to teach for a year, and I decided to come to Canada; getting a visa was fairly straightforward. I also wanted to be far from my family, as well as Switzerland itself. I felt that if I stayed there, I would just die. It's a very conservative place and I felt that if I wanted to be who I really was, I had to be elsewhere. I wanted to be in a French-speaking country, but France was too close. I had visited Quebec the year before and I loved it, so it seemed like the place to go. I came in 1975—a lot of things were happening in Quebec at this time. I really didn't know that I'd end up in a creative profession, but I just knew that I had to change things in my life, that I had to move on.

I find that interesting, because your films often deal with transition, geographical as well as personal.
When I shot *Strass Café* [1979], my first film, it was really the land-

scape of Montreal that inspired me. It was so strange to be in Canada and not Switzerland. And it seemed like much of Montreal was falling apart, like it was a city after a war. I was in a new country, but it wasn't so new after all.

What first led you to filmmaking?
When I applied for my visa to live in Canada, I applied to study at the University of Quebec at Montreal, where I studied communication arts. I had done some photography. It really wasn't something I set out to do, it was something that my friends and I just got into in the evenings and on the weekends.

Can you tell me about the genesis of your second film, *Anne Trister* [1986]?
Roger Frappier had a group at the NFB [National Film Board of Canada, a government film agency], that included Denys Arcand. [Frappier and Arcand have gone on to become two of the most important figures in Canadian cinema: Frappier as one of Quebec's key producers, and Arcand a screenwriter-director with an Oscar win for *Les Invasions barbares* (*The Barbarian Invasions*) (2003).] Roger asked if I was interested in joining this group; the only condition was that I had to make a personal film, not an adaptation, about love. I began to work on the idea of someone from Switzerland who was getting over the death of her father. At first it went well, then it seemed to go off in a different direction. But one day I heard the song, "De la main gauche" ["With my left hand"] by Danielle Messia, and suddenly [the film] became very clear. Music is often very important for me.

Anne Trister enjoys a huge cult following.
There was a lot of excitement in Berlin when it played at the festival [1986 Berlin International Film Festival], and then it circulated in the local cinemas for some time. It also played in Paris for a whole year. People still talk about the film now. My film *Emporte-moi* [*Set Me Free*, 1998] is also one that lingers with audiences.

Would you call *Anne Trister* your coming out movie?
It was one of the first on that subject. Now it's not such a big deal, but back then, twenty years ago, *Anne Trister* and *A corps perdu* [*Straight for the Heart*] [1988] were really considered big deals. Especially *A corps perdu*, where you have three people making love and

two men kissing. When the film played at the Venice International Film Festival, the press was divided—the right wing hated it and the Italian community at the time was quite upset by it. The radical left, interestingly enough, said I didn't go far enough. "Well," I said, "that's where I wanted to go."

[However, thirteen years later,] when *Lost and Delirious* came out in 2001 in Berlin, the film was seen as quite soft; yet the same-sex love and also the suicide made the film a very difficult release in the US. When I did interviews there, they talked on and on about the sex scene [which was between two teenage girls]. That was what everyone wanted to talk about. There was a glaring difference between the European and American reactions to the film.

A *corps perdu* seems to reflect Montreal so well, in particular the issues surrounding identity, given the city's two main languages and its cultural diversity.
Montreal was very inspiring for me, especially in my early films. It's not necessarily the most beautiful city, but it's a fascinating place. There's a lot of history and a lot of contrasts. It's also a very cinematic place. Montreal is not that big of a city, but there's a lot of feeling here. If I'd had to film *A corps perdu* in a Swiss city, I don't know that I would have done it. Questions around identity arise [in the film] because I too came to the city where no one knew who I was, and I had the opportunity to reconstruct my life as I wanted. Obviously, the death of my father had a profound impact on me too.

Emporte-moi was another breakthrough for you. How autobiographical is this film?
It was very close to my own story. There was always conflict in the house. My father was the kind of person who wanted us to be Jewish. He was a writer who didn't write, so it was my mother's responsibility to bring money home. We didn't grow up with much, as my mother worked in clothing factories. My mother and brother saw the film and they connected with the story; it's always strange to show such a personal story to family members. But even though *Emporte-moi* was very autobiographical, it was also inspired by my Jean-Luc Godard fascination.

What then led you to *Lost and Delirious*?

Mattias Habich (left), Johanne-Marie Tremblay (center), and Michel Voita in A corps perdu *(1988), courtesy Toronto Film Reference Library*

Piper Perabo and Jessica Pare in Lost and Delirious *(2001), courtesy Toronto Film Reference Library*

Cité-Amérique [a Montreal-based film production company] offered me this project, which was written by Judith Thompson, a well-known Canadian playwright, and based on the Susan Swan novel [*Wives of Bath*]. When I read the screenplay, I thought, "Why not?" It gave me an opportunity to shoot in English and that seemed another feather in my cap. Plus I like to work with young actresses, so I decided to do it.

You've discussed various fears around making *Lost and Delirious*.
It was difficult for me to jump from a very personal way of working on a film—one that I've originated myself—to one that's offered to me and written by someone else. I wasn't sure I would be able to handle it. I always saw myself as being very involved in the entire process of filmmaking, from the original idea right through to the end. But I thought it was a good opportunity, so I jumped in, knowing I had to find another way to connect with the project. My daughter was only about two years old at that point, so I couldn't write then, and the film was a good opportunity to do something different.

And the shift from French to English?
The shift at first was difficult. I speak only French with my daughter, and I live in an entirely French-speaking milieu, and I usually express myself best with the French-speaking crews. Making *The Blue Butterfly* [an English-language film made in 2004, after *Lost and Delirious*] was easy, because William Hurt speaks French, so when I grew tired of speaking English I would just speak French with him. So making an English-language film slows me down a bit. Ultimately I prefer to work in French.

The reviews of *Lost and Delirious* were very divided. How did they affect you?
The reviews were really polarized. Half the critics liked it, half didn't. And when the review was bad, it was really bad. Yet, some found the film very moving. At the beginning, you have the impression that it's a story about schoolgirls, possibly a lighter film. But fifteen minutes into it, it's not that at all. It got released widely in the US, and that generated a lot of interest in my previous films. So I think making *Lost and Delirious* was a good career decision in that respect; it helped to open up my work to audiences in other countries.

What prompted you to then make the children's film *The Blue Butterfly*?

It was already written and [the producers] had the money to do it. At the time, I was looking for films that my daughter would like. She was then seven years old and beginning to be interested in what I was doing, and it would have been hard for her to understand *Lost and Delirious*. Also, it was a good time in my life to make this project—I knew it was something I'd be comfortable with.

Do bad reviews torment you?

The moment I release a film I am very fragile, and that's normal because I work so long on each one. I'm always sensitive about a bad critique—I need to know that my work has been understood. For me, *Lost and Delirious* is a better film than *Mouvements du désir* [1993], but a lot of critics prefer the latter. Very often with a film, there are parts I'm very proud of and other parts I simply want to fast forward through.

How much of a role do you think your sexuality plays in your work?

I see a thread from my first film right through to *Lost and Delirious*, I think, that is becoming more and more clear. When I look at these films, I see myself growing more and more. When someone asks why I didn't "go further" with a film, I say that it's because it was where I was in my life when I made it—not just in terms of my sexuality, but my identity. My films act as a mirror, reflecting who I am. I have grown, and it's all there in my films.

What's the main way you've changed as a filmmaker over the years?

Certainly, I'm more conscious of the audience, of critics, of money. When I began to make films, I just did them. Now it's difficult; I have to prove to others that a film will make money, that people will go and see it. I try not to think about it. Each film has its own challenges. I know my work better now—the acting, the composition. I bring everything I've learned with me to each new film. I'm more confident—at least I hope so.

Each director has his or her own persona. Spielberg is essentially an optimist, Hitchcock was menacing and cheeky. What would you say are your chief characteristics as a filmmaker?

I'd say I'm pretty dark, but there's always some hope in my work. It's a difficult world, but it's a world that I love and care for. I like life, even if I'm not blind about what's going on. We have to be careful about a lot of things, but I still have the impression that life is wonderful. I'm not dark in my own life, but there's no doubt we're going through a difficult period. Art is a wonderful way to bring light into the darkness.

FILMOGRAPHY

The Blue Butterfly (feature) (director), 2004

Lost and Delirious (feature) (director), 2001

Emporte-moi (Set Me Free) (feature) (director and co-writer with Nancy Huston and Isabelle Raynault), 1998

Gabrielle Roy (feature) (director and co-writer with Micheline Cadieux and Diane Poitras), 1997

Mouvements du désir (Desire in Motion) (feature) (director and writer), 1993

La demoiselle sauvage (The Savage Woman) (feature) (director and co-writer with several writers), 1991

Montréal vu par (Montreal Sextet) (feature, "Rispondetemi" segment) (director and writer), 1991

Hotel Chronicles (feature) (director and co-writer with Laurent Gagliardi), 1990

A corps perdu (Straight for the Heart) (feature) (director and co-writer with Marcel Beaulieu), 1988

Anne Trister (feature) (director and co-writer with Marcel Beaulieu), 1986

La femme de l'hôtel (A Woman in Waiting) (feature) (director and co-writer with Robert Gurik and Michel Langlois), 1984

Strass Café (feature) (director and co-writer with Luc Caron), 1979

Laurent Lamerre, portier (short documentary) (director and writer), 1978

Wakefield Poole: Revisionist Pornographer

Wakefield Poole is a legendary gay porn director whose classic films in the 1970s and '80s consistently broke new ground. The way in which Poole became involved in pornography is the stuff of legend; one night in 1969, he and a few friends ended up at a porn theater and watched a movie that was so degrading and dreadful that it inspired him to attempt to make his own.

Poole, a dancer who had worked extensively in Broadway productions and on television, had recently been given a 16mm camera by his boyfriend, and had already made a ten-minute short film, *Andy*, a tribute to his friend Andy Warhol. He then ventured to Fire Island and, amid the gorgeous natural setting, shot his first porn feature, *Boys in the Sand*. Upon its release in New York in 1971, it became an instant sensation. Shot in bare bones, cinéma vérite style and with touches of magical realism, *Boys in the Sand* expresses the unabashed hope, joy, and optimism of gay-liberation-era sexuality. It was the first gay porno film to have a display ad in *The New York Times*, and drew strong praise from *Variety* while making a superstar of its protagonist, Casey Donovan.

Poole immediately took the profits from the film and put them into other projects, including bankrolling the early rehearsals of a show his friend Michael Bennett wanted to take to Broadway—a show that would ultimately debut as *A Chorus Line*, one of the most successful and long-running musicals in Broadway history. Poole followed up *Boys in the Sand* with *Bijou* (1972), a much darker feature—and arguably more of a cinematic breakthrough with one of the first gay orgy scenes ever captured on celluloid. Poole's next projects included a straight erotic comedy, *Bible!* (1973), an erotic short film, *Roger* (1977), and a sequel to the film that started it all: *Boys in the Sand II* (1984), which also starred Donovan.

But Poole's work and life took a harsh turn in the 1980s, when an addiction to cocaine took its toll. Worse still, he found himself increasingly isolated career-wise, due to the stigma he faced as someone who had made pornography without the protective veil of a pseudonym. Poole was also emotionally devastated as he watched many of his friends die during the AIDS epidemic, including Donovan and Bennett. Ironically, as he tells it, his cocaine addiction may well have saved his life by preventing him from having an active sex life.

When he felt his film career was over, Poole turned to a new passion, training to become a chef and working at various restaurants before becoming a manager for food services at Calvin Klein Cosmetics corporate headquarters.

But in recent years, there has been a renewed interest in Poole and his work. In 2000, Alyson Books released his autobiography, *Dirty Poole: The Autobiography of a Gay Porn Pioneer*, and in 2002 the Anthology Film Archives in New York screened a retrospective of his early works. That year also marked the release of a two-disc DVD package, *The Wakefield Poole Collection*, which includes *Boys in the Sand, Bijou, Andy, Boys in the Sand II*, and an extensive interview with Poole as well as commentary tracks for each film. The DVD package is a fitting tribute to a survivor who made what could be termed revisionist pornography—uplifting, invigorating, and truly erotic—creating a porn aesthetic free of the pre-Stonewall era of shame, degradation, and remorse.

I interviewed Wakefield Poole in the spring of 2006.

What was your childhood in Jacksonville, Florida like?
It was very normal as far as being a dancer is concerned. I went to ballet school after school every day and then every Saturday we would meet from about nine o'clock until about five. I was very active in school; I was a little better than your average student. And of course I took part in all the school's theatrical productions—it was a very nice childhood. Very normal. I went to dances and was very popular. My father was an automobile salesman, my mom stayed at home, and I had two sisters, both older. Jacksonville was a very nice place to grow up.

I love the story of how you first got a camera and decided to make a film.
I was really into filmmaking—from the first time I put my eye to the camera, it was unbelievable. I had an 8mm camera that I always played around with. My lover at the time was Peter Fisk, who would be in some of my movies. For my birthday, Peter gave me a 16mm camera and I just started doing a lot of fun things with it. I had the inspiration to make *Boys in the Sand* [1971] when I was directing an American Federation of Television Art showcase. It was a Friday night and [my colleagues and I] wanted to do something after rehearsal. We couldn't get in to see the movie we wanted to see so we went to a porn theater and saw a film called *Highway Hustler*. It was so bad. [There is a scene where] a guy held a knife to

another guy's throat while he raped him. Peter fell asleep during the movie, and Martin Sherman, the playwright [and screenwriter], and Drey Shepperd, a writer and lyricist, were laughing throughout. Afterwards we were talking and asking ourselves: why can't somebody make a good porno movie? Why can't somebody make a movie that's pretty, that's hot, and with nice people in it who have clean feet?

How was the experience of making *Boys in the Sand*?
It took a while to get *Boys in the Sand* off the ground. Two friends had agreed to appear in my little movie but backed out the day before [we started filming]. That was the first time that someone had said that to me, "Oh, I can't wait to be in a movie," and then chickened out. I financed the first section of the film on my credit card. When I showed the short version to people, they said it was the best thing they ever saw and [encouraged me to] make it into a full-length movie—and because of this lark, I turned into a pornographer. Of course, once you're a pornographer, you're always a pornographer. I approached my manager, Marvin Schulman, to be my business partner and he agreed. It was a great decision. He had great taste and [understood my vision]. So we made *Boys in the Sand* and rented the theater ourselves for its premiere. The theater, the 55th Street Playhouse, was across the street from Marvin's apartment. Andy Warhol had shown all his films there and at the time it was showing Chinese films. We did all the advertising, treating it like a real movie, even if it was porn. I think that's what attracted people to it. It had a lot of class. It premiered the Wednesday after Christmas, and on the following weekend, we put an ad in the Sunday *New York Times*, right next to the ad for *Nicholas and Alexandra*. Everyone in New York was talking about it. That's what made the film a success—besides Casey Donovan, of course, who was a big factor. The way we promoted and advertised it gave it legitimacy. We got reviews in *Variety* and *The New York Times*—no porno film had ever done that before. I was interviewed for [the documentary film] *Inside Deep Throat*, even though I didn't end up in the movie. But the main question in the interview was, "How do you feel for not getting credit for what you did for the sex film industry?" They were alluding to the fact that *Boys in the Sand* was released before *Deep Throat*, which came out one year later, insinuating that [*Deep Throat*'s producers] couldn't have made their movie without mine.

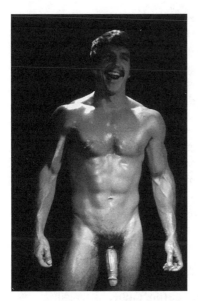

Roger in Roger *(1977), photographed by Peter Fisk*

Wakefield Poole, photographed by Peter Fisk

Was there a stigma about gay porn at the time you released *Boys in the Sand*?

Oh my God! Well, there *still* is. [At the time, gay porn theaters] were nothing but little holes in the walls. Some of the films that ran were called "loops," which were just sex films; no story, with music playing in the background [instead of dialogue]. They would play "June is Busting Out All Over" or Beethoven's Fifth Symphony, it didn't matter.

What was your reaction to the film's success?

My film got the kind of attention that had never been [accorded a gay porno] before and we were very surprised. When it premiered, we thought we would have maybe fifty people there and God only knows how many for the shows after that. When the doors opened, people started pouring in with their five-dollar admission ready in their hands—they had them ready in their hands because they didn't want to stop [in the queue and be recognized] at the box office, that's how much stigma there was about porn. They were scared that somebody would see them.

In the film, how did you arrive at the scenario of the characters having sex in the wilderness?

It just sort of happened. It was very easy, like doing a ballet. I'd choreographed a lot of ballets. In fact, I was at a screening for a film I am in, the *Ballet Russes* [a 2005 documentary on the history of the Ballet Russes dance company], and a woman in the audience asked, "Why did you make porn movies? Why didn't you stay with the ballet?" And I said that I equated it to being a ballet dancer: you work hard and you sweat, then you have this creative, beautiful thing at the end of it. Afterward, I read the woman's blog and she wrote, "I think I was the only one who was offended by it," due to the fact that I had equated making porn movies to ballet. I'm grateful that I'm in *Ballet Russes* because it's given me a little bit of legitimacy in the later years of my life and it's brought me back to my roots [as a dancer]. I'm very honored to be in the film because I wasn't in the [ballet] company for more than two years, and I wasn't a soloist. When they asked me to be in the movie, I told them that I made pornography but they said, "That's why we want you to be in the movie, because we want to show a diversity of what happens when people leave the ballet."

Was it difficult for you to work in the theater after *Boys in the Sand*?

Oh yes. When I was coming off my drug habit [in the 1980s] I was called back to New York to work in theater. About halfway through the previews of [the musical *Bring Back Birdie* in which I was assisting director Joe Layton] the *New York Post* said, "Wakefield Poole, Joe Layton's right-hand man listed in the program, [said] that he did art films when what he did was male pornography." It was tough because I'd been working with kids [during the production]. [All of a sudden] everybody knew about it, everybody read about it, and then all of the mothers thought I was going to take their little children and make porn stars out of them. I was very discouraged because I thought this was my chance to come back, I wasn't making movies anymore. Right after that, I bottomed out. I gave up drugs, went totally cold turkey, and decided to permanently move back to New York with only twenty-five dollars in my pocket. It was quite the experience.

What did you think of that period in the 1990s when porn looked like it was going mainstream?

I'm not sure. When I left the film business, I totally lost contact [with the industry] and I became a chef. I entered culinary school when I was close to fifty. I was the oldest one in the institute, but I had to make a living. I had been totally unemployable, I didn't want to make any more films, Broadway had turned its back on me. What was I going to do? I realized I liked to cook, so I went to cooking school, and eventually got a job at Caravelle, the best French restaurant in New York at that time. Then I went to work for Jackie Kennedy's chef in her catering company, making five-course meals for stockbrokers. I found a whole new life. Suddenly film was just not a part of my life anymore. I became celibate too.

Why did you become celibate?

The last year that I was sexually active I was also very much into coke, so when [my partner and I] had sex we really didn't have sex. It was impossible to have erections with all of the cocaine we were doing. So, being a coke addict actually saved my life because that was when all the HIV infections started happening; all my friends got sick, and my lover at the time was dying of liver cancer. Suddenly I was losing all my friends, people were dying all around me. But I had no intention of giving it up forever. Plus, I couldn't force myself, as promiscuous as I was, to play that type of suicide. I stopped [having sex] and I just never got back into it. I have always just followed my instincts. I've done that all my life and that's probably why I made *Boys in the Sand*. I'm very happy that I did it. I'm happy that I gave a little self-esteem to people that left us too soon. I can't tell you how many people have come up to me and said, "Do you know I came out after I saw *Boys in the Sand*?" I'm talking about hundreds: [on the set of] the last movie I did in San Francisco, *Take One* [1977], there were five people who told me they'd come out after seeing *Boys in the Sand*. I can't deny the effect that I've had on gay people in my time.

You made *Boys in the Sand* in the wake of the Stonewall riots of 1969. How did that influence your film?
It was the same year. It's amazing how it all fell together. We could go on about Stonewall and the whole effect that it had on me, how it made me want to make a beautiful movie. Anybody [who lived through] that period, who had any gumption at all, stood up for their rights.

Do you watch gay pornos today?
Very rarely. I have been looking at some films because I think I'm going to do a new movie. I had TLA Video send me half a dozen of their most popular films so I could see what was going on today. I was a little taken aback by them, and I honestly don't know if people would want to watch my kind of films today. Not that there aren't some good [contemporary gay porn films] out there. With *Boys in the Sand*, I wanted to make a beautiful movie, with beautiful actors and no feeling of degradation. That is exactly what [today's gay porn directors] are doing, so I have no right to complain. It's just that they don't want to put any thought into it. There is no story, no titillation, no suspense—only sex. Even the sex is not there, because you know what they are going to do next. In the 1970s, my friend Jack Deveau said, "If you can do it, then I can do it!" So I said, "Do it, Jack!" and he did. He made *Left-Handed* [1972], which played at the 55th Street Playhouse right after *Boys In the Sand* closed, and he kept it running there until my next film was ready to be released. People [like Deveau] started making films because they saw that I did it and it titillated them. The '70s was the peak

of gay filmmaking, because we had *filmmakers* making films, not cameramen. People were interested in the process, not just the outcome. It was a very exciting time for pornography. My photo appeared in the gay press a lot, and people would recognize me [on the street].

It must have been very gratifying to revisit your films with the DVD compilation release.

Yes. The DVD compilation got wonderful reviews and we are getting ready to do another one. We are going to re-release *Moving* [1974], which is the third movie I made, and *Take One* [1977], which is the last movie I made, about ten men talking about their sexual fantasies. It's very much like today's television [talk] shows. There is going to be a re-release of the only straight movie I made, *Bible!* [1973]. It's called *Wakefield Poole's Bible*. The film wasn't very successful; [the reaction was] the opposite of our experience with *Boys in the Sand*. We had a very tongue-in-cheek ad for *Bible!* with the Virgin Mary in a vampy dress holding baby Jesus with shades on to let people know that the film had a sense of humor to it. The *New York Times* refused to print our ad unless we took out the halos. In fact, all religious references had to go, so that the ad made no sense at all. And the MPAA [Motion Picture Association of America] gave us an X-rating even though there is no hardcore sex in the film. There is one shot of a dick in the whole movie. They gave us an X simply because it was a softcore porno about religion. We had put $130,000 into a film that we couldn't advertise and that nobody was coming to see. [As a result,] I lost all the money that I'd made on the other two films. But making films is a narcotic—you learn so much making them that you can't wait for the next one to use what you've learned.

Do you feel that the film industry has come a long way in terms of representations of gay culture?

Oh God, yes. Except you have to remember now, *Brokeback Mountain* arrived just at the right time. They did the same thing in 1982 with *Making Love*. That's a mainstream movie that had nudity, not necking but full kissing, between two men [Harry Hamlin and Michael Ontkean]. It was a very sensitive movie. It ruined Harry Hamlin's career until he got into television. Both [Hamlin and Ontkean] had to go to television because they couldn't make any more movies. So the stigma was there for the actors, for sure. We've come along way.

You must feel gratified by the legacy of your films, which have altered gay men's attitudes toward their sexuality.
Yes, I feel very good about that. It is a good time to look back at those films we made so long ago. Things have really changed, but the work remains as a testimony to that time. I'm glad that much of the work can have a new life on DVD.

FILMOGRAPHY

Wakefield Poole is director and writer of the following which are features unless otherwise noted:

One, Two, Three, 1985
Boys in the Sand II, 1984
The Hustlers, 1984
Split Image, 1984
Hot Shots, 1981
Roger (short film), 1977
Take One, 1977
Gay Parade San Francisco (short documentary), 1974
Moving, 1974
Bible!, 1973
Bijou, 1972
Boys in the Sand, 1971
Andy, 1970

Ian Iqbal Rashid, courtesy Ian Iqbal Rashid

Ian Iqbal Rashid: Film as Refuge

Growing up in Toronto in the 1970s has clearly shaped Ian Iqbal Rashid's cinematic sensibility. During his adolescence, this Tanzanian-born, Canadian immigrant found solace in Hollywood film fare from the 1950s and '60s to escape from racist bullies in his neighborhood at the same time he was realizing he was gay.

In his twenties, Rashid had an inkling of his creative potential, writing poetry while working for repertory cinemas and arts groups. In 1990, he moved to London, England, where he continued writing, eventually making several short films and writing for British television, including the cult show *This Life*.

Rashid made his first feature in 2004 when, after years of struggle, he managed to secure funding to shoot the delightful *Touch of Pink*. The film is the tale of a young gay Muslim man (played by Jimi Mistry) living in bliss in London with his sweet boyfriend (Kristen Holden-Ried). Trouble is, Toronto-based mom (Suleka Mathew) has no idea that her son is gay, and when she comes for a visit, her son is nowhere near ready to break the big news to his mother that grandchildren just might not be in the picture. The plot could have easily descended into contrived slapstick, but Rashid keeps his script suitably quirky and surprising, making *Touch of Pink* one of the best of the spate of romantic comedy-family melodrama hybrids that appeared in the late 1990s and early 2000s (among them *My Big Fat Greek Wedding* and *Bend It Like Beckham*). The film's self-consciousness also helps it break through the clichés of the genre, becoming many things at once: an homage to Hollywood romantic comedies, a coming-out movie, an exploration of race in postcolonial England, and a family melodrama. Tossed into the mix is the film's sublime running gag: protagonist Mistry is haunted by the ghost of Cary Grant, who follows him throughout the movie, offering him bits and pieces of advice. It's an hilarious conceit, and Kyle MacLachlan is perfect as the late matinee idol. In his 2006 book *The Romance of Transgression in Canada: Queering Sexualities, Nations, Cinemas*, Thomas Waugh praises *Touch of Pink*, expressing relief that someone has "finally [created] an excellent queer subversion of the oppressively heterocentric diasporic wedding cycle of the 1990s and 2000s."

But *Touch of Pink* is fascinating for another reason. The Thatcher-era films of the 1980s depicted Great Britain as a grim, unwelcoming place for immigrant communities. Films like *My Beautiful Laundrette* (1985)

and *Sammy and Rosie Get Laid* (1987), collaborations between director Stephen Frears and screenwriter Hanif Kureishi, point their lens
towards a British pressure cooker, a toxic combination of old-school
British racism and at times less-than-ethical immigrants willing to do
anything to climb the capitalist ladder to success. Rashid, who continues to live in London and has recently completed directing a new
feature film (a teen dance movie titled *How She Move*, 2007), makes no
apologies for his outlook: "As I've changed, my scripts have changed,"
he says, adding that his outlook is essentially one of optimism.

Rashid spoke to me in December 2006 from his London home.

**You've stated that you've always had a powerful connection to
film.**

When we first came to Canada, things were pretty tough. My parents worked a lot of jobs and we lived in a really rough Toronto
neighborhood. My brother and I were bullied quite a bit. My earliest memories of the movies are of coming home from that violence
and turning on the television to watch old movies. They became
a haven for me. There would be the 1950s and '60s bedroom comedies, very early screwball films, the kind of old movies that would
be shown on television in the afternoons. They became a source of
comfort even more than a source of escape, actually. Those movies
were an idealized version of the culture we'd expected to come to,
not the version we were actually experiencing.

Was it racially-based bullying?

Yes. When we immigrated in 1971, there were very few South
Asians in Canada at all. It was pretty extreme. We moved to Flemingdon Park which was then a mostly poor, white working class
neighborhood. It was the beginning of the big wave of immigra-
tion under the Trudeau government. There was a pretty heavy
backlash in Toronto against the new immigrant populations then,
and we were on the front lines in Flemingdon Park.

**What was it like growing up in a strict Muslim household and
realizing you were gay?**

I'm from an Ismaili Muslim background which isn't, relatively
speaking, that strict a Muslim community. But yes, it was difficult.
It's a culture which doesn't even have a name for homosexuality
that isn't pejorative. I didn't really know what I was feeling. The
word "faggot" was often used on the school playground, but it was

just a generic term; it had no kind of association with sexuality for me. It's really odd, because in a way it was helpful that there were no associations to what I was feeling, because it sort of normalized it for me. I knew well enough that I couldn't talk about my feelings, but back then it wasn't okay to talk about any kind of sexual feelings. What I didn't know was that there was this practice out there called homosexuality. At the time, it just was an attraction that I felt and it wasn't demonized for me—yet. By the time I was twelve or thirteen, homosexuality had a name and a context, and that is when it started to get difficult. I came out to my parents quite young. I was sixteen when I told them. At first it was very, very hard and they didn't accept it. It took almost a decade of work on both our sides for acceptance and now things are pretty good. They love my boyfriend; my boyfriend loves them. I feel like the other woman in this relationship sometimes. It's all good. You'll see in [Touch of Pink, 2004]—the spirit of it is pretty autobiographical.

Can you tell me about the beginning of your career in film and television?

I think the origins were in Canada, but I didn't really start practising until I got to England. I volunteered at a place called the Euclid Cinema in Toronto. It was a community cinema and theater created by DEC, the Development Education Centre. It was the mid to late 1980s and the most amazing stuff was being programmed—from experimental film and video to community- and activist-based initiatives. I was on a committee that organized events and festivals; some of the early projects that I worked on included the Inside Out Festival and Race to the Screen (both Toronto film festivals). I also founded a festival and organization called Desh Pardesh with a gay South Asian group called Khush, which became a big South Asian cultural event for many years, which also had its origins at the Euclid. Being a community-based organizer and activist who worked with film and video seemed like an effective way to connect with people and initiate discussion about the fantastic work being made at the time. I became close to people like [Toronto filmmakers] Richard Fung and John Greyson—artists who were making some of that exciting work, and who were also activists and also affiliated with the Euclid. I made a short video promoting safe sex in the South Asian community in Toronto with Gita [now Kaspar] Saxena called Bolo! Bolo! [1991].

But I was practising as a poet then and had a couple of books published. When I moved to England, I landed in the film community too, working in distribution at the London Filmmakers' Co-op, which had a huge library of experimental film. The film and video work that I was promoting was much more conservative—at least in terms of content—than the work I was used to dealing with in Canada. Then in the mid-1990s, BBC Television was looking for writers. They were offering an internship program and intensive workshops, where you had the opportunity to develop a television script in six months and work with BBC script editors. Most importantly, they gave out a small bursary. So my boyfriend, who thought he was going to be supporting a poet for the rest of his life, suggested I apply. I thought he was nuts. I was new to the country and thought, What could I possibly have to say that would mean anything to British people? I was just finding my own feet here. But he sent in a short story that I was working on, along with one of my books of poetry, and I got an interview. And it was brutal. These people grilled me, trying to make sure I'd be invested in the program. I don't know what the rationale was, but maybe it was a tough-love approach, preparing me for the harshness of working in the TV and film industry. I found myself getting really passionate about why I should be a television scriptwriter, even though I had gone to the interview feeling quite blasé. And I got it—I got one of four internships offered. I wrote the very first draft of *Touch of Pink* in that workshop.

I understand there was pressure to edit the gay material out of your script.

The BBC really liked [the script] and optioned it. But it never got made. Over the next five or six years, the project came to life and died several times as either a TV movie or a feature film. Each time, a new producer came on board, and each time they would want to reinvent it. On two different occasions, producers came on board and told me, "Great idea. Very charming. Cut out the gay stuff. Keep the Cary Grant/fairy godfather figure alive and we'll have something commercial that we can put on the air."

They wanted to turn the couple heterosexual?

The script was so different in those days. What was interesting was that they liked the mother character through all the different versions—that was the one constant. Originally the script was auto-biographical, in that it was about a young gay man who had come to London from Canada, retracing his mother's footsteps. It was a mediation between the mother and son through this ghost figure of Cary Grant, which is still there to a certain extent, but that was very much the center of the script in its early versions. Originally, the mother was as much an active protagonist as the son was, but became more of a reactive character as the years went on. Also, in the beginning, the protagonist was not in a relationship. He was promiscuous and continually looking for sex. But as my life changed, the script changed along with me—as my relationship deepened, so did my protagonist's. The script kept catching up with my life.

It's interesting how the tone changed. In the beginning, it was darker and much more contemporary. Then it became lighter and lighter and started to take on the same frothy tones as those bedroom comedies from the '50s and '60s I used to watch. [The transition] probably had to do with my own circumstances. I felt more hopeful and optimistic the more I insinuated myself into British life. There is a lot here that is despairing still, of course, but my multiracial, multi-class community gave me lots of reason for hope. That may just be my own little bubble, I don't know. The London that I live in is challenging but a very hopeful and exciting place.

How is it for you as a Muslim living in London?
Whenever I'm in North America, I'm struck by the Islamophobia in the media. The reporting is just so slanted, and seeing how much goes unreported is also stunning. In terms of life here, yes, it has become more difficult for Muslims, and I expect it is worse outside of London than it is in the city. You know, there is a feeling I get in London where immigrants and people of color walk around like they own the turf; there isn't this beaten-down, eyes-to-the-ground kind of culture you get elsewhere, or what I felt growing up in Flemingdon Park. Of course, in the larger scheme of things, immigrants and people of color own nothing, relatively speaking. It's not like there isn't crime and poverty, and the threat of identity cards isn't having an impact—it is. But there is a strength of purpose that is transcending all of that. I feel like the people here don't act or behave like they are on the margins of life. They are

front and center of their own lives. Life here is tough, but it is less tough than the places that many of them come from, and so they keep moving forward and finding ways to heal. Again, it may just be a small bubble in the London that I live in, but I take a lot of hope and comfort from it.

Why do those of us who live in cities feel like we're living in a bubble? Aren't people who live in rural areas in their own special little bubbles?

In a way, I felt like the romance of *Touch of Pink* was for the people that I live with and amongst. So many gay Muslim men have come up to me and said they loved the film for not making them an issue—for just making an old-fashioned, Hollywood-style romantic comedy with characters who might be them. That really wasn't my initial intention—I was trying to challenge Hollywood film in which whiteness gets idealized and the culture of "happily ever after" messes with our heads. But it was the romance, and the happily-ever-after, that people cling to; that could be my failure as a filmmaker, but people still seem to need and want that stuff, in the same way that I did when I was growing up and took what I needed from those old romantic comedies I watched on TV.

What was the inspiration for the Cary Grant ghost?

I love so many of his movies. To me, he was just perfection. He was either the man I wanted to be or the man I wanted, I wasn't sure—a familiar gay conundrum, I think [*laughs*]. He was a dreamy white man and quite the opposite of the brutal, inarticulate, and violent white men and boys that I came across at school and on the street when I was growing up. There was something incredibly gentle, warm, and accepting about Cary Grant. He was the hopeful face of white masculinity and I gravitated toward his persona. He was a model of how to dress, how to be, how to look, the manners—everything. He was my mum's favorite movie star. She also thinks that my Dad is like Cary Grant [*laughs*].

The films produced in Britain while Margaret Thatcher was in power were often full of bitterness and resentment. A few years ago, you said that if George W. Bush was re-elected, films would get very dark.

My own work has become darker. One of the projects that I'm developing right now is called *YYZ*—it's about Toronto. It is about the

Kyle MacLachlan (as Cary Grant) in A Touch of Pink *(2004), courtesy Ian Iqbal Rashid*

Jimi Mistry, Suleka Mathew, and Kristen Holden-Ried in Touch of Pink *(2004), courtesy Ian Iqbal Rashid*

time when my family first came to Canada when racist violence was so prevalent, and how the brutality of that early racism continues to inflect and infect our lives years later. I suppose it's sort of the flip side to *Touch of Pink*. It's interesting that this is what is surfacing for me now. I just finished directing a film, *How She Move* [2007], which, in spite of being a teenage dance film, is imbued with darkness—both aesthetically and thematically. It's as much about the scars of migration experienced by a Jamaican-Canadian family as it is about a young woman who's gotta dance.

I am also getting asked a lot, especially here in the UK, to write about Islam. There is a British television project that I've been working on called *Don't Panic, I'm Islamic,* about a young, Westernized, feminist British-Asian woman who chooses to wear burqa, even though burqa isn't imposed or sanctioned in any way by her family. I do a lot of writing workshops with kids, mostly young writers of color, and I'm seeing this kind of situation again and again, with African-Muslim girls as well. In the face of Islamophobia, they want ways to proclaim their Muslimness, they want to be proud of who they are. I think they see their parents' generation as suffering from shame. Racism casts such a long shadow on the first generation of immigrants—so many humiliations, big and small, so many attempts to make them feel lesser, inferior. My schoolteachers made me adopt "Ian" as my first name when my family first moved to Canada, for example. But the second generation doesn't want to take any of that on. Young women are covering themselves to announce their Muslimness, proclaiming it loudly, and young men are finding their own forms of proclamation as well. So I want to explore that but not to present it as a sociological issue. I want this to be something that young kids of color would gravitate toward.

Filmmakers appear to be at very different points, depending on where they're located. Where do you see the state of queer film now, in the post-*Brokeback Mountain* world?
It leads to that old chestnut of a question, what is a queer film? I think *How She Move* can be identified as a queer film even though it doesn't name any queer characters. We are at an interesting point with coming-out stories. But do we need them anymore? I think where these stories are incredibly valuable are in places like

the Middle East, parts of Asia, and other places where being gay is still very dangerous. I think gay people are starved for positive coming-out stores in such places. *Touch of Pink*, for example, is being screened by gay groups in some of those countries. People in Pakistan are holding screenings of it at parties, and DVDs are being smuggled into some Gulf State countries. The film also did well in Latin America and India.

That must make you very happy.
It does. We are so privileged, and maybe a little smug, in our urban centers in the West. There are a lot of people who roll their eyes at the thought of—yet again—one more coming-out story, but I think there are places in the world where they are still desperately needed and valued.

FILMOGRAPHY

How She Move (feature) (director), 2007
Touch of Pink (feature) (director and writer), 2004
Stag (short film) (director and writer), 2001
Surviving Sabu (short film) (director and writer), 1998
This Life (TV series, two episodes) (writer), 1997
London Bridge (TV series, various episodes) (writer), 1995
Bolo! Bolo! (short film) (co-director with Gita Saxena), 1991

Don Roos: The Opposite of the Norm

Like so many gay filmmakers, Don Roos has a knack for conjuring up powerful women. Many will recall the girl-on-girl rivalry in *Single White Female* (1992), the suspense film that Roos wrote in which Bridget Fonda takes in roommate Jennifer Jason Leigh, only to discover that Leigh is insane and obsessed with taking on Fonda's identity. He also wrote the critically-savaged remake of *Diabolique* (1996), in which Sharon Stone plays a (surprise!) scheming murderess. And in *The Opposite of Sex* (1998), which he directed and wrote, an embittered Christina Ricci manipulates those around her, including her gay half-brother and his boyfriend whom she seduces.

Roos began his film career as a writer, taking a screenwriting course at the University of Notre Dame when he was in his early twenties. In the 1980s, he contributed to a number of popular television shows, in particular *Hart to Hart* and the *Dynasty* spin-off *The Colbys*. Roos also earned a reputation as a script doctor, working to improve screenplays others had already written. (Roos says he is too much of a gentleman to name the films he's been brought in to doctor.)

A turning point for him came in 1998 with the release of his directorial debut, *The Opposite of Sex*, the ensemble comedy that made many critical top-ten lists that year. After this success, Roos expected that getting studio support for films featuring gay characters—or even heterosexual characters who happened to be complex—might get easier. But not so, according to Roos, who says that studio executives interfered with his follow-up film, *Bounce* (2000), starring Ben Affleck and Gwyneth Paltrow, which resulted in its box office failure. This made his next feature film, *Happy Endings* (2005), all the more difficult.

His experience thus far has been somewhat disappointing to Roos, not only because of how studios treated him, but also by the critical and public reaction to the kind of narrative complexity and character ambiguities common in his films. He now lives in Los Angeles with his partner, actor-writer Dan Bucatinsky, and their adopted daughter. A conversation with Roos is much like one of his films: insightful, intelligent, sometimes digressive, and always sharp and witty. Sadly, even in the post-*Brokeback Mountain* Hollywood, Roos still sees problems getting gay characters portrayed honestly on the big screen.

In interviews, you've talked about the fact that when you were growing up, homosexuality was a huge taboo. Some of the film-

makers and writers that I've spoken to said they began writing precisely because they were gay. Was that your experience? Did part of the act of writing have to do with wanting to talk about something?

No, it didn't for me. I think I became a writer because I felt very different and strange, and writing gives you a sense of control. When you're writing, you're not playing ball, you're not with people; you're very much alone. I think writing is a good refuge for misfits of all shapes and sizes. Being an outsider or a minority or an oppressed person in the kind of society that I grew up in—which included my own home—I think I wrote just to get some kind of power, just to make a little world for myself where I could punish people or make them do things. Of course, it's connected to being gay, but I didn't start writing to talk about gay issues, at least not consciously.

Was your home life tough?

I grew up in a Catholic family in the 1950s, which was a very rough environment for a child to grow up in. Morality permeated every-thing, as did group thinking, discipline, and lessons about appro-priate and inappropriate feelings—you know, your typical repressed '50s household.

You've talked about the importance of gay images on the screen and what that can do for people. Do you remember the first gay character you saw on film or television?

No, but I remember Peter O'Toole with his shirt off in *Lord Jim* [1965]. The first gay image ... that's really hard. I don't know what that would be aside from the camp images or the mysterious im-ages that have a lot of power over gay men, like from *The Wizard of Oz* [1939] or *Peter Pan* [1960]. Mary Martin playing Peter Pan is a very strange image for a kid to hang on to, but I was obsessed with the yearly broadcast of *Peter Pan* on television. I couldn't have been more than four or five. But an openly gay image ... my God, was there one? There were a few people who appeared on talk shows, like Truman Capote, and Paul Lynde, who made me uncomfortable.

Why?

Because I sensed that he was something different or maybe like me. There was a lot of disapproval of how he was—my mother would laugh at him, my father would frown.

Both of those examples are people I grew up with too. They were both entertaining figures who were also train wrecks, in a way. Both Capote and Lynde died alcoholics.

There's a lot connected to those kinds of images. They suggest not only a sinful lifestyle, but an unhealthy one too. It's a strange feeling that leads people to sense their own damnation and extinction. That was what was so awful about AIDS. It seemed to some of us like, "This is the nightmare of our childhood come true," that being gay leads to death.

You began your career as a screenwriter. Can you tell me about your first writing gig?

My very first one was for *Hart to Hart* [1979–84], a television show in the early 1980s [starring Robert Wagner and Stefanie Powers] with quite a camp sensibility. I wrote four spec scripts, meaning scripts that aren't commissioned. I got to meet the producer who happened to be Mark Crowley, who wrote *The Boys in the Band*, the very important early gay play. He took an interest in me and gave me some assignments, so I suppose the gay mafia helped me in the very beginning. I wrote for television throughout the '80s, mostly for undistinguished shows, because I was very shy and didn't feel confident pitching to better shows. I also thought I wasn't capable of writing for cop shows or medical shows, that I was more soap opera. So maybe that was my own internal homophobia at work, or maybe it was my natural shyness or insecurity. I don't know. Finally, I wrote a script on my own, a feature-length film called *Love Field* [1992], and managed to get it to two producers who liked it, and then Michelle Pfieffer got on board [who was nominated for an Oscar for the role in 1992]. After that I forgot about television for a long time.

You talk about internalized homophobia, but personally I'd rather be writing for *Dynasty* than a cop show.

I wrote for *The Colbys* [1985–87], which was a *Dynasty* spin-off, and a series called *Paper Dolls* [1984] that was a drama about two young models. I wrote for shows that dealt with human emotion and interaction—the things that people said or did to each other rather than gunshots or legal cases or medical problems. I was really attracted to soap opera. A lot of people call my movies soap operas.

Soap operas have such a bad reputation, but shows like *The Sopra-

nos or *Six Feet Under* are essentially soap operas.
Absolutely. When I started doing film, the powers that be didn't
care what I'd done in television. I thought making films was going
to make it easier for me to write about things that I cared about.
The television censors were crazy and the networks were timid.
Television, I think, is a terrible, terrible place to work even today
because of stupid people telling you what you can and can't say to
America. I just think that the people working in television aren't
very intelligent.

**Like a salivating gay dog, I recently purchased the first, pre-Joan
Collins season of *Dynasty* on DVD. There is some really interesting stuff in that show, including the gay son who's an outcast and
getting drunk all the time. I'm sure the writers went through a
terrible meat-grinding process to get that character on the show.
It's a really interesting cultural artifact, a reflection of America in
the '80s.**
I agree. I think television shows can't help but be a reflection of
the age in which they are made because they have to be popular
to succeed so they have to somehow speak to the masses, even if
it's unconsciously to the desires of the public at the time. Television can't help but be a great way to look at a culture, and what the
values of that culture are. For someone who is in opposition to the
culture, though, again, television is not the greatest place to work.
Although I watch an awful lot of television and I love shows like
The Sopranos, Six Feet Under, Sex and the City, and *24.* There's a lot of
great British television too. But in general, American television is
pretty much unwatchable. Characters are never deeply unlikable or
deeply complicated.

**Going back to your writing, you speak of camouflaging gay char-
acters in some of your screenplays.**
I did that a lot in the beginning. But I may have to go back to it,
just because sometimes putting gay characters out there hurts you.
The studio will say, "Oh, there are gay characters, it's a gay film, we
have to market it a certain way," which is very frustrating. I don't
know how *Brokeback Mountain* got made. It will probably do us
more harm than good because it will be pointed to as an example
of the fact that Hollywood is open and that things are changing,
but believe me, on the frontlines they aren't changing, they are

getting worse. It's harder to put gay characters in a film now than it was ten years ago when I did *The Opposite of Sex* [1998]. Camouflaging gay characters can take many forms. A popular way is making the lead character's best friend sassy, but female. Or the lead can be an outcast who is not a happily accepted member of traditional heterosexual Christian society. A black character can also masquerade as a gay character, as well as any character who is out of step with the mainstream.

Of course there is the popular theory that many of Tennessee Williams' characters, particularly his strong women characters like Blanche DuBois, were in fact gay characters.
I don't know if they were for a fact, but they probably were. I think Williams probably drew out their internal spiritual life and soul from his experiences as a gay man. Of course, if they were actual gay characters, their experiences would be quite different, and they would be perceived quite differently. But camouflaging is a way for the gay writer to get inside his characters and to tap into a little of the anger and anxiety that you feel as a minority person.

The fact that you wrote *Single White Female* [1992] makes sense to me, seeing as a character is murdered by getting a high heel in the head.
That was all kind of unconscious. I thought, "Oh, that will be fun." I was thinking, "What is the most dangerous thing about a woman?" She wasn't going to hit him over the head with her vagina, so I thought, "Well, she'll hit him over the head with her high heel shoe."

Were you conscious of other issues—I mean, it's about these two powerful women.
Well, I was conscious that none of the straight white men in the film were good guys. The only man who survives is the gay neighbor upstairs. The characters who had power, compassion, or intellectual ability were either gay or female. That [characterization] was very consciously done. I was tired of those movies where the girl is just a victim to be offered up to the evil person, where women are stupid and weak and teetering in high heels.

In *The Opposite of Sex*, you bring a lot of these sexual issues to the fore. I've always felt that Christina Ricci's character was your

voice, was the voice of a gay man at the center of the film.
Yeah, I think you're right. I can talk about her being a real character in her own right. If you look at it, she is a woman defined by
her sexuality. [In the film], Christina's character doesn't really have
any sexual appetite, but she is defined by society as what she is because of her sexual attributes, because of her breasts and because of
her attitude, independence, and unwillingness to obey convention.
She's defined by society because of her sex or her interest in sex—or
what they presume to be her interest in sex—and, of course, that is
very gay. Gay men are defined [in that way] by people all the time.
They think that the most important thing about a gay man is that
he wants to sleep with another man. So in that way, Christina's
character is a gay man. She's also very thoughtful and confused
about sex. She's unconscious about it in the beginning and over
the course of the film it begins to trouble her, which is very much
like my experience of being a gay man: what's this thing that
separates me from everyone else? Where is it located? What does it
mean about me that I want to be with a man instead of a woman?
Why does that define me, because my taste for chocolate or vanilla
does not define me nor does my taste in sports? What is it about
my desire for the same sex that totally separates me? What is everybody's desire? Christina's character is a rebel, she's impatient with
a morality she doesn't really understand, and in that way she's a
very brave character; unlike myself through most of my life. She
also does what she wants to do and doesn't spend too much time
in any kind of moral argument, but I don't think that's very gay. I
think gay people spend a lot of time agonizing over the things they
do.

**I think that's why she's so refreshing. That's wish fulfillment, be-
cause so many gay people would like to say, "Fuck off."**
She's very powerful that way. That's what I liked about her. In fact,
that's why we wrote the character. I wrote all the voiceovers for her
narration before the movie began. We shot the film without her
voiceovers, though, and I directed everything as straight scenes.
I've discovered that characters behaving honestly can be funny.
We shot everything without pushing for laughs, so it didn't seem
to us to be a comedy at the time. I knew it was, but we were more
concerned with the internal lives of the characters. When I finally
edited her voiceover narration into the picture, it was really, really

shocking because I had come to treat these characters very intently and lovingly, but there she was in her voiceover making fun of them, being very bold and not being particularly discriminating in her hostility and not really taking an empathetic view of anybody. I thought, "Oh my God, I hate her! She doesn't know anything, she's a kid, she's a punk. This is complicated." I grew to love it, but it was a shock in the beginning. I do think she says some horrible things and her language is terrible. She's pretty awful. But I appreciated her spirit more and more.

I was really struck by the film when I first saw it. We talk about how far we've come, but there's still something radical about a film where gay and straight characters are given equal time and equal respect.

It's hard to pull it off. There was this time during the 1990s when movie people weren't paying a lot of attention and you could get an independent film made quite easily. And let's face it: Christina Ricci is a very cinematic person. She's very beautiful and compelling. I think people thought it was going to be a "funny" comedy, but once we got the audience in there, we started dealing with difficult things like sex and death and being gay. In that way, it was kind of a stealth bomb. It's very hard to surprise audiences now. I think audiences are more alert to signs of gay culture, signs of what they don't want. I think every year the audience gets stupider and stupider and that they've been trained to get that way. I mean, what can you say about a country that re-elected Bush? How much can you admire their intelligence? Seriously, it's not fun.

I was in shock on election night.

It's a deeply stupid country. I think when we grow up we think everybody is like our family or like our neighborhood block and that they're all smart and they all care. Well, they're not. They're very difficult, and a lot of them are dumb. And the ones who are smart are distracted by what's fashionable and in vogue. I think it's difficult for thoughtful films to get a good reaction from movie audiences in America because they want to be soothed by movies; they don't really want to go to the movies to think. You get a highly praised film like *Pride & Prejudice* where not a single real disturbing thought or feeling occurs in the entire film. That's America's idea of a thinking-man's film today. Maybe I sound bitter, but as you grow older you lose a little of that sense of, "It just takes a good film and they will come." I don't think that's true. There are some barriers in the business that work against that. The principal one is really the culture as a whole. Where is this culture going? A culture that is based on fear, one that is controlled by its fears, and is not going to be open to anything challenging in their entertainment? As for films with gay characters or content, studio types will say, "Well, it's not that I don't want to see that," and ask, "Do they have to be gay?" After I made *Happy Endings* [2005], which took two and a half years to make and fell apart several times, my own producer told me, "In the next movie, don't put a gay person in it. It's so much harder." So, even your own team will dissuade you, just because it is so impossible.

I don't know how Ang Lee got *Brokeback Mountain* [2005] green-lit, but he is an award-winning director who can do what he wants. The problem with *Brokeback Mountain* is it will take up the space that a lot of smaller independent films could've taken up. There are people in the business who will point to it and say, "We're not big-oted, we made *Brokeback Mountain*." So it'll work against us for the next ten years. I think a lot of gay filmmakers are consumed with jealousy that he was able to do it. "Why could he do it and I can't?" And they are also aware that it will be used against us for years and years.

I think another part of the reason Ang Lee was able to make
Brokeback Mountain was because he's straight.
He's the gayest straight man I ever met. *The Wedding Banquet, Sense and Sensibility*, and *Brokeback* … and I think he's a very open guy in terms of what appeals to him. I wish he was gay. I would love to claim Ang Lee for our team, but he's not. That is one of the reasons it's safe. In order to put a gay thing over in this country, it helps if it's shepherded through by a straight person. In fact, one of the ideas I had for *The Opposite of Sex* was, "I have to make this lead character a buxom, beautiful, blonde straight girl who hates gays, or has the normal contempt for gays that most Americans have, and she will shepherd the gay themes and characters through this film and people will trust her."

It was interesting to see how *Brokeback Mountain* played in more conservative parts of North America. It was shot in Alberta, Canada's most conservative province.

I don't think you're going to fool a straight audience by putting the gay leads in cowboy shirts and putting a buffalo on the poster so that they'll think, "It's just two cowboys chewing the fat sitting on the fence talking about their cattle." You know, for a gay man, as you grow older, you come to understand just how threatening homosexuality is to others. When you're a child, it seems that people are very, very stupid and limited. But the depth of the hatred and the fear is something you realize when you grow older. The basic biological fear that many people have is very daunting.

It's not only a difficult time to be gay in America, but simply to stay sane, given what's happened in Iraq and Washington.

The Christian part of America is getting increasingly harder to deal with because it is so intrusive and aggressive. The Republicans' use of homophobia to galvanize voters like they did in the 2004 election was very discouraging. On the flip side, I've never been able to live my life more freely than I have in the last ten years. I'm a citizen of California, which has my loyalty, not the United States—I'm not what you would call a patriotic American, but I am a patriotic Californian. I'm not discriminated against in my business for being gay. They don't care if I'm a gay writer or a gay director at all, they really don't. They don't discriminate against me socially or in terms of awarding me jobs. They couldn't give a shit about my sexual preference. My partner and I have a home together, our doctors and lawyers are quite accepting of us, as are our neighbors and the people who work for us. It's not a problem. We also have a daughter. I have a very free and full life as a gay man in California. It's a weird feeling to be that free and open in your daily life. When I was fifteen years old, if I could have thought that one day I could have all these things as a gay man and be out as a gay man, I would not have believed it. On the other hand, we live in a society that is so vocal about its dislike for who I am and how I love, it's tough.

After the success of *The Opposite of Sex*, I understand you were inundated with gay screenplays.

Yes, but I don't direct other people's work, so it was all for naught.

Then you chose, as you say, to write straight.

I wrote *Bounce* [2000] immediately before I made *The Opposite of Sex* to prove that I could do straight. I had never done a movie where I had a straight man for a lead. *The Opposite of Sex* was very, very gay, and I wanted to write in the mainstream and I wanted to write a movie without irony. *The Opposite of Sex* was so easy to write because it was ironic, which is a natural tone for me, and I wanted to see if I could hide and do a straight tale in every sense of the word, about straight people told straightly—a straight love story. The script wrote itself quickly, but it was a very difficult movie for me to make. Originally, I wasn't going to direct it, but we couldn't find the right director. Then *The Opposite of Sex* came out and because it was successful, the studio said, "Well, would you like to direct this?" I thought, "Yes, I can make it edgier." But the studio wouldn't let me make it as edgy as I wanted and in the end the test audience wanted it to be even less edgy. The two stars, Gwyneth Paltrow and Ben Affleck, were wonderful—I just love them both. It was a thrill to work with them. When the film was finished, the studio took it to New Jersey to test screen it. Miramax was very responsive to the test audiences, who didn't like the dark parts of Ben's character. They loved Gwyneth's character because she's a victim throughout the entire movie, like a lucky victim, that's the role. But the complicated guy who lies and who's divided and who's dark and responds very humanly and who has weaknesses and strengths—they didn't like that. They wanted him to be one thing or the other. Can he be either a bad guy or a good guy? That was very hard for me to see. The net result was that the film made no more money than it would have if it had retained the integrity of the first cut—in the quest to make characters less objectionable, you lose as many people as you gain.

You weren't very happy with the process of making that film.

I'll never do a studio movie again. Never, never, never. That's how much I liked it. I would also never work on a commercial television network show again, ever. I'm not the kind of person who's like, "It was a horrible experience, but I'll go in there again and make it work." I know these people are never going to change. I'll kill myself on the wheel trying to get it to work. It's not for me. Your voice is not respected. They don't really want to hear from you. So why do it?

Don Roos, Ben Affleck, and Gwyneth Paltrow on the set of Bounce *(2000),*
Miramax/Photofest

Christina Ricci and Ivan Sergei in The Opposite of Sex *(1998), Columbia TriStar/*
Photofest

I really liked *Bounce* and put it on my top ten list that year. I was very drawn to what I saw as your sensibility because it felt like an ode to Douglas Sirk. I liked seeing Ben Affleck cry and I recognized the dark elements. And I could feel you in it too. You and I had talked earlier about substance abuse and there's a scene where he breaks down publicly and I felt there were a lot of personal elements in it. Of course, I didn't know what went on behind the scenes about the audience testing, but I want you to know that a lot of your intentions actually did come through.

Thank you, that's nice to hear. I have a very fond memory of the film because of Gwyneth and Ben. Directing Ben was really a joy, because he's the kind of actor who will do it a million times and be very game and committed and open and willing and ready to go there, and that was a ball for me. And Gwyneth is a deeply admirable person. It was great working with those guys and I'm fond of the movie for that reason. But the film was, for me, an artistic disappointment and it informed my choices over the next couple of years. I didn't want that to happen again. I'm not really a corporate in-fighter. That just doesn't appeal to me. You just never win. If I know they don't want to hear from me, I won't go there because I find that process very, very painful. To make a film and then have an audience in New Jersey tell me what to do with my baby, I couldn't handle it. [Miramax] had a little focus group [in which] some idiot in acid-washed jeans stood up and said, "I didn't like him when he did that." I felt like saying, "No one has ever lied to you in your life? Someone lied to you when they said you looked good today. People lie." I didn't have the balls to say that, or, "Before you take care of my movie, please take care of your hair."

You're hilarious.

It's tough to make movies because they cost so much money so you have to get a lot of people to see them, and I am not a person who loves the American populace. I would be happy if only a few people saw my films, especially the people who need to see my films, like gay teenagers. But it's a really expensive art form. That's a real conflict for me.

The hope will be that the DVD market is changing that. I read recently that what's successful on DVD is not necessarily the big blockbuster, it's mid-range or low-budget movies, like *Happy Endings*.

Thank God for DVDs. As a filmmaker, you say that every time you have an opening weekend. Because on DVD, the movie exists in a form that is available to anybody at anytime. That is very encouraging for all of us. Because if you're like me and you're writing in order to speak to yourself at a younger age, it's important to have that available to kids through Blockbuster or Netflix.

It must have seemed logical after your experience with *Bounce* to go back and do a lower-budget film like *Happy Endings*.
Absolutely. I wrote *Happy Endings*, which I finished in July 2002. Because it's an independent film, very much like *The Opposite of Sex* and very much in the same genre, I thought in my deluded, egocentric perception of myself that there would be a feeding frenzy for that script. The timing seemed right to me. But nobody wanted to do it. We bounced the project around a bit and then a deal we thought we had fell through. Finally, we ended up at Lions Gate, a studio I did not want to go to because they had blown the release of a movie my boyfriend had written and starred in a couple of years before called *All Over the Guy*. But we finally ended up at Lions Gate, which made the movie. In that respect, I'm very grateful to them. We had a really magical time making the film. It was the happiest I've ever been professionally in my life during the six weeks we shot it. It was great, but the release was an absolute disaster.

Why?
First of all, it was not a summer film, it was a May or September film. But they released it in July opposite *Charlie and the Chocolate Factory* starring Johnny Depp and *Wedding Crashers*, the only weekend in the summer that I was afraid of. They opened it in only forty-four theaters and didn't do any television advertising. They simply didn't support the film. It was an appalling release. I was never as angry as I was in that summer. There were wonderful reviews, but they wouldn't take out ads that quoted any of them. It was an appalling, disgraceful, and shameful release. It took a lot out of me. It was a new fear. I'd had fears before: what if I can't write the script? What if I have no ideas? What if I have an idea but I can't write the script? What if nobody likes the script? What if nobody wants to act in it? What if nobody wants to make the movie? What if I blow it while making the movie? You have all of those fears. I

never had the fear of, what if you make a movie and you love it but
the studio blows its release? That had never happened to me. Now
I have a new fear about what can happen to you when you make
a film. The actual experience of making *Happy Endings* was truly
wonderful, deeply wonderful. Like you said, the DVD market will
keep that film alive and available, and in that respect it was a wonderful experience. And studios make mistakes, but the thing is they
make mistakes with three years of your life. I'm just emerging from
that whole period.

That sounds like it was really painful.
It was painful, but the movie I loved. I never had that experience
before of loving something that I made. I think one of the reasons
why is because I let go on that film and let the actors be much
freer, let the DP [director of photography] be much freer, Clark
Mathis, who is a wonderful DP. We all just had a really joyous time
making it and I'd never had that experience before.

Even with *The Opposite of Sex*?
With *The Opposite of Sex*, I was a nervous wreck. It was my first film
and I didn't know what the hell I was doing.

**In *Happy Endings*, that confidence comes across. It's interesting
that in the script, you seem to arrive at a rethinking of the abortion issue.**
I'm always right down the middle of the line about abortion. I've
no idea which side of myself is right. On one hand, as adoptive
parents, as people who require a supply of unwanted or unable-to-
be-cared-for children, it would be great if there were no abortions
and all of a sudden there were a lot of kids who we could adopt.
On the other hand, the idea of society being so invasive into a
woman's life as to say, "You must carry this child," is so deeply sex-
ist and troubling that I will fight to the death to expand the rights
of women to have abortions. What's happening in this country
right now is really just awful—it's very difficult for people who
are not wealthy to get abortions. You have all of these kids who
are unwanted being raised, and the cycle continues. The church
is involved far too much in this question. But in terms of *Happy
Endings*, it's not really a rethinking of the issue; just about all of
my films have children or pregnant women in them. That's a very
strong and powerful figure for me: a pregnant young woman. Also,

as a gay man, I feel this kind of camaraderie with women who are being told by straight white men what to do with their bodies. I have felt that oppression and I have felt people who have no understanding of my situation telling me how to do the most important things there are [in life]. Telling me how I can do it, or when I can do it, or that I can't do it. I'm politically pro-choice, entirely. If you talk to women who've had abortions, there is a range of different feelings about it. It's a huge [decision], but there are many things that we have to have the right to do, even if they trouble us.

Don't you have a funny story about how the TV reality series *Queer Eye for the Straight Guy* played a role in your adoption?
We were in the market to adopt a baby. How it happens here in California is you contact a lawyer who has contacts all over the United States and then the women who are pregnant contact him. Our lawyer called us and said this girl's going to call you. She did and she was a wonderful person. She's from the Midwest, from a very conservative part of the country, and I was very curious and asked her, "Why do you want to have two gay men raise your child?" She said, "My mom and I just love *Queer Eye for the Straight Guy*. We think any one of those guys would make a fabulous dad." I don't think she said fabulous because I say fabulous and that's how I tell the story, but it was something along those lines. She said, "Would you mind naming the baby Kyan if it's a boy?" Kyan is the cute one who does all the grooming. I said, "No, no, sure we will." But it was a girl. We named her Eliza.

That's a great story.
That is an example of the power of media and the power of television to get inside those homes. That didn't happen to me in the '50s and the '60s. I wasn't receiving any messages from the outside world about being different. I do think people today are able to learn about the world and that there are options through their televisions. I don't know if we will win or not. The battle will grow larger, and there will be people who will be saved by this knowledge of the world out there. I'm always worried when I hear about gay teens committing suicide. I think we lose a lot of Christian people that way too, because it's very tough growing up in a Christian family being gay. It's a funny thing to say, but I do think that the variety of images that television offers young people offers us some hope.

FILMOGRAPHY

Happy Endings (feature) (director and writer), 2005
Bounce (feature) (director and writer), 2000
M.Y.O.B. (TV series) (writer), 2000
The Opposite of Sex (feature) (director and writer), 1998
Diabolique (feature) (writer), 1996
Boys on the Side (feature) (writer), 1995
Love Field (feature) (writer), 1992
Single White Female (feature) (writer), 1992
The Colbys (TV series) (writer), 1985–87
Hart to Hart (TV series) (writer), 1979–84

Phillip B. Roth, photographed by Melissa Timme

Phillip B. Roth: Family, Spirituality & Jewish Sex Work

Phillip B. Roth's bone-dry sense of humor runs throughout his short but spirited body of work. Specializing in short films, he asks repeated and pointed questions for audiences to ponder the complicated intersections of sex, family, and spirituality.

Roth's only feature film to date is a documentary, *I Was a Jewish Sex Worker* (1996), which garnered strong critical praise on the international film fest circuit for its often-hilarious collapsing of seemingly disparate issues. As well as expanding Roth's favorite themes, it also incorporates footage from Roth's earlier short films. The film opens with a montage of images of Roth, who worked as an erotic masseur, interacting with various clients, set against a soundtrack of Roth's phone messages: one is from a relative, another from someone who requests his underwear, and yet another from someone who clearly thinks they have reached the home of the celebrated novelist of the same name. While *I Was a Jewish Sex Worker* is endowed with a sharp sense of humor, it is also bruising emotionally; in it, Roth searches for emotional intimacy, both as a neophyte filmmaker (he has an affair with director Rosa von Praunheim early in the movie) and as a sex worker. He also interviews family members; his grandmother is a standout: in one scene, she recites a proverb, "Only those who can see the invisible can accomplish the impossible," which she then reveals she read on a plaque in her dentist's office. Along with Super 8 footage of himself as a child, Roth includes a brilliant array of media clips, including his nude appearance on a New York cable-access show and his love scene with porn star Annie Sprinkle from one of his earlier short films.

With its fusion of themes on family and sexuality, *I Was a Jewish Sex Worker* is emblematic of the kind of intimate, first-person style of documentary filmmaking that emerged in the 1980s and '90s.

Roth has been working as a yoga instructor in Los Angeles in the past few years, though he has continued to make short films. He is now working on a documentary about the complex relationship between American Jews and Israel. He spoke to me from his Los Angeles home in the winter of 2007.

Tell me how you first became involved in filmmaking.
In the late 1980s, I finished college at University of California at Berkeley, where I'd studied film theory. I moved to Germany where I learned about classic films, like the French New Wave, studied

some documentaries, and also met Rosa von Praunheim who encouraged me to take up personal, more radical, filmmaking. He told me to do my films in first-person, using voiceover to express my personal perspective. I moved to New York later that year [1988] and worked as a soundman on one of Rosa's films called *Survival in New York* [released in 1989]. I had this subject in mind—the contrast between the freedom that I felt in gay sex clubs and my fear of being affectionate with men on the streets. New York seemed a lot less tolerant than Berlin—there was public taunting of gay people in the street, like people yelling "faggot" out of car windows, and other anti-gay violence, which made me afraid of being affectionate with other men in public. And so I thought I'd make a film about this. I did it exactly as Rosa encouraged me to, not thinking about production values, not waiting for money or grants or anything—just go out and do it. I had a friend who sold me a Bolex camera for cheap. So I got a cameraman, James Wentzy, and organized a sex party in his basement loft. I had everyone sign releases. We also did a scene about public affection, which some guys from the Radical Faeries [a gay men's organization mainly interested in the spiritual dimension of sexuality] helped me out with. I edited it at Millennium, an East Village film cooperative, and titled it *Boys/Life* [1989]. It was Rosa who suggested I submit it to the New York Gay and Lesbian Experimental Film Festival, which is now the MIX Festival. I showed a rough cut to Jim Hubbard and Sarah Schulman, the festival organizers, and they loved it, which was very gratifying. They made it one of the closing night films. The funniest thing about *Boys/Life* for me was that I didn't realize it was a comedy until I watched it with the audience on that closing night. From the first line of my voiceover, the audience burst out in raucous laughter. I was floored by that! When I was editing, I didn't think the film was funny at all. I thought I was being very serious, speaking from the heart about my fears and my messy sexual matters. But they just kept on laughing. That night, I realized that part of my appeal as a filmmaker is that I take myself so seriously, which winds up being funny. After it screened in New York, it was invited to the Berlin International Film Festival in 1990 and from there, it got a lot of invitations to other film festivals.

So this was a sign, and you continued along in this vein?

Yes. Another thing that I was very interested in was pansexuality.

I had dated a number of women, and decided I wanted to explore that subject, I wanted to have sex with a woman on film.

Why?

Because I'm nominally bi and a sexual adventurer.

So you're gay but a little bit straight on the Kinsey scale.

Yes. Does "six" on the Kinsey scale mean you're totally gay? If so, then I think I'm a Kinsey "four." Perhaps it was a bit of a precursor to the reality-TV era, but I felt like whatever experiences I had, they weren't worth having unless I filmed them. In 1990, I met Annie Sprinkle, who had been a porn star in the '70s and '80s. I told her I wanted to do a movie where I fucked a woman for the first time and she was like, "Yeah, I'll do it!" [*Laughs.*] Now I guess she's a full-on lesbian, but at that time I think she considered herself mainly straight. She was very kind and really great to work with. We spent two full days shooting the film, which I called *25-Year-Old Gay Man Loses His Virginity to a Woman* [1991]. Interestingly, Sarah Schulman found it offensive, but wanted to show it at the [New York Gay and Lesbian] Experimental Film Festival anyway, perhaps to stimulate discussion. The audience loved it, but it got a scathing review in *Outweek*, calling me a male chauvinist, presumably because I fucked Annie in the missionary position. Gay and feminist politics were a little different back then. This was around the time that GLAAD [Gay and Lesbian Alliance Against Defamation] was protesting against the release of *Basic Instinct* [1992], which most of my friends now consider a gay classic.

Your scene with Annie Sprinkle is very funny; you later incorporated it into the *I Was a Jewish Sex Worker* [1996].

It's funny because it's just Annie and me being the way we were. It was genuine—not part of an act.

Your films, especially *I Was a Jewish Sex Worker*, are great examples of the "personal is political" style of documentary filmmaking, which became popular in the late '80s and early '90s. Filmmakers started retrieving their home movie footage, dredging up various family anecdotes, then adding their own voiceover. You've said that Rosa pushed you in this direction. Were there other filmmakers that influenced you that way?

Around the time I was making *I Was a Jewish Sex Worker*, I was very

Annie Sprinkle and Phillip B. Roth in I Was a Jewish Sex Worker *(2003), photographed by Kim Hansen*

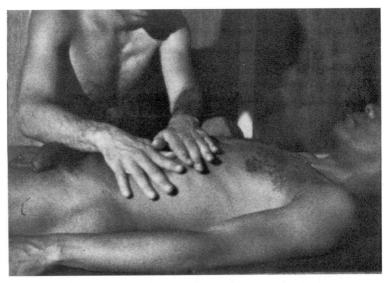

Still from I Was a Jewish Sex Worker *(2003), photographed by Billy Quinn*

influenced by Ross McElwee's *Sherman's March* [1986], and the films of Andy Warhol, which I saw at a retrospective at the Museum of Modern Art in New York following his death. I also remember studying Jean-Luc Godard's *Masculin-Feminin* [1966] and Jean Rouch's *Chronique d'un Été* [1961], both of which continue to influence me, especially in my current film project.

There's been so much talk of compartmentalization, the idea that people can put their sexuality in one area of their life and put their work in another, and so on. What I loved about *Jewish Sex Worker* is that you seem to work against that idea.
Yes. I made my films specifically as an attempt to decompartmentalize my life. I think it stemmed from a deep-seated feeling of shame about my sexuality, and making films was a way to work that out. I was already out, but by showing myself having sex with other men, I came out in a way that was beyond just talking about it. It affected me greatly. It made me feel like more of a whole human being.

When I did *Boys/Life*, my mother and brother came to the screening at Outfest in Los Angeles. There's a shot in the film which begins on my face and then pans down to my hard dick. I remember standing in the back of the theater and thinking, "What the hell was I thinking inviting my mother to this?" And just then, I saw her whisper something in my brother's ear. Afterward, when she came out of the screening, I asked her what she thought of the film. She said, "It was about what I expected." And I said, "What does that mean? What were you expecting?" And again she said, "It was about what I expected." That was it. So I asked my brother if she had said something to him, and he said, "She didn't say much, but halfway through the film she leaned over to me and said, 'He's *so* conceited!'" We stopped talking about the film that evening, but the next day, she said, "I heard a rumor that Richard Gere had to be taken to the emergency room to have a gerbil removed from his anal cavity. Tell me—do you do gerbils?" So I guess the film opened up a frank discussion between us about my sex life.

So do you do gerbils?
After the Gere rumors, I had to stop. [*Laughs.*]

***Jewish Sex Worker* ends with this extended questioning of your**

father. I must say, that scene is so complex and moving. In one moment, I feel sympathy for him, and then in another I feel angry with him. On one hand, he was from a different generation. But on the other, I think parental love should be unconditional.

For me, I was happy just by his appearing in my film and speaking the way he did. For a guy who's fairly conservative and uncomfortable discussing any aspect of sexuality, at least with me, he really put himself out there. He certainly would have preferred to keep our discussion private, but he allowed me to film him, even knowing that his interview might be seen by family, friends, and co-workers. I was extremely appreciative that he agreed to participate. I've come to realize that "accepting" and "liking" are not the same thing—I don't need to have my parents or anyone else like what I do. I don't think my dad necessarily likes that I'm gay, but nowhere in the interview does he condemn my choice.

Does he see it as a choice?

I do.

You do? I don't. I guess you're further along the Kinsey scale than I am.

I know most gay people would vehemently disagree with me on this point. My feelings may not be a choice, but I choose whether or not to act on those feelings. I think the "It's not a choice!" litany that pervades gay politics makes gay people seem like weaklings and victims of genetics. It plays right into the shaming scenario that we've been trying to rid ourselves of. Instead of pleading, "Please accept me because I couldn't help myself," I'd much rather say, "I chose to stick my dick in that guy's ass and I'm proud of my choice!"

But getting back to your father, I didn't mean to seem like I was attacking him, I just felt a complex range of emotions as I watched that final interview in the film.

A lot of people felt the same way you did.

You seem annoyed while you were interviewing him.

At the time, I felt more like you. I felt frustrated because I wanted him to not just accept, but to embrace my sexuality. Watching that interview over and over again when I edited it made me realize that I was actually being a much less tolerant person than he was. He accepted my homosexuality even if he didn't like it. I, on the other had, was trying to force him to like something about me that he didn't like. As a gay man, I would have hated it if he was trying to change me, but at the time, I was doing my darnedest to change him. Learning to accept my parents as they were was a hard lesson for me, one which I learned mostly by doing that film. I've come to realize that the fact that he wanted to continue our relationship and continue to spend time with me, despite something major about me that he didn't like, was a true testament of his love for me. Many gay people are not so lucky to have a father like mine. In the years since that interview, I've learned to accept the things I don't like about him, and love him in the same way that he loves me.

Certainly, I think what you've just said can be a major point of reconciliation between gay people and their families. The scenes with your grandmother are simply incredible.
She's still alive. She's just celebrated her ninety-third birthday. Sadly, my Aunt Lynn, the outspoken one who rants about racial issues and abortion, passed away in 2005.

Why isn't this film available on DVD?
I may try to release *Jewish Sex Worker* on DVD when my current film projects come to fruition. But I actually enjoy the fact that it's an underground film. I love talking to people after the screenings. When I do screen it now, I get great turnouts, precisely because it's not available on home video

What are you working on now?
I'm working on a film about the relationship of American Jews with the state of Israel. Again, it's coming from a very personal place. I'm approaching it from that same motivation of trying to understand myself better. I'm interested in how the looming presence of Israel, a country which I've never visited, affects my identity as an American Jew. I've already done several interviews, including one with my grandmother, who was born in America and did not visit Israel until she was in her sixties. My parents were very strong supporters of Israel, as was the synagogue we attended. I learned very little Hebrew, but I studied a lot about the history of Israel and the Jewish people in Hebrew school. Later, though, I realized that I had received a very one-sided perspective during my childhood.

Everything was presented to us as simple fact, reinforced by what I read in newspapers and saw on the news. When I was young, there weren't suicide bombers, but there were bombings and other violence like that horrible incident at the Munich Olympics [at the 1972 Summer Olympics in Munich, Germany, a Palestinian organization took the Israeli Olympic team hostage and killed eleven of the athletes]. The message from my family and Hebrew school teachers was always, "All Israel wants to do is live in peace. Why won't the Arabs leave us alone?" At college, I started to read alternative books and newspapers with different perspectives, and suddenly felt that I had not been given the complete picture. I don't want it to sound like the people who taught me as a child were trying to mislead me—I think they presented things as best they could, and as they saw them. Although I'm critical of many of Israel's actions, I don't consider myself an Israel basher.

Some people may label you an Israel basher when you come out with this film.
I know they will. It's interesting that many American Jews have such a hard time hearing any criticism of Israel. There's actually much more criticism of it in the Israeli press than in the mainstream American press. I think it's highly problematic that non-Jews who criticize Israel are labelled as anti-Semites and Jews who criticize Israel are labeled as self-loathing. It's a good way of silencing people and ending discussions before they can get started. I also feel that many American Jews define their Jewish identities in terms of victimhood, a notion that I strongly reject. That's the essence of what I'm exploring.

FILMOGRAPHY

Phillip B. Roth is director and writer of the following which are short films unless otherwise noted:

Cuddler, 2003
Fancy-Boy, 2003
Glad I'm Not Straight Anymore!, 2003
Hammer of Hope, 2003

Rikki Dee, 2003
Weaker #2, 2003
Hanky Code, 2001
Tit Torture, 2001
I Was a Jewish Sex Worker (feature), 1996
Latex Saves Lives, 1993
25-Year-Old Gay Man Loses His Virginity to a Woman (short
    documentary), 1991
After the Piss Club (short documentary), 1990
Boys/Life (short documentary), 1989

Patricia Rozema: The Mermaid's Song

Patricia Rozema's 1987 feature debut *I've Heard the Mermaids Singing* is a rousing, poetic film about a misfit dreamer who lives vicariously through another woman. Full of magical realist touches and winning performances (the cast includes Sheila McCarthy, Paule Baillargeon, and Ann-Marie MacDonald), the film incited such intense buzz at the 1987 Cannes Film Festival that it set off a bidding war, which was won by Harvey Weinstein and his new company Miramax. As a result, Rozema became a critical darling and a cult heroine among lesbian moviegoers; feminist theorist Camille Paglia has repeatedly praised the film, calling it one of her all-time favorites.

Unfortunately, Rozema's obtuse second feature, *White Room* (1990), starring Kate Nelligan and Margot Kidder, was a disappointment, and led some critics to declare Rozema a one-hit wonder. But five years later, she won over critics and audiences once more with *When Night Is Falling* (1995), a romantic fable about two women (Pascale Bussières and Rachel Crawford) who fall madly in love. This film, which features some of the most erotically-charged same-sex love scenes ever captured on the big screen, brought Rozema back into the popular fold, and reestablished her permanent lesbian-cult-icon status, despite efforts to resist being labeled by her sexuality.

After the success of *When Night Is Falling*, in 1999 Rozema took on the daunting task of adapting Jane Austen's novel *Mansfield Park* to film. Her risky version, which pushes the theme of slavery to the foreground, received solid reviews, even from diehard Austen enthusiasts.

Aside from her part in a growing queer contingent of filmmakers, Rozema's work stands out for its defiantly optimistic and rosy tone at a time when independent North American filmmaking was overwhelmingly violent and dark. Film critic Geoff Pevere notes in the 2004 book *Take One* that "there are no unhappy endings in the films of Patricia Rozema." It is perhaps surprising to learn that Rozema began her career as a journalist; her cinematic work is marked by expressionistic flourishes that are brazenly not part of the real world.

Rozema and I spoke in her Toronto home in the spring of 2006.

You grew up in a strict Christian environment. What was that like?
Well, it was just my life, I didn't find it conservative or liberal; in fact, I thought we were mavericks. We were radicals because we

couldn't drive the car and buy things on Sundays, and in later years we were allowed to go to the beach, but only on Sundays. It was just my life—church twice a day on Sundays. I came across my Bible recently and it's full of my handwritten comments and cross-references. I was obsessive about my religion in my teens. I converted people to Christianity. I couldn't go out with boys if they were heathens so I converted them, or so they had me believe. To me, fiction is conflict and those who come from highly conflicted situations can still function well [in society]. I also believe that fiction is a kind of religion. [I believed] the fantastical stories of the Bible which were, to me, quite natural. A number of the filmmakers have had these same experiences. Denys Arcand once studied to be a Jesuit priest, I believe. When I went to Calvin College, I studied English and philosophy, but we had a lot of core courses about theology.

You've cited Ingmar Bergman as a major influence.
He's the first filmmaker I remember really being moved by. I was dating my philosophy professor at the time, which was not allowed, and he introduced me to Bergman. I watched a double feature of Bergman's *Persona* [1966] and *Face to Face* [1976]. I had seen nothing like it; his films appealed to the dour, sober side of me. I wasn't the first to notice Bergman's relationship to Canada [and my upbringing]: the cold, unforgiving landscape and a lovely Calvinist God who decrees that you can devote yourself to Him, but if you aren't what He likes, one of the "elect," you're not getting into the Kingdom of Heaven. [Calvinism] is a great faith in a way, though, because it's non-touchy-feely, non-praising, non-loving, and non-demonstrative. It's a great place to come from as a filmmaker because it cultivates some kind of internal drive [which allows you to survive] devastating criticism. Atom [Egoyan] and I talked about how it's good to come from a family or an environment where you aren't constantly being told that you're the best. We also don't get [much affirmation] from the Canadian film industry either. It's not the Canadian way. And I don't mind that.

But you've done so well in Canada, as well as internationally.
Sort of, but it's not like the American film industry. In America, you're called a genius every time you turn around. [They all say] they adore you; you know it's bull, but it's still nice.

In addition to Bergman, you say you were greatly impacted by the Maysles Brothers' 1975 documentary *Grey Gardens* [about two heiresses living in a derelict mansion in the Hamptons].

I saw *Grey Gardens* the year it came out. I just couldn't get the relationship the [main characters] had to the camera out of my mind. I couldn't get over my guilt as an audience member. The notion of their exposure and that intimacy, I couldn't shake it. I felt like there was [an ethical] barrier crossed in that film, which is not something I could advocate. There's an implicit seduction on the part of the filmmakers that says, "I'm going to make you famous and follow you around and let the camera fall in love with you." I feel that it was an abuse of power, but to have fictionalized their stories would have been interesting.

That is a surprising point of view, though, since you began your career in journalism.

I always thought I would write because I loved making up stories, but then I thought, "How am I going to make a living writing?" I also loved theater, but then I didn't really like acting and I didn't think I was that good at it. I thought I was good at writing reviews—so I thought, okay, I'll go for journalism. I took a journalism minor and then was offered an internship in Chicago at an NBC-TV station called WMAQ. I wrote public service announcements for them [during the day], and in the evening, I was exploring gay bars to see if I might like that scene. The bars were mostly dreadful. I remember thinking, "Hmm, I like women but I don't like lesbians." I took another internship at WNBC New York in Park Plaza. Working there demystified New York and famous people for me, though, and [soon] I wanted to get back to Canada.

When I moved back to Canada, I was hired at *The Journal*, a nightly newsmagazine on the CBC [Canadian Broadcasting Corporation] television. I had a crush—I should say a platonic professional crush—on [late Canadian TV personality and *Journal* host] Barbara Frum. I couldn't believe how every story mattered so intensely to her. I watched her reporting every day and expected to hear at least one snide or dismissive comment, but not her. She was a very generous person.

Then I got fired. It completely derailed me. I was used to overachieving. There were a ton of cutbacks at the CBC, and even though *The Journal* was a popular program, I was the [least important] producer. And I was a bit of a wild card for them—pushing for interviews with Laurie Anderson and the like. Someone reminded me that I proposed a story about this disease that gay men were getting called "GLAD" or something.

GRID, the first name for AIDS: Gay-Related Immune Disorder.
[The producers] said, "Oh no, [that story is] too American." They felt [GRID] didn't have broader implications. No one knew. Overall I'm very happy I had that job at *The Journal*. But I felt that with fiction I could get a more delicate story.

Can you tell me about your first film?
At the CBC, everyone liked my editing because I completely dove into it— cutting images together and putting music and sound together. Through that job at *The Journal*, I met Beryll Fox and Don Owen. Don was directing something, and Beryll was producing the last film by [late gay Canadian filmmaker] Claude Jutra. I asked her out for coffee and got all the names I could from her [for industry connections] and asked her for her support. Then I got a job as Don Owen's assistant.

What did you learn from Don Owen?
Don was much more from the hip than I would ever have been because of the way he started in the film industry. He worked in a cinéma vérité style which I'm coming to appreciate much more now. I wasn't crazy about his film, *Unfinished Business* [the 1984 sequel to Owen's landmark 1964 film, *Nobody Waved Good-bye*]. But perversely, it gave me confidence in my cinematic taste. I had an opinion about each take in *Unfinished Business* and I felt I could tell when the acting was good and the blocking was good and what was false. So I took a night course in filmmaking at Ryerson University in Toronto. We were supposed to do a one-minute film about someone waiting for a bus—a study in elongating time. I decided I had to make it about someone waiting for an idea. It was such an interesting exercise to me—the temporal plasticity of film was exciting. Then I repeatedly applied for [Canada Council for the Arts] grants. One rejected film proposal was called *I'd Probably Be Famous If I Wasn't Such a Good Waitress*, based on a Jane Siberry song about a superhero waitress. Another one was called *The Look of Genesis*, about a sperm bank owner. I felt that the script would

envision new ways of procreation, but everyone thought it was too wacky. Then I had this idea of a film that was a letter to somebody, which I finally got to make called *Passion: A Letter in 16mm* [1985]. Being in the closet at that time defined the structure of this film for me because I was jealous of those who could write a song or a poem to someone they loved without saying who that someone was. I didn't want to reveal the true object of my affections, interests, and passions.

So the form was dictated by the need to be under the radar?
You could say self-loathing was [its inspiration]. I don't know if I would've been pushed to do something that unusual if I felt I could explore both sides of the relationship. But there were other things I was interested in at the time—[Eugène] Ionesco and [playwright Luigi Pirandello's] *Six Characters in Search of an Author*. And Beckett, I loved Beckett.

What drew you to Beckett?
To me, his stories are almost biblical and they really excited that side of me. I grew up thinking that Moses came down the mountain with tablets that God had given him. It's great imagery, right? Even though I don't think [the biblical stories] are literally true now, the message they convey has some sort of truth. I think Beckett does that in his plays, but not in a didactic way.

That's an inspiring work.
And funny too. I need funny and I need kindness wherever I can find it.

Can you tell me what inspired *I've Heard the Mermaids Singing* [1987]?
I had been criticized for *Passion: A Letter in 16mm*; I was also praised for it too, but I just focused on the criticism. *Mermaids* was in reaction to those criticisms. Truffaut [François Truffaut, one of the founders of the French New Wave movement] once said that we make films in reaction to the last one. *Passion* was about a successful career woman, so I wanted to depict an unsuccessful career woman in *Mermaids*. I had a vision of this character, "Polly," which was the film's original title. I knew [all about her character]; I would see people on the bus and I knew they were like her. They are the kind of women who are very moving to me; not confident,

Sheila McCarthy (as Polly Vandersma) in I've Heard the Mermaids Singing *(1987), Mirama/Photofest*

Rachael Crawford and Pascale Bussières in When Night Is Falling *(1995), October Films/Photofest*

rarely hit upon, and with no sexual or intellectual power in our culture. And I just think that Polly's, and those women's, dreams are as big as anybody's—Polly's need for wonder, joy, sexual ecstasy, and artistic thrill is probably bigger than anyone else's. And her grief is as poetic as the most celebrated poet's. I really love this idea that I can give somebody like that the sense that she is [important].

Knowing her character was the best starting place for the script. The Coen Brothers say that too, that they knew how the character Marge in *Fargo* talked right away; they had the language down. I could hear Polly's philosophical naiveté combined with her desire to approach big subjects.

Structurally, I wondered what other media I could use as the basis for a film. The last one was modelled on a letter, so for *Mermaids* I thought about a confession. Polly thinks that she has committed some heinous crime, so why not have her make a video confession of her alternate fantasies? And having the paintings that glowed was a way for her to confront art that she found fantastic. I heard someone suggest that Quentin Tarantino stole his glowing-suitcase idea from me. [In *Pulp Fiction*, a suitcase is opened and it glows.] Who knows?

How do critical responses to your work affect you?
I try not to listen to what people say about my work, or to get caught up in whether or not I receive awards. I started filmmaking without any expectation of accolades. I experienced a real innocent pleasure making my films and a real Calvinist desire to never do it for trashy, vain reasons. If filmmakers believe that the main rationale for their work is the sheer pleasure of making it, then they will have a freer [experience]. But after the first film, it is hard to maintain that pure motivation, that ability to not anticipate [critical] reactions.

You had a fantastic reaction to *I've Heard the Mermaids Singing* at the Cannes Film Festival.
It was really heavy. I can't even say it was beyond my wildest dreams, because I hadn't let myself dream anything.

After Cannes, I understand you had seven companies bidding on its distribution?

Yes. [The producers] and I were sitting there with Harvey Weinstein who was just starting up Miramax. He said things like, "Okay, I can offer you this, and you can answer yes or no, but you can't leave the room." And I'm thinking, "Okay, is this how it's done? Whose rule is that?" So I said, "No, we're going to leave the room and we are going to come back and talk to you." But he wanted the film badly enough that he set a figure that was higher than the budget of the film and higher than anyone else, so we took it. It was all very silly. You know, when you're young, you just kind of trundle through the big events in your life a bit stunned. When you're older, you recognize them as big events more as they are happening. I've come to realize how lucky I am that I often have delayed reactions to things because I can keep a cool head in chaotic moments. I can handle pretty much anything. Later, alone, I fall apart.

Many of us read the central character in *Mermaids* as lesbian. But you didn't necessarily intend it that way?

I read her as "just born," really; like she's two years old and fascinated by sexuality in general. In her mind, I think, [her sexuality] is kind of all mixed up together. As it was for a long time in me. I think that my life has demonstrated that I'm definitely way more interested in female romantic sexual partners than men. But I've been with several men in the past and often fantasize about them. I love blurred gender roles. I feel like at the time I came out with that film, the gay community was a bit angry with me that I wasn't more overtly out personally and that I wasn't more strict about the barrier between gay and straight in the film. On the one hand, I might have been a bit cowardly [about discussing my sexuality], but I just couldn't bear the thought of it with whatever creep decided to bring up the subject in an interview. Now I feel like the gay community has caught up to me—if I may be so arrogant—and that queer culture has recently allowed for a lot more fluidity of emotional sexuality. What we need [sexually] from each other is so much more complicated than we could ever think. Tidy dialectics like "gay" and "straight," "dominant" and "submissive," and even "male" and "female," don't reflect the real world. I am often excited by images of men and women or images of men and men. People talk themselves into a corner too often because there is comfort in clarity. But sexuality is so much deeper. I think that people do eventually have to make a choice in their lives of one type of partner, unless they want to be extremely promiscuous and try everything under the sun. But if you're not like that, and I'm not, then I think you have to pick a lifestyle, and for me, that is living with a woman. But emotionally and artistically, the world is a rich place, and if I had several other selves that I could experiment with, they would be doing all kinds of interesting stuff. Thank God I'm an artist and I can play with scenarios—play at being a man, being a woman, being a child. My life doesn't have to be torn apart every time.

You have said you were bisexual.
You know what I dread? Greasy guys saying, "So tell me about your first experience with a woman!" That's what you leave yourself open to. I'm not a good enough dancer to evade questions. So if I didn't actually put my sexuality on the table in an interview then I didn't have to deal with it. I will now because I'm old and strong enough, but at the time [that I said I was bisexual] that is what I was worried about—people feeling like they had the right to discuss something so delicate and so important to me.

***White Room* [1990] deals with the issue of voyeurism, in which a man witnesses the murder of a female rockstar. How was that experience?**
I was feeling fragile about [being a public person and having my sexuality questioned] at the time. I think again that I was in the idea that when people are closeted, they become two people: the real you and the one that people think is you. I think the more personal a work is, the more successful it is—the more people will respond to it. It's not trying to sell or promote something, it's just being honest. At the time of making *White Room*, I felt very much like I was two people. But I realized that it wasn't safe to hide behind my public or private self. It was a strange dance between the watcher and the watched, both internally and externally. With the film, I also wanted to play with what it was to be a male. I still like doing that, being able to play every side of the story—being the man who is attracted to the woman and the woman attracted to the man. *White Room* began as an urban comedy, then became a thriller mystery, then a pastoral romance, and then a fairy tale. This unsettled audiences, but there wasn't enough of the familiar to hang on to. It's not as free or as warm or as funny as *I've Heard*

the Mermaids Singing, but I really like it. It's more complicated [than *Mermaids*], it has more dark mixed into the light. My life was very complicated when I was making it. My life was in turmoil. I felt very observed. There was a ton of pressure on what *White Room* should be. I think everyone was expecting this nice, warm, funny, surprising film like *Mermaids*, but I didn't feel like all of my skills were on display in the first film.

When I watch *When Night Is Falling* [1995], it's impossible not to think about your Christian background. How much of Pascale Bussières' character, Camille, is you?

She is like me, but I also lead a circus of a life just like Petra's character. If I can't find myself in a character, then he or she is not convincing enough. I just play both sides of them in those scenes and see if they fit. For the side of me that is reckless and aggressive and daring, that's Petra. For the side that is terrified of intimacy and never makes the first move and is awkward, that's Camille. But I'm also the guy. It was really important to me that the Henry Czerny character [Martin, whose wife Camille falls in love with Petra] was not a prick. When [Czerny] came in to audition, he was the best actor for the part, but he was still carrying a bit of hostility from his role in *The Boys of St. Vincent* [a Canadian TV miniseries] where he played a pedophile priest; he had overtly said that the role had been a very upsetting process for him. But for *When Night is Falling*, I wanted him to be a really decent human being because I didn't want to depict the cliché that a woman becomes a lesbian because her husband is terrible to her. That is so psychologically shallow.

Were you worried that *When Night Is Falling* might be perceived as another coming out movie?

I have wondered sometimes why so many gay films were about coming out. When I was making *When Night is Falling*, I knew that another coming out film was not what the gay community needed or wanted. I felt like the world wanted a sophisticated *Go Fish*, but a bit more crafted. I knew it would be my most classic, yet least formally adventurous film—there is no framing device, just a story simply told. The end has a wacky twist, but the rest is a very standard love story. [We even picked classic story colors]—gold and burgundy and warm woody colors, and the lighting, as much as possible, was incandescent and warm, not cool or harsh. It was radical for me to make it conservative. I also knew I could get more of an audience for a formally straight-forward film then I could for an experimental one.

At the time you were promoting *When Night Is Falling* in Montreal, you didn't want to acknowledge your sexuality. I found it odd, because the film was so brazenly about two women getting together, with autobiographical overtones.
We all want to see other people fucking. Our curiosity is endless, and if someone is going to give [their intimate details] to us, we're going to take it. That was partly what *White Room* was about. Kate Nelligan shares stories of sexuality, violence, and abuse because those are the best interview anecdotes. I think that as a person who wants to have a private life, then I can't go there [in my interviews], even though I know it would make them more interesting. I know that people would be more inclined to write about me if I was to come flat out about everything. Maybe it's a form of cowardice, but I attribute it more to Calvinism and to my lack of, or disinclination, to discuss my sex life, which is what it is, with other people.

***When Night Is Falling* was financially more successful than *Mermaids*. Then you were approached by Miramax to do the adaptation of Jane Austen's novel *Mansfield Park*.**
For some reason Harvey [Weinstein] and I have gotten along really well and always have. He approached me [about the adaptation] and at first I wasn't interested. It seemed too dainty. But then when I read the novel and some essays about it, I discovered a political subtext to be brought out that I hadn't seen in other Austen works. Her writing is so well observed, wry, and very funny without ever showing how she is thinking at that time. At first I thought, "Who am I to be doing Jane Austen?" I have no authority on the subject, but I could identify with the Fanny Price character who is like me—from a small town, and brought to the world stage while not really being qualified to be there, and everyone lets her know that. I was attracted to the idea of exploring how people can be thought of as possessions; like blacks as possessions of whites, or women as possessions of men. Have we really outgrown that idea? I find that amazing territory.

You had no trepidation about the Austenphiles, the purists who

would accuse you of tampering with her work?

If you have trepidation about anything then you can't do it. On some level I like to leap into things without looking. When I look back upon the choices I made in making *Mansfield Park*, I feel they were pretty ballsy. I just thought there has to be a reason why I was doing a period piece. I wanted to say, "Look, we are rich because of slavery. We *stole people* and made them into slaves. Nothing comes for free." I didn't want to do another English dance party. The result is a kind of example of cubist filmmaking, with many sides at once. I wanted the audience to get a better understanding of what Austen knew by showing a bit more of the debate that was raging in British parliament at the time of the novel's publication. Lori Moore recently wrote a piece in *The Atlantic Monthly* called "Five Great Novels Made Greater by their Adaptations," and she included my film *Mansfield Park*, specifically because I brought the slavery issue to the fore. I have to say, that one pleased me.

FILMOGRAPHY

Tell Me You Love Me (TV series, various episodes) (director), 2007

Suspect (short film) (director), 2006

Happy Days (TV short film) (director), 2000

This Might Be Good (short film) (director), 2000

Mansfield Park (feature) (director and writer), 1999

Bach Cello Suite #6: Six Gestures (short film) (director), 1997

The Hunger (TV series, one episode) (director and writer), 1997

Yo-Yo Ma Inspired by Bach (TV series, one episode) (director and writer), 1997

When Night Is Falling (feature) (director and writer), 1995

Montreal vu par (feature, "Desperanto" segment) (director and writer), 1991

White Room (feature) (director and writer), 1990

I've Heard the Mermaids Singing (feature) (director and writer), 1987

Urban Menace (short film) (director), 1986

Passion: A Letter in 16mm (short film) (director and writer), 1985

David Secter: Queer Pioneer

Perhaps what is most striking about *Winter Kept Us Warm* (1965) is that the movie exists at all. Shot by then twenty-two-year-old filmmaker David Secter on the University of Toronto campus in the winter of 1964, it stands as a magnificent achievement that offers an unapologetic—if subtly told—story about two young college students who fall in love. The fact that both of them are men hardly seems to matter, as Secter saw their mutual attraction as so innocent that this sentiment is reflected in the film's tone. Secter recalls that the actors weren't even entirely sure they were in a gay movie—which would be understandable, seeing as there was no popular notion of what a "gay movie" was back in the 1960s. David Cronenberg has said that *Winter Kept Us Warm* inspired him as a young director-to-be, given its thematic audacity and the fact that a Canadian filmmaker with few resources was able to create a good movie at a time when there was not an established Canadian film culture or industry. In the book *Cronenberg on Cronenberg*, the internationally-renowned director states: "Secter had somehow hustled together a feature film that was intriguing because it was completely unprecedented. And then the film appeared, and I was stunned. Shocked. Exhilarated. It was an unbelievable experience. This movie was a very sweet film."

And *Winter Kept Us Warm*, as it turned out, had legs. It was the first English-language Canadian film to be invited to the Cannes Film Festival, where it was warmly received, then went on to have theatrical runs in several cities across North America—all astonishing parts of the story, given the fact that the modern gay rights movement was still in its infancy. Secter's next film was *The Offering* in 1966, one of the first Canadian movies to depict an interracial relationship. But sadly, Canada's then lack of support for the film and TV industry meant that Secter felt compelled to move to the US to further his career. "I had developed a [television] series that had gay characters in it, and I was in discussions with the CBC [Canadian Broadcasting Corporation] about it, but nothing came of it," Secter recalls. "Back then, there was really just the CBC and the NFB [National Film Board, a public agency that supports the production and distribution of Canadian films]." When he moved to the US, he worked in the theater and continued to make the occasional film project in New York. (He had been slated to direct Sonny and Cher in their first feature film, but Cher became pregnant, so the project was cancelled.) Later, Secter migrated west to California, where he settled in Long Beach.

Forty-plus years after its release, *Winter Kept Us Warm* has been embraced by a new generation. David Secter's nephew Joel has made a thoughtful documentary on his uncle's unusual and celebrated place in film history, *The Best of Secter & The Rest of Secter* [2005], which has made the international film festival rounds, drumming up more interest in Secter and *Winter Kept Us Warm*. And he's still making movies; his latest is *Take the Flame!* (2006), a feature documentary about the history of the Gay Games.

When did the renaissance for *Winter Kept Us Warm* [1965] begin?
In the early 1980s, [Montreal author and Concordia University film studies professor] Tom Waugh wrote a piece in *The Body Politic* [a now-defunct Canadian gay magazine] praising the film. Then I got a number of calls from gay film festivals across Canada. I hadn't actually even seen the film myself in about twenty years and it wasn't even on video, so we had to transfer the film to VHS [in order to show it at film festivals].

What struck you most as you watched it for the first time in twenty years?
That it's even show-able! We were all so green when we made it. I still cringe [when I watch certain scenes]. The fact that it seems to resonate with an audience today is very rewarding. The other thing that amazes me, to this day, is *plus ça change*—so much remains the same, kids grappling with their sexuality.

Forty years after your film was released, *Brokeback Mountain* was hailed as a cinematic breakthrough. Does it feel like there have been forces working to keep this kind of story off the big screen?
For many years, the kind of money required to produce and circulate a studio film turned off a lot of people [from making any film]. Producers had to justify the millions of dollars they had riding on their films. But now, the burgeoning independent scene is allowing filmmakers to get into every nook and cranny [of the market], with a lot of variations. I'm surprised that there are so many movies out there about the transsexual experience. Talk about a niche audience! Suddenly there's a whole genre around it.

You've said one of your major influences with *Winter* was French cinema's Nouvelle Vague [French New Wave] from the 1950s.
The one place you could go for arthouse cinema in the 1960s in To-

David Secter, ca 1966

Joy Tepperman, John Labow, and Henry Tarvainen in Winter Kept Us Warm *(1965), courtesy Varsity Films*

ronto was the New Yorker. There were a lot of foreign films shown there and I was reviewing them for the [University of Toronto student newspaper] *Varsity*. I loved it. I was really knocked out by [Jean-Luc] Godard and [François] Truffaut—it was much easier for me to relate to their films rather than Hollywood studio films. Certainly, the first time I saw Ingmar Bergman's *The Seventh Seal* [1957] made a huge impression on me—I had never seen anything like it before. In Canada, Don Owen's *Nobody Waved Goodbye* [1964] was a strong influence too because I knew the film's lead actor, Peter Kastner, who was also at the University of Toronto. Seeing these films gave me the idea that making *Winter* was actually possible. They made movies, I figured, so why shouldn't I?

And in the end, *Winter* was the first English-language Canadian film to be invited to the Cannes Film Festival.
Sophia Loren chaired the jury that year and I sat with her at a dinner party. That was a heady experience, one I'll never forget. Cannes made me feel the closest to levitating that I'll ever get.

When you were making *Winter*, the University of Toronto authorities questioned you.
Definitely. Some were taken aback by the sheer audacity of us making a movie, but people in the theater scene were very enthusiastic. I had to get permission from the university to do the shoot, and some bureaucrats could see through the carefully worded synopsis, which was loaded with euphemisms to fly under everyone's radar. One dean whose permission I needed said, "There's nothing like that here! How dare you bring the university into this!" But I was pretty good at finding my way around people like that and simply finding another route towards getting things done. The theater department was very helpful in terms of recommendations for casting. So I also got a lot of cooperation, amid some pockets of resistance.

Your script was so covert that even the actors weren't quite sure what they were up to.
I thought I was clear with them about what the film was about, but to this day a number of them say they had no idea their character was to be perceived as gay. It was a different time, though. A lot of people didn't really even have terms for [being gay].

You wrote a sequel to *Winter*?

I called it *Memory and Desire*, which, like the title of *Winter Kept Us Warm*, is also from T.S. Eliot. I had the main characters meet up thirty years later, and both married [women]. One day, one of the wives arrives home to find them in bed together and the men ultimately have to come to terms with their sexuality. One guy becomes quite homophobic, but ends up having a gay son. There's a divorce, but there is also reconciliation. It would have been a great sequel. If we were to make anything now, of course, we'd have to update it entirely because I wrote this over a decade ago.

Are you surprised at how far the gay rights movement has come, both in terms of social acceptance and legal equality?

Oh yes, absolutely! If someone had told me when we were making *Winter* that gay marriage would be legal in Canada within forty years, I would have wondered what they'd been smoking. It's amazing that Canada has become so progressive because there are still conservative people there. I wish to hell that some of that [liberal] attitude would permeate this side of the border. I'm quite frightened by the influence of the religious right here, people who think that the Bible should be read literally. How do you talk to people like that? I can't move back to Canada, though, because I've become too acclimatized to California.

FILMOGRAPHY

David Secter is director and writer of the following:

Take the Flame! Gay Games: Grace, Grit and Glory (feature documentary), 2005
Pacific Passions (short documentary), 2002
Burn Too (short documentary), 2001
Burn (short documentary), 2000
CyberDorm (feature), 1997
Getting Together (aka *Feelin' Up*) (feature), 1976
BlowDry (under the pseudonym Laser Scepter) (feature), 1975
The Harrowing Tale of the Haunted Lighthouse (feature), 1968
The Offering (feature), 1965
Winter Kept Us Warm (feature), 1965
Love With the Proper Guppy (short film), 1964

Annie Sprinkle: Sexual Chameleon

Annie Sprinkle first became known as an actor in porno films. Since the 1970s, Sprinkle has appeared in a number of erotic movies, from *Streets of Sin Francisco* (1972) to Doris Wishman's *Satan Was a Lady* (1975) to *Oriental Techniques in Pain and Pleasure* (1983). But beyond her prolific career as an actor (appearing in more than fifty films), Sprinkle has also worked extensively as a performance artist, author, sex educator, and filmmaker. In 1981, she drew attention for her directorial debut, the feature-length *Deep Inside Annie Sprinkle*. In it, she tinkers with the traditional porn formula, envisioning women as being sexually in charge—which was then a rarity. Based on her stage act, the film includes elements of burlesque, and at times, Sprinkle directly addresses the viewer.

By the mid-1980s, however, Sprinkle had her fill of the mainstream heterosexual porn industry. Seeing friends stricken with AIDS, she attempted to introduce the use of condoms in porn films, with little or no enthusiasm from most of the industry. As a result, she moved away from mainstream porn and instead pursued her own unique path of open sexuality, expressed in performance art, filmmaking, and writing. Her stage performances included acts like *Strip Speak* and *Deep Inside Porn Stars*, and often involved breaking down the myths and stereotypes of sex workers.

In 1990, she stirred up more controversy with *Linda/Les & Annie: The First Female-to-Male Transsexual Love Story*, a thirty-minute docudrama that she wrote and co-directed. In 1992, Sprinkle wrote, starred in, and co-directed (with Maria Beatty) a fifty-two-minute how-to video, *The Sluts and Goddesses Video Workshop or How to Be a Sex Goddess in 101 Easy Steps*. Sprinkle, endowed with her sense of humor and gentle nature, introduces viewers to a smorgasbord of various sexual acts, offering advice on how to improve sexual performance.

In the late 1990s, Sprinkle created a retrospective one-woman stage show that looked back at her career in porn: she adapted it into a feature-length film, *Annie Sprinkle's Herstory of Porn: Reel to Real* (1999). As well as being an excellent primer on Sprinkle's life and work, the film captures the energy of her live performances. She has also written numerous articles and books, among them her memoir *Annie Sprinkle, Post-Porn Modernist: My 25 Years as a Multimedia Whore* (1998) and *Hardcore from the Heart: The Pleasures, Profits, and Politics of Sex in*

Annie Sprinkle, photographed by Joegh Bullock

Performance (2001). In 2006, Sprinkle co-directed (with Sheila Malone) *Annie Sprinkle's Amazing World of Orgasm*, in which she interviews numerous authorities about orgasms and how to improve them. In 2002, she received her PhD in Human Sexuality from the Institute for Advanced Study of Human Sexuality in San Francisco. (Her dissertation topic was "Providing Educational Opportunities for Adult Industry Workers.")

Sprinkle has worked hard to forge her own path as a feminist and erotic artist. She seems constantly optimistic, and sees the increased public discourse on sex and sexuality as hugely positive and transformative for our culture as a whole. While there appears to be a sweet naïveté about Sprinkle, she is in complete control of her work and art, and can command a live audience like few others can. She spoke to me from her San Francisco home in December 2006.

How did you first get involved in sex work?
It was 1973. I was a shy, young hippie who left home at seventeen and lost my virginity. When I was eighteen, I fell into prostitution when I got a job at a little massage parlour in a trailer. Just lucky, I guess.

Where were you when that happened?
Tucson, Arizona, but I grew up mostly in Los Angeles. For the first few months [I was prostituting], I thought I was simply a very horny masseuse. I also had a job in a porno movie theater selling popcorn for the showing of *Deep Throat*. It got busted [for obscenity] and I had to appear in court. Right away, I learned that sex was very political. [As a result,] I got to meet the director, Gerard Damiano. He was the biggest star I'd ever met. I was like, "Wow, a movie director!" I liked him a whole lot, and I became his mistress for a year and a half. We're still in touch today, over thirty years later.

I started out in porn films working behind the scenes for a few months, but then decided I could do a better blowjob than the actresses and I wanted to prove it! Besides, doing porn was kind of a young, hippie, political thing—it wasn't the big mega-billion-dollar business that it is now. I was raised by my parents to be a political activist of some sort. No one would have predicted what kind I would become!

Did your family have issues with it?

They were concerned that I was on drugs or that someone was forcing me—those were the main issues. My mom and dad were both feminists, so porn seemed like it went against their politics. My mom was protesting Rolling Stones album covers while I was making porn. Eventually they came to see that what I was doing was a political and feminist thing, and it still is. My mother took a women's studies course, and my work was studied in the class. She realized then that I was a feminist, and from that time on, she was more accepting.

When I read interviews with you, your experiences in sex work sound so positive, which I find surprising. Mainstream culture tells us that sex work must be negative and degrading.

Anyone can have an experience with anything and it can be positive or negative. I just went through breast cancer and all the treatments—surgery, chemo, and radiation—and I have to say that I had a positive experience. I am just the kind of person that always has had a positive experience. I always feel that if I can learn from it, then I come out a winner. I've also never been a drug addict or alcoholic, which helps. From what I've seen, that is where you really get into problems. I'm only a cookie monster, but that does have its challenges too.

You've said that you have always been interested in film. What are your early film experiences?

As a family we went to the theater and to movies a lot. We liked to see musicals. When I was twelve, I saw the film *Gypsy* [1962], about Gypsy Rose Lee, the stripper. That blew my mind. And of course *Damn Yankees* [1958] and *West Side Story* [1961], those were probably the three family favorites. I just loved films and going to the theater. But I saw [the stage musical] *Hair* when I was twelve and I was horrified and embarrassed. I couldn't believe people could be naked on stage. But obviously it had a profound effect on me.

Really? Why?

Oh, naked men, ewww! I was just shocked. My dad was a playwright and tap dancer in his youth, very creative. In fact, my dad was basically bisexual. He was darling. A wonderful, gentle, yet strong man.

So there was an open attitude in your home?

No, sex just wasn't really talked about. But at the same time, they were open-minded. In the late '80s when I was about thirty, I brought my first girlfriend home and they didn't bat an eye. I was pretty much heterosexual up until then. I adored men, and sex with men. I loved cock. I had dabbled in being with women sexually but when I started meeting F-to-Ms [female-to-male transsexuals] they transitioned me. I made the first F-to-M porn [*Linda/Les & Annie*, released in 1990] as far as I can ascertain. I'm very proud of that.

Were you surprised by the reaction to *Linda/Les*?
The thing that surprised me the most was that a group of F-to-Ms in San Francisco got pissed off at me. They said that my film made them look bad because I interacted with Les's vagina, and F-to-Ms at that time were very uptight about having vaginas. I got shit for that, but then eventually they all started making porn and using their vaginas too. So I figure we were just ahead of our time. Being avant garde isn't always easy, but it's fun and exciting.

You worked as a porn actor on both male-directed porn and female-directed porn. What do you see as the biggest difference when a woman is in the director's chair?
Well, there are some women who are more misogynist than men and there are men who are more feminist than some women. So it all depends. But to generalize, I would say that men largely go for the hardcore sex and women want sex that's more holistic—more of a whole range, the emotional, the sensual. Women want an erotic story context; they don't want just the genital sex.

So generally, there is more depth to pornography created by women?
I don't know about depth. One isn't necessarily better or worse. Women want more than just the sex. They somehow want to transcend the animalistic, raw sex. I describe it as seven-chakra sex. Man-made porn for men is generally two-chakra sex. But I am generalizing when I say this. Plenty of women like seeing the in and out too.

It's not that women in general are against the raunchy porn, because a lot of them love it. Some women especially love gay porn. It is just that when you get a chance to direct yourself, you want to transcend, you want to go beyond what is out there and explore something new rather than the same old in and out—at least me and my friends do. Like Candida Royalle, Bridgette Monet, Veronica Hart, and Scarlot Harlot. But hey, there are lots of women that love the same porn men love. Some lesbians have been great innovators in porn. I was very inspired by *On Our Backs* magazine for years—and I loved doing photography work for them because I could really experiment.

Why do you think there is still this kind of phobia around the representation of sex in mainstream film?
In the '70s and '80s, I thought that porn was eventually going to become more like Hollywood films. But when video came out, porn went in a totally different direction. Porn became more separate, more about just the sex, which is fine. It is surprising that more Hollywood films haven't gotten into it. Some of them have dabbled; you do see more nudity. You certainly see more sex, though you just don't see hardcore.

My new work is all about love, which I think is more transgressive than the sexually oriented work. Beth Stephens, my partner and collaborator, and I made a film called *Kiss* where we are both bald and androgynous-looking. We kiss for an hour straight; it's very Andy Warhol-ish. We took the raw, explicit sex act and instead of filming the bottom end, we only filmed the top end. It's hot. We have shown it in art galleries on nine monitors at a time as an installation. People find it mesmerizing.

Do you think that your experience of battling breast cancer changed the way you look at intimacy?
I was heading in the intimacy direction anyway. I love intimacy. Yum. Especially with Beth. Our work is about love, but it is also still about sex. I've been touring a new performance art piece called *Exposed: Experiments in Love, Death, Sex, and Art*. It's about love, but it's got sex in it too. We go under the covers on stage and have sex while filming it with a closed-circuit video camera, so the audience can watch us. They can see and not see us because the sex is happening live on stage but they only see it via the projected images. Our performance was super hot; we had, like, days and days of sex.

Do you ever get into trouble for doing it on stage?

Annie Sprinkle, photographed by Richard Sylvarnes

Annie Sprinkle, photographed by Leslie Barnamy

No, not yet. But with my last two shows [that toured mainly in the 1990s], *Annie Sprinkle's Herstory of Porn* and *Post Porn Modernist*, I encountered a lot of censorship. Being censored has been a way of life for me, actually. For example, in Australia, you can have sex on stage, but you can't show films of it. So I suppose we'd run into problems there with this new show.

What you think of the state of culture right now?
Obviously there is definitely a conservative backlash, and there is a response to all the new-found freedom and the diversity, and the porn and gayness, and all that jazz. Two steps forward, one step back. It's all part of the fun. No problem—we can handle it. But honestly, sometimes I'm a little worried. I could be busted at any moment. My film *Annie Sprinkle's Herstory of Porn* [1998] has things in it, you know, like fisting, golden showers, rainbow showers, SM mixed with sex, that could potentially bring some legal trouble. It has stuff that could irritate somebody who doesn't want other people to see those things. But I think of it as an art film, a historical document, not a porn film per se. I worked in the mainstream sex and porn industries for many years, and my films aren't mainstream porn. They are simply too arty for porn. You can't jerk off to them, really. But museums play them, as do galleries and film festivals. I don't sell a lot of films, but they get a lot of play in the art world, especially in gay film festivals, bless them all.

You've always spoken very optimistically about things, but I'm wondering how you feel about images of women in our culture right now.
Somebody just emailed me an article from a scientific journal suggesting that rape is down eighty-five percent and this academic guy attributed it to there being so much porn. I agree with him. I think the world is a better place for women. I think women are more educated sexually than ever. I was recently with some students at the University of Denver for their anti-rape, Take Back the Night week, which they also wanted to be sex-positive. So here we were marching to stop rape and the next day we were, like, "Let's find our clits and have big orgasms." I think we've come a long way. I don't think it is worse, I think it is better than ever for young women. I wouldn't have been invited to a Take Back the Night march ten years ago. I'm very anti-rape. And I'm also an enthusiastic fan of sex.

As Allen Ginsberg told me, "It's most important that we have candor and honesty."

Pat Califia [a bisexual transman] said something like that too. I'm paraphrasing, but she said something like, "In a world where there is so much ignorance and fear about sex, it is better to be honest than to be correct."

What do you think of the mainstream flirtations with pornography, films like *Boogie Nights*?

Porn is a very intriguing subject. I think a lot of people are trying to understand what pornography is and why it is so popular and how they feel about it. They can't put their finger on it, no pun intended. I think it is wonderful when the mainstream takes a look at it. A friend of mine says that porn is really folk art. It is by the people, for the people, it is not highbrow. It is something that is useful. You can jerk off to it, and just like a pot that you can put water in, it has a purpose. Sometimes you find that it is well-crafted and sometimes you find that things are really funky.

Some people argue that pornography remains very oppressive to women and that feminist pornography is a contradiction in terms.

There have been images of sex since the beginning of time, since cave paintings. People have done drawings and paintings about sex forever, just as they have about love or war or fear or daily life. For me, women making porn is a totally feminist act. It is taking over something that men have been doing and saying, "Let's try it this way, let's do it a different way. Our way." The problem is people try to lump together rape issues, exploitation issues, and violence with the porn industry and depictions of sex. I agree there are porn films that show women being really and truly humiliated, being taken advantage of against their will. But 99.9 percent of porn I've seen is just women having a pretty good time fucking and sucking and being paid for it. No biggie.

Did you see the anti-porn documentary film *Not a Love Story* [1981]?

I did. It's funny because Marc Stevens, who was one of my best friends, was in the film. My recollection of the film is that he looked silly. There is a lot of positive stuff in the sex industry and there is some stuff that is really ugly. But pornography is a reflection of our society and in our society there are women having a great time sexually, learning more about their bodies and even being slutty. On the other side there is rape, abuse, coercion, and people killing women and filming it in their garages. So, again, the criminal sex acts are lumped together with the joyful, fun, playful sex acts, and I think that those are two very different things.

Do you now identify as lesbian?
Yeah, lesbian/bi. We like men a lot; my girlfriend and I cruise guys but we are in a committed lesbian relationship. A really great relationship. I adore her.

Was there a conscious choice for you to be with a woman or have you always been bi and you just ended up with a woman?
I think I was very heterosexual, and then I was bisexual. Then I was a lesbian separatist for a brief time. I was a tranny chaser. I love androgyny. I call myself metamorphosexual because I'm always changing. I like F-to-Ms a lot sexually. And M-to-Fs too. Frankly, after 4,000 men, it was just time for a change. I have a fantastic partner; this is my longest relationship and I'm just thrilled to death. I finally found all the love I was looking for. Beth and I are committed to doing seven years of art projects about love, called the Love Art Laboratory. Part of the piece is that we have a wedding every year, based on the theme and color of each chakra. We then put all the documentation of our projects on our website, www.loveartlab. com. We're doing our part to make the world a more love-filled, sexy, compassionate, and queer place.

FILMOGRAPHY

Annie Sprinkle's Amazing World of Orgasm (short documentary) (writer and co-director with Sheila Malone), 2006
The Art of the Loop (short documentary) (writer and co-director with Jeff Fletcher), 2002
Annie Sprinkle's Herstory or Porn: Reel to Real (feature documentary) (director and writer), 1998
The Sluts & Goddesses Video Workshop or How to Be a Sex Goddess

in 101 Easy Steps (short documentary) (writer and co-director with Maria Beatty), 1992

Linda/Les and Annie—The First Female-to-Male Transsexual Love Story (short film) (director and writer), 1990

Rites of Passion (feature) (writer and co-director with Veronica Vera), 1987

Deep Inside Annie Sprinkle (feature) (director and writer), 1981

Monika Treut, photograph courtesy First Run Features

Monika Treut: Gender Outcast

With her remarkably unusual oeuvre, German filmmaker Monika Treut has managed to explore themes of sexual transgression through the metaphor of geographical boundary crossing. In her first film, *Seduction: The Cruel Woman* (1985), co-directed and co-written with Elfi Mikesch, Treut examined the imaginary netherworld of an art gallery owner who plays out her sadomasochistic fantasies in front of paying audiences; with this film the two directors created their own strange universe, applying literary references to an MTV aesthetic. Three years later, in Treut's first solo effort, *Virgin Machine* (1988), she follows a journalist who leaves Germany for San Francisco, where the journalist falls in love with a sexually liberated stripper. Then in *My Father Is Coming* (1991), arguably Treut's funniest film, a German actress living in New York pretends she is married to her gay roommate in order to fool her visiting father. But the fun begins when her dad ends up getting cast in a New Age erotic film. Enter porn film star Annie Sprinkle, who is cleverly typecast and who eventually becomes romantically involved with the father.

Treut's next film would continue the filmmaker's fascination with American women and with gender and sexual transgression. Four gender outlaws are profiled and interviewed in *Female Misbehavior* (1992), including self-styled gender iconoclast Camille Paglia, sex guru and porn star Annie Sprinkle, an SM enthusiast, and a female-to-male Native American transsexual. In 2001, Treut focused on activist Yvonne Bezerra de Mello, a human rights champion who works with homeless children in Rio de Janeiro, in *Warrior of Light*. She continued to broaden her international scope with *Tigerwomen Grow Wings* (2005), about the lives of Taiwanese women in the context of rapidly changing gender roles in East Asia. Treut became fascinated with Taiwanese culture after attending a film festival there, where a retrospective of her work was screened.

As Alice A. Kuzniar convincingly argues in her book, *The Queer German Cinema*, Treut's films often involve the literal journeys of her characters overseas which effectively reflect their sexual journeys. Kuzniar states that Treut's own German-ness—and her "other"-ness as a lesbian—allows her to explore the issues that she does so freely. But Treut has also suggested in interviews that post-World War II West Germany was a fairly open place to explore alternate sexual paths, seeing as the German people became very self-conscious about treating outsiders respectfully. Being a lesbian in a strange land has meant that Treut clearly identifies with outsiders, with women (and men) who have stepped out of the rigid confines of gender and sexual conformity.

Treut and I discussed her filmmaking career in the summer of 2006.

What was your childhood in West Germany like?

The provincial town I grew up in [Möndengladbach] was once Paul Joseph Goebbels' [one of Hitler's closest associates] hometown. In the 1950s and '60s, the town was very Catholic and most people voted for the Christian Democrats. My parents were somewhat more liberal and tended [to support] the Social Democrats; at least they had learned their lesson from the horrors of Nazi Germany.

As a kid, I was a little tomboy; I had short hair, wore boys' clothes, and loved to play soccer. I went to a girls' high school and, at fifteen, became some kind of a rebel, a left-wing hippie. I was sexually quite naïve, though—I had close relationships with a few classmates without realizing that lesbians existed. My coming out came later. At twenty-four, after a period of sexual experimenting with all kinds of boys and girls, I fell in love with a woman.

You have talked about watching films on German television as a child. What are some of your formative influences?

In the '60s and '70s, public television in Germany had excellent programming—they showed a lot of films of the New German Cinema and the French New Wave, including Werner Schroeter, Rainer Werner Fassbinder, Alexander Kluge, Jean-Luc Godard, and [François] Truffaut. I also watched films by Rosa von Praunheim. Since my parents were not so strict, I was allowed to watch them and found them quite fascinating—we didn't have a single art house in [Möndengladbach], so we had to rely on seeing movies on television. When I was sixteen, the first film which made me think and didn't allow me to sleep for a few nights was Roman Polanski's *Repulsion* [1965].

How did prominent German queer filmmakers like Fassbinder or von Praunheim affect you?

Their impact came a bit later when I was studying literature, art, and politics at university in Marburg. A group of other students and I ran a student movie theater, and I would travel to the Berlin film festival every year to look for new films by women filmmakers such as Ulrike Ottinger, Elfi Mikesch, Yvonne Rainer, and others.

Your first film was *Seduction: The Cruel Woman* [1985]. How did this film come about?

In the early '80s, I was finishing my PhD thesis on the writing of [the Marquis] de Sade and [Leopold von] Sacher-Masoch when I showed Elfi Mikesch's early films at a women's movie club in Hamburg. There I met Elfi, and she expressed interest in my thesis and asked me to write a screenplay with her. In the course of writing we became lovers, made the film together, and set up a production company.

You've stated that you wanted to clear up the myths surrounding SM sexuality. What exactly did you want to clarify?

Especially in Germany, there was a lot of misunderstanding surrounding SM—it was connected with the cruelty of the Nazis. There was little understanding that it is a playful sexual practice between consenting adults, so *Seduction* was received with a lot of misunderstanding in Germany. It is still officially banned in Germany and cannot be aired on television. Next year will mark its twentieth year of being banned, which means we can finally try to get it off the so-called government list of "media which is dangerous to young people's mental and psychological development."

In the 1997 documentary *Lavender Limelight*, you state that you don't believe in the concept of sexual identity. Do you still believe this to be true?

I believe that we are defined by more identifiers than simply sexual orientation; for example, by class, nationality, cultural differences, age, and body image, to name just a few.

You also stated that you prefer documentary over dramatic filmmaking. Why?

The great thing about documentary filmmaking for me is that the budgets are smaller, therefore it's faster to find the money for production. Also, the work is more flexible; you can work with just a handful of people. The down side is the editing, though; it takes longer and as the director, you need to be there all the time, which can be quite draining. This is one of the reasons why I'm now planning to do a dramatic feature film again.

Some have said that gay and lesbian artists flourished in post-World War II West Germany because the country had no national identity after the fall of the Third Reich. Do you agree?
Though West Germany was a very conservative country in the 1950s until the late '60s—we still had many ex-Nazis in parliament and other prominent places—the cultural climate was mostly "politically correct" in the sense that hardly anybody, even if they were very homophobic, dared to openly attack gay people, probably out of fear of being identified with Nazi ideology. Especially after homosexuality was officially legalized in the '70s, Germans had to accept it, and the cultural climate changed for the better.

Do you feel part of a global queer community? I know that you've suggested your work is appreciated more in Canada and the US than it is in Germany.
Yes, I feel especially connected to queer filmmakers, artists, and activists all over the world, probably because I've been traveling internationally quite a bit and was able to befriend wonderful queer people from different countries. Recently, [I have been connected to filmmaking] more in Asia and Eastern Europe, where my older films are now being discovered.

Are you ever surprised by the range of interpretation of your work?
Well, it is strange that there is not enough connection between queer and non-queer academics and artists. As a filmmaker, I'm also not fully aware of many themes or discussions in academic or other film circles since I'm so caught up in making and distributing my films. I seem to have less time to travel to cinema conferences. I hope that will change, because I really like interdisciplinary exchanges.

You profiled feminist theorist Camille Paglia in a segment of your film *Female Misbehavior* [1992]. What do you think of her views on gender now, more than ten years later?
I feel that her views on women and power, and especially on transsexuals, were and still are right on target. She sometimes gets taken away by her own personal taste, and sometimes people dislike her for her exaggerated public personality which occasionally overrides her ideas. I still like her ability for stirring things up.

Still from Female Misbehavior *(1992), courtesy First Run Pictures*

Still from Seduction: The Cruel Woman *(1985), courtesy First Run Pictures*

What led to your fascination with transgendered people and the transgendered community?

Partly probably because I never felt at home, even as a child, in mainstream definitions of femininity. Early on I was a socially transgendered child; I remember I used to play "house" with four neighborhood children, where I always played the father and the oldest boy played the mother. I also played soccer; I looked like a boy and was accepted as a boy. Later on, it was a revelation to meet female-to-male transsexuals; I could easily identify with them without wanting to go through the biological changes myself.

Your 2001 documentary *Warrior of Light* [about a woman who works with street children in Rio de Janeiro] is especially powerful, full of hope and despair at once. Was this your most difficult film to make?

It wasn't a film that was difficult to shoot and to edit; rather, it was difficult to win the trust of the main protagonist, human rights activist Yvonne Bezerra de Mello, who was initially not sure if I was the right person to portray her work. She had seen my previous films and probably would have liked a more mainstream filmmaker to tell her story. Later on in the process of making *Warrior of Light*, she understood that I have a strong interest in marginalized people, whether they are transgendered or street kids in Brazil. I will always feel connected to the project; this was not a film which I could separate myself as the filmmaker—I'm still in close contact with Projeto Uere ["Children of Light," the organization dedicated to these children].

In your film *Didn't Do It for Love* [1997], your feelings for the central subject, sex symbol Eva Norvind, are somewhat unclear. I like the ambiguity, but some critics, like Stephen Holden in *The New York Times*, wondered what your perspective on her was.

Before I answer this question, I have to say that Eva died about two months ago in Mexico, while taking a swim. It's very sad news, as she just was about to finish her first feature-length documentary film on Jose Flores, a Mexican musician. I still cannot believe it, Eva was so full of life and plans. We had become really good friends after *Didn't Do It for Love* was finished. We traveled to film festivals together and met many times thereafter. I admired her stamina and her courage to be able to start new lives in different cultures, but I also thought that sometimes she was her own worst enemy. I'd say that Eva had a very complex personality with lots of stark contradictions. The portrait I made of her in *Didn't Do It for Love* tries to mirror the many faces of Eva, who was a likeable person, while still allowing the audience to piece together its own view.

Canadian filmmaker Anne Wheeler, who went from documentary films to dramatic, has said that dramatic filmmaking is less complex, in that the exploitation of subject is not an issue.
Every documentary film is an intrusion into people's lives and mostly subjects have little control over what is going to be presented in the end product. The audiences have to trust the filmmaker and the filmmaker has to trust their subjects. I never worried about the exploitation issue because with every documentary film I made, I knew that the subjects and myself alike would gain a great deal from the experience. Of course, there are always some conflicts during the process as we get to know each other's boundaries, but that's the exciting part of the work.

Is there a current documentary filmmaker who you feel is doing standout work?
There are many documentary filmmakers whose work I like a lot, for example Kirby Dick [*This Film Is Not Yet Rated*]. I appreciate the ones who work for years on the same subject and go back again and again and keep editing and shooting, until finally they have an intriguing film. Unfortunately, I don't have that kind of patience.

Recently, gay and transgender themes have worked their way into mainstream films. How do you think this movement affects marginalized or fringe film and video?
I don't think it's bad at all. It shows that the perception of queer people in Western societies is changing for the better. There are many other subjects we can work on, because so many subjects have fallen through the cracks of the mainstream media's attention.

FILMOGRAPHY

Monika Treut is director and writer of the following which are feature documentaries unless otherwise noted:

Madchengeschichten (TV series, drama, one episode), 2005
Tigerwomen Grow Wings, 2005
Axensprung, 2004
Jump Cut: A Travel Diary, 2004
Begegnung mit Werner Schroeter (short documentary), 2003
Warrior of Light, 2001
Gendernauts: A Journey Through Shifting Identities, 1999
Didn't Do It For Love, 1997
Danish Girls Show Everything (feature anthology, one segment), 1996
Erotique (feature anthology, one segment), 1994
Female Misbehavior, 1992
My Father Is Coming (feature), 1991
Annie (short documentary), 1989
Virgin Machine (feature), 1988
Seduction: The Cruel Woman (feature) (co-director and co-writer with Elfi Mikesch), 1985

Rose Troche: The Trouble with Labels

At the Sundance Film Festival in 1994, Rose Troche made one of the most auspicious feature directorial debuts a filmmaker could hope for with *Go Fish*, an unexpectedly fresh and funny delight about a group of lesbians and their struggles to find love and happiness. The black-and-white, low-budget film—which stars Troche's then-girlfriend, Guinevere Turner, who co-wrote the screenplay with Troche—immediately won over critics and audiences for its keen style and charm and largely novice cast. But the indie success of *Go Fish* came at a cost for Troche; she was promptly proclaimed *the* Lesbian Filmmaker, a label that came with great expectations. At a time when gay male directors were garnering major awards and the attention of the mainstream industry—Todd Haynes, Tom Kalin, Gus Van Sant, and John Greyson among them—Troche was the one female director who had managed to create a lesbian feature that verged on widespread interest, becoming a source of inspiration for lesbian audiences everywhere who craved stories about themselves.

But Troche then confounded audience expectations by choosing to direct a film based on someone else's screenplay—*Bedrooms & Hallways* (1998) focused on the messy lives of a group of male characters, with a central protagonist who was gay. A droll romantic comedy, the film drew some positive reviews, but—as Troche has conceded—left much of her fan base disappointed.

Troche then changed gears yet again with her third ambitious feature, *The Safety of Objects* (2001). Based on a complex series of short stories by A.M. Homes, Troche's screenplay collapsed and connected these tales into one sprawling meditation on a devastating car accident and its effects on a suburban community. She assembled an astonishing ensemble cast, including Glenn Close, Mary Kay Place, Patricia Clarkson, and Dermot Mulroney, who provided an example of what film theorist David Bordwell calls the "Network Narrative"—a film in which a diverse group of characters are brought together by a single catastrophic event. *The Safety of Objects'* subplots include Close coping with the care of her comatose son and Clarkson dealing with the fallout from a divorce. The film received mixed reviews from critics who were arguably suffering from a meditation-on-suburbia overdose following the huge success of *American Beauty* (1999).

Since then, Troche has continued to hone her craft by directing various episodes of television series, including *Six Feet Under, Touching Evil,*

South of Nowhere, and the hugely popular lesbian soap *The L Word*, including its 2004 pilot.

Troche is a warm and engaging person, gifted with an incredible sense of humor. We spoke in the fall of 2006.

What first got you engaged with the cinema?

I would have to say it was my mom. Movies had influenced her so much. I was fascinated by her knowledge of them; she could tell you who starred in what film and when. It's interesting because I'm first-generation Puerto Rican and even though my mother worshipped the life [she saw] on the screen, it was considered a life beyond our reach. When I was growing up, it was impossible to say, "I'm going to be a filmmaker," or "I'm going to be an actor." My parents considered that for someone like me, becoming a filmmaker was a pipe dream. They wanted me to be a nurse, something tangible, realistic. When I went to college [the University of Illinois], I studied psychology, like almost everybody else. I was actually certain this was my calling, but when I had to decide whether I was a Jungian or a Freudian or something else, I quit. I secretly changed my major to industrial design. It had the word *industrial* in it, and to my mother, it sounded official; that's how I was able to finally break into something creative. When I switched to industrial design, it required a year of art foundation, which led me to photography, then to video, and finally to film. When I got my degree in film, we were still working with celluloid, so for me, film was about the merging of photography and movement, it was an ongoing experiment. As you can see in *Go Fish*, we shot and processed our own film and did our own optical effects—I did all the Super 8 to 16mm blow-ups and motion effects.

Hans Schaal [a professor at the University of Illinois] was instrumental [to my interest in film]. On the first day of class, he held up twenty-four frames of film and said, "I can make a feature out of this." In the early 1990s, people were making experimental films that involved repeating images and dyeing, burning, and scratching stock to turn the film experience upside down. It wasn't necessarily about the pleasure of viewing. I would go to students' thesis shows and be like, "That [film] was painful [to watch]. I guess it was really good."

Tell me how *Go Fish* began.

It came out of a desire to fill a void—to do something different. I thought that narrative film was no longer art. I believed that if you were doing straight narrative, you were selling out, and that experimental aspects needed to be included in films in order to elevate them. I had made six short experimental films and felt that I had hit a dead end. I found my audience was very limited; apparently people do want to have fun in the cinema. So I wrote and shot my first narrative, which was a twenty-minute film, and it was, wow, terrible. That's when I learned the lesson: just because you make it doesn't mean people should watch it. Shortly after, I made a thirteen-minute narrative, but let someone else shoot it. Around this time, I had met Guinevere Turner in ACT UP [AIDS Coalition to Unleash Power] and we started dating. Soon we decided to do a film together. Our desire was two-fold: we wanted it to be a feature-length film, but we also wanted to include the activism that we were both involved in—we had been involved in Queer Nation [an activist group founded by ACT UP members in the early 1990s] and doing kiss-ins and lesbian-visibility activism, and then it dawned on us, what way to be more visible as lesbians than to make a film?

You and Guinevere Turner broke up during filming of *Go Fish*. How did that affect the filmmaking process?

It was very tricky. There were a lot of bad feelings, more on my part than on hers, but we were both really ambitious and pushed past it. What was difficult was that we shot scenes in our friends' apartments, as well as our own apartment. After about twenty days of shooting, we ran out of money [and had to raise more]. Our relationship dissolved before the second half of shooting started. Even though I moved out [of our apartment after we broke up] I couldn't take any of my belongings for continuity's sake [in the film]. There was an eight-month gap between shooting, so that was really 'fun' for me.

When was the last time you watched *Go Fish*?

If you would've asked me that question a few months ago, I would have said more than ten years, but recently Guin proposed the idea of making a sequel to the film, called *Go Fuck Yourself*. I said, "Don't you think that sounds a little bitter?" She said, "So? That's what we are." Fair enough. We gathered in Paris with our friend V.S. Brodie, who played Ely in the original, and watched the film. I was literally cringing at how obviously green I was [as a director]. I had no idea how to do coverage [a filming technique used to make the editing process smoother] or get performances out of non-actors. But I did notice a commitment to the idea of incorporating experimental elements into narrative film, something I would later lose in my work. As I continued to watch the film, its clunky charm started to draw me in. By the time it ended, I was crying, not because the film was a cinematic achievement, but more because of its hopefulness, its lack of cynicism, its heart. I wasn't sure a bitter sequel was a fitting follow-up. It felt antithetical to the spirit of the original film.

Fans of *Go Fish* like me are ready for *Go Fuck Yourself.*
True, but we do grow. Grow up, grow old. And after several meetings, Guin and I decided to make it a film about the families we make, and the ex-lovers who stay in our lives for fifteen years, still spending holidays and crazy nights together. Basically, as with the original, we decided to make it about our lives.

As a gay man who identified with the lesbian characters in *Go Fish*, I felt a great sense of euphoria around this film because of the realistic, positive depictions of lesbians.
I have always found what Tom Kalin [the producer of *Go Fish*] had said about the film poignant. He loved the way it celebrated life and love in a time when so many gay men were affected by the AIDS crisis. *Go Fish* became an escape for them, a work that was almost immediately nostalgic.

When *Go Fish* was a big hit at the Sundance Film Festival, you became the "It Girl" of lesbian filmmakers. How did that make you feel?
I wasn't immediately aware of the pressure or the implications of the success of *Go Fish*. It was a fairy-tale ride, and I think that I would've appreciated the experience much more now than I did then. It all happened so quickly and I had no point of reference. I had no place to put it. I just thought, "It's always going to be this way when you make a film. There is always going to be this much press and this much attention." It's funny, because of all my films *Go Fish* is the one that has received the most attention, that is until *The L Word.* [At the height of the buzz with *Go Fish*,] I met with every major studio [to discuss my next film], but I really didn't have

a finished follow-up script to show them. So I missed the opportunity to say to them, "This is exactly what I want to do." Instead, I went to these pitch meetings saying, "I have these five ideas and this other script that's kind of done." At the time, I didn't realize what an amazing position I was in. I never owned my success. I enjoyed it, but I didn't capitalize on it. I think part of that has to do with growing up not feeling entitled [to success], and thinking that if I got anything at all that it was either a miracle or a mistake. To this day, it's difficult for me to say, "I've earned this, it's mine."

So you were perhaps too modest about your success?
No, believe me, I turned into the monster that is the first-time filmmaker. Full of all that bravado that causes you to claim in every interview that, "Yeah, I did it all myself." Luckily, it wore off pretty quickly. I've had a bunch of friends who've had success with their first films, then turned into monsters and stayed that way. It's very difficult to have the experience not affect you, turning that childhood fantasy of being a rock star [into reality]. Suddenly people care about what you say. It can be very intoxicating. Fortunately, when I continued with my career, I learned to be more modest about my talent—filmmaking is a craft and it is always a collaboration; when you realize that you become a better leader and, in turn, a better filmmaker.

When you met with the studios after the success of Go Fish, did you ever experience any kind of homophobia?
Quite the opposite. I felt like what the studios were looking for was a bigger, better version of Go Fish. You have to remember it made 200 times what it was made for. It proved there was an audience for lesbian films. The problem was, at that time I didn't want to be labeled as a *gay* director. I wanted people to see me as a filmmaker who could do anything. Twelve years later, The Safety of Objects [2001] is the only straight film I've made, and quite honestly I don't think of it as very straight. Ultimately, as a filmmaker I want to be loved and respected by my peers, and I want to be judged for my talent. Unfortunately, when a filmmaker is gay or lesbian, there are few who can see outside the box.

Do you mean you told yourself you shouldn't make another gay film?
After Go Fish, everyone in my life advised me not to make another

gay film: "You'll be pigeonholed." There wasn't a single person, straight or gay, who said, "You know, Rose, you made a great lesbian film. Make another one." I grappled with that advice for a long time, but in my heart I thought I could make a complete and total career out of lesbian filmmaking—I could do lesbians on the moon, the lesbian cowboy movie, the lesbian period piece. There was a market then and it is still alive and doing very well today.

I really enjoyed your second film, *Bedrooms & Hallways* [1998].
I just watched it again the other night. It's one of my brother's favorite movies. I thought I did a much better job with that, in terms of filmmaking. However, it was rather middle of the road comparatively, but that was where I was at in my life at the time. I was in this place where I believe—and still do—that just because a lesbian sleeps with a man doesn't mean she's not still a lesbian. [*Bedrooms & Hallways* is about a straight man who has an affair with a man.] And just because a gay man sleeps with a woman doesn't mean that he's heterosexual. Sexual identity is not just based on who we fuck but who we philosophically, emotionally, mentally feel connected to, and who we imagine spending our lives with.

Are you suggesting that sexuality is more fluid than many would argue it is?
I think it is, and I don't think it should dictate our lives. I see people who worry so much because of the sex of the person they just slept with. We make too much of this fucking thing. It's a tough world. Crazy things happen. Ultimately, we know one thing, this a short life, connect [with who you want to] when you can.

On the release of *Bedrooms & Hallways*, you were already known as a lesbian director. Did you take heat for doing a story about gay men?
Lesbians thought I left them in the lurch. They questioned me: "Gay men have already so many films, why are you making one [about them]?" I still remember the premiere screening in Paris. There was a journalist there who'd had quite a bit of champagne— that's the night I learned what a magnum was—and she raised her hand and said, "What happened to you? You were so good and this, this is such shit." What do you say when you are standing in front of 500 people and that happens? I just said, "I'm sorry you didn't like it." I think it was the beginning of my losing a lesbian

audience; when I realized the audience I had built was not really interested in my work, but rather in lesbian representation. It was and remains understandable, but disheartening to me as a film-maker who has many stories to tell, with some that do not include girl-on-girl action.

Do you feel that identity politics stigma has waned, in part because people like you have made films about gay men or straight suburbs?

I suppose a bit. But I'm concerned that many gays and lesbians are vying for a spot in the middle—a place to blend in. No one wants to be on the edge. There is fear and danger there. I see so many of us trying to live out different versions of heterosexual social models. "Look at me, I'm not so different than you. I have a part-ner, a house, kids." We are living under the Bush administration, where "the other" is vilified, arrested, or disappears. This is a time of fear-mongering; conform or pay the price. It is not a wonder that queers, for the most part, don't want to stick out. Hate crimes are making a comeback. Kevin Aviance, an amazing drag per-former here in New York, was gay-bashed by a group of teenagers. The man is close to seven feet tall in heels. He's formidable. If he gets bashed, what chance do the rest of us have? And it's not just queers who are victimized, race-based hate crimes are on the rise. It's frightening. Sometimes we act like the outside world doesn't impact us, but within the lesbian community I've noticed certain trends. Among femme dykes there has been a mass exodus of wom-en going back to men. Among butch dykes, many are becoming transgendered. Both are ways of blending in, of disappearing into the majority. It speaks volumes about the world we are living in.

A lot of gays and lesbians think that labels damage us.

I have gone back and forth on this. Sometimes I want the freedom to say, "Fuck it, you can't slap a label on me." Then another part of me realizes that in the world we live in we have to stand up and be counted. I would love for it to different: after all, I haven't lived my life feeling absolutely homosexual. There are times in my life that I would have loved the opportunity to not be publicly known as a gay person. So yes, I do feel the burden [of being labeled as a les-bian filmmaker]. But I understand the label and why it is still used and why I have to be stamped. This is a country that still elects politicians on anti-abortion and anti-gay platforms.

Guinevere Turner and V.S. Brodie in Go Fish *(1994), Samuel Goldwyn Company/ Photofest*

Rose Troche (centre) and Jennifer Beals (right) on the set of The L Word, *Showtime/Photofest*

How did you become attached to *The Safety of Objects*?
In 1993, my roommate, V.S. Brodie, handed me a collection of
short stories called *The Safety of Objects*, suggesting it would make a
great movie. I read it and loved it. Shortly after, I met A.M. Homes
at a mutual friend's Christmas party and pitched her the idea of
combining the characters and stories into a cohesive feature script.
The idea intrigued her and I began to develop it. But then A.M.
decided she wanted to write a book based on one of the key stories in the collection, what would later become the novel *Music for
Torching*. After she pulled that story, I no longer wanted to make
the film, so I withdrew the offer. I went on to make *Bedrooms &
Hallways* but could never get *The Safety of Objects* out of my head, so
I called my producer and told her I wanted to make it. Thus began
the three-year road to adapt it to film.

**I thought of Robert Altman's *Short Cuts* [1993; based on Raymond
Carver's short stories] when I saw *The Safety of Objects* because of
the way that you meshed these stories together.**
I did more collapsing and combining of character and story than
Altman did in the adaptation of the Carver stories. I thought of it
like shuffling a deck of cards. I took seven stories with twenty-five-
plus characters and merged them into four families with approxi-
mately sixteen characters.

***The Safety of Objects* had a larger budget than your first two fea-
tures. Some filmmakers have told me that when that happens, the
filmmaking process changes.**
That's not always the case. It's amazing that even though a film
has a larger budget, you still find yourself struggling to make ends
meet. *The Safety of Objects* had 220 scenes in it. It was an insane
undertaking for thirty-three days of shooting and the amount of
money we had. During production, we spent a lot of the budget on
overtime because we never faced [the amount of shooting required]
for this movie. So everyday was a complete and utter challenge. I
made the film with Killer Films, who operate on a certain level of
suspension of [dis]belief. That's how they get impossible projects
done. They set a date and go for it. It's effective, but extraordinarily
difficult.

***The Safety of Objects* definitely divided audiences. Some critics
said that it came too soon after *American Beauty* [1999].**

I tend not to read reviews. I think it can be incredibly damaging to a filmmaker to read all their press. Some people build a career on being cruel and it's difficult to know who those people are when the press starts to come in. I learned that on *Bedrooms & Hallways*. People were kind of brutal and got personal: "In a mind-bogglingly bad career move, Troche makes *Bedrooms & Hallways*." It is shocking the first time when someone crosses the line between critiquing your film and critiquing your life choices. Honestly, I don't have a lot of respect for reviewers. At the end of the day, they too are entertainers serving an audience that would much rather read about a public hanging than trudge through a fair trial. So I made a promise to myself not to get caught up in it when *Safety* was released. However, when there is an amazing review, people tend to get it to you, and I recall being alerted to the *Variety* and the *New York Times* reviews for *Safety*. They are possibly two of the best reviews I will ever get in my career.

You've done well with *The L Word*, a show that's been a huge success. How does the experience of doing television compare with filmmaking?

After completing *Safety*, I wanted to direct more and work on my craft. If I'm doing a film every four years, it's not enough. I talked to my agent about doing television pilots and hour-long programming, but I wanted to maintain a degree of control. It was really great to do the pilot of *The L Word* because along with Ilene Chaiken [creator, writer, and producer of *The L Word*] I got to basically establish the tone of the show, and that is really fun. After my experience on *The L Word*, I felt like I could direct anything; it gave me a lot of confidence. I now know how not to let my own fear derail me. I've been through so many different situations on set and on location that I feel like I'm up for anything.

Do you now see positive representation of lesbians in the industry?

No.

Really? Even shows like *The L Word* don't give you the sense that we're moving forward?

Okay, I'm sorry. Yes. But you know what? I want to be edgy again. I don't mean that I want to fuck someone up the ass on television, I mean I want to not give a fuck again. I want to be irreverent. I want to be political. Gay has become so superficial, it's become, "What am I going to wear to this event?" To an extent, *The L Word* has helped to perpetuate this. Someone said to me, "Don't you think it's really great that gay women can be concerned about what they're wearing tonight?" My answer, frankly, is no. This is a time when we need to be focused on larger issues. Instead, I feel like gay people with their gay television channels and gay fashion are being like the rest of America. Shopping rather than protesting. Writing on some gay blog rather than sending a much-needed letter to a congressperson. We pretend things aren't falling apart, but they are. I don't feel comfortable thinking our progress in visibility has brought us to a better place. I love that there is more representation out there, but I worry about [its quality]. I see *L Word* clones everywhere. Suddenly, reality is following fiction and that is problematic. *The L Word* is a show, not a way of life. And so it appears we've arrived—[lesbians] are the next big thing. But does that mean we are as vapid, shallow, and empty as the rest of the world? I hope not.

FILMOGRAPHY

The L Word (TV series, various episodes) (director and writer), 2004–present
South of Nowhere (TV series, various episodes) (director), 2005
Touching Evil (TV series, one episode) (director), 2004
Six Feet Under (TV series, one episode) (director), 2002
The Safety of Objects (feature) (director and writer), 2001
Bedrooms & Hallways (feature) (director), 1998
Go Fish (feature) (director and writer), 1994

Robin Williams, Gus Van Sant, and Matt Damon on the set of Good Will Hunting *(1997), Miramax/Photofest*

Gus Van Sant: Big Film, Small Film

Of all the filmmakers profiled in this book, perhaps no other has scaled the extremes of filmmaking styles than Gus Van Sant. This writer-director has not only worked on big-budget studio pictures with stars like Nicole Kidman, Matt Damon, Ben Affleck, Sean Connery, and Robin Williams, but also on no-budget, no-frills films featuring unknown actors; what's more, Van Sant appears comfortable leaping back and forth between the two approaches, seemingly without effort.

His first feature, *Mala Noche* (1985), is a strange, low-budget wonder about an American man in love with a Mexican immigrant who speaks not a word of English. Based on the autobiographical novel of the same name by Walt Curtis, the film depicts the same-sex relationship brutally and honestly, and earned a cult following.

But Van Sant's breakthrough film came in 1989 with the release of *Drugstore Cowboy*. Based on James Fogle's novel, it chronicles the story of a group of addicts who roam the country, knocking off drugstores to get their next fix. Like *Mala Noche*, *Drugstore Cowboy* is a bleak yet stunning film, and became noteworthy for the performance of Matt Dillon, who proved that he was much more than just a handsome face. Van Sant would again combine stories of outcast youth and stunning male beauty in *My Own Private Idaho* (1991), a film many still regard as his finest work, about the close, homoerotic relationship between two young hustlers played by River Phoenix and Keanu Reeves, who turn tricks and do drugs on the streets of Portland, Oregon. The one-two punch of *Drugstore Cowboy* and *My Own Private Idaho* established Van Sant's reputation for documenting the lives of alienated youth, while subtly blurring the distinctions between what constitutes a gay or a straight film.

In 1993, Van Sant took the first of several unexpected deviations from his career trajectory, with the adaptation of *Even Cowgirls Get the Blues*, Tom Robbins' surreal novel that many had suggested would defy translation to the big screen. They were right. The film, about a woman born with enormous thumbs that make her a natural at hitchhiking, failed spectacularly, both with critics and audiences, despite an eager cast that included Uma Thurman, Angie Dickinson, Keanu Reeves, and John Hurt. But in 1995, Van Sant re-established his ability to reach a wide audience—without sacrificing intelligence or depth. His film, *To Die For*, was inspired by the true story of a school teacher who becomes sexually involved with one of her students and then, with the assistance of the student, plots the murder of her husband. In the screenplay, penned by Buck Henry, the woman is an aspiring weather newscaster, hoping to claw her way to the top of the television business. Again, Van Sant shows a terrific ability at casting, putting Nicole Kidman in the lead as the weather girl gone mad (for which she won her first Golden Globe Award) and Matt Dillon as her unsuspecting, doting husband. As well as being hugely entertaining, *To Die For* is a scathing depiction of blind ambition.

In 1997, Van Sant stepped further into the mainstream with *Good Will Hunting*, noteworthy in particular for its screenplay written by two then-little-known actors, Ben Affleck and Matt Damon (who went on to win an Oscar for it). *Good Will Hunting* depicts a young working-class man (portrayed by Damon) who works as a janitor at a university while trying to hide his mathematical genius. This moving yet conventional film earned Van Sant his first Oscar nomination for best director, yet was something of a disappointment for fans of Van Sant's earlier, grittier work. The following year, the director attempted another seemingly inexplicable experiment: a scene-by-scene remake of Hitchcock's landmark 1960 suspense movie *Psycho*. Van Sant returned to more commercial filmmaking with *Finding Forrester* (2000), a *Good Will Hunting*-style feature about a struggling teen prodigy who learns from an aging mentor, played by Sean Connery.

In 2002, Van Sant shifted gears yet again. With very little crew, two actor friends (Matt Damon and Casey Affleck, Ben Affleck's brother) and no script except for an idea, Van Sant headed out into the desert and shot the largely-improvisatory *Gerry*, about two men apparently lost in the desert; it features very little dialogue and no conventional plotline. In 2003, Van Sant continued on this experimental path, making the disturbing *Elephant*, inspired by the Columbine school shooting massacre. The film's naturalistic approach to such a horrific event won Van Sant three awards at the Cannes Film Festival, including the prestigious Palme D'Or, yet puzzlingly was largely ignored in the US. In 2005, Van Sant cast Michael Pitt as a rock-and-roll star veering towards suicide in *Last Days*. The character is clearly based on Nirvana front man Kurt Cobain, and the film provides an intriguing speculation about his final hours.

Throughout his career, Van Sant has never denied his homosexuality, but unlike some other gay filmmakers, he's never declared it particularly loudly either. With the exception of *To Die For*, his films are decidedly uncampy, but at the same time they all possess a degree of gay aesthetic, in particular the way Van Sant's camera appreciates the youthful beauty of many of his male actors. The director has often fostered close friendships with his male stars, and has spoken about his devastation in 1993 when River Phoenix, then twenty-three years old, died of a drug overdose. In 1997, Van Sant wrote the novel *Pink*, about a filmmaker who becomes obsessed with a handsome young infomercial star after he has passed away, which Van Sant has acknowledged was inspired by his own mourning for the lost Phoenix.

For such a careful, brilliant, and accomplished filmmaker, Van Sant is remarkably casual and easygoing in conversation. I have had the pleasure of interviewing him numerous times over the years; what follows is a conversation we had in March of 2006.

How did you first get involved in filmmaking?
In the 1960s, there was a professor that I had in middle school when I was fourteen who showed us various films. [We watched] short films from the Canadian National Film Board, generally eclectic, experimental films; and then there was *Citizen Kane*. I remember Arthur Lipsett's *Very Nice, Very Nice* [1961], and [Robert Enrico's] *An Occurrence at Owl Creek Bridge* [1962], which is a short story that had been made into a film. [The class] even made a few films back then, but I kept doing it.

You grew up in a middle-class household, yet in several of your films, including your first feature *Mala Noche* [1985], you've focused on street life or those grappling with poverty.
When I was in college [in Los Angeles], I lived off Hollywood Boulevard. It was like Times Square, and it was where I went every day to get something to eat. There were about ten theaters along Hollywood Boulevard at that time showing first-run films. I think just being there [on that street] influenced the first film that I made, which was a feature that I cut down [to a short]. It was a film about [street] people who lived along Hollywood Boulevard. In those days, I didn't really know much about the street life, I was an observer, I didn't get involved with the drama on the street. There was this place near my home called the Gold Cup which was a little Chinese restaurant which had a counter and chairs, and I passed by it but I never went in there. Then one night, I was watching *60 Minutes* and it showed the Gold Cup as a center for both male prostitution and child prostitution; some of the hustlers were

only ten years old. Much later, I wrote [the first version] of *My Own Private Idaho* [1991] about these male street hustlers who lived off Hollywood Boulevard. I still didn't really know [about hustling], so I was just using my own imagination [when I wrote the script]. Then I read John Rechy's [novel] *City of Night*, part of which is set on Hollywood Boulevard, and it was pretty extreme [The Gold Cup is actually a location in *City of Night*]. It was so well done, I realized that I either had to adapt it or abandon my project, which I did at the time. Later, I read Walt Curtis's book *Mala Noche*. It was a very small book, something quite small and contained. I decided I would try and use it as source material [for my first film]. It wasn't until after [I made] *Mala Noche* that I wrote another version of *My Own Private Idaho*. There were many versions of *My Own Private Idaho* [as it evolved over ten years].

Do you see your films as making political statements?
Yes, but I think more socially, which can involve politics. I can see my work being reactions to different administrations, it's usually something against the grain of whatever the [political] climate has become, whatever I perceive the norm to be. I usually try and balance it out and become interested in [the absence of things,] in the things that are not there [on screen].

You're inspired by absence?
For instance, stylistically, if [the trend in] films is to have really fast cuts, then I tend to make films that don't cut at all. I see it as an answer to the way we look at films. I feel that the style is part of [filmmaking]. I don't think it's something that just ushers a way to tell a story; I think that the story is part of the style. I don't think that there is a standard, I think there are just so many ways of looking at [subjects]. *Brokeback Mountain* is made in a certain way [i.e., like a traditional melodrama]; if it were made in another style, like some Russian movie from the 1930s, moviegoers would say, "That's not a movie," because stylistically it's not what they're used to. In some ways the style is more important than the story itself.

In some respects, *Brokeback Mountain* [2005] has been largely embraced because of its traditional style.
I think that the style really helps. It's a plain, non-confrontational way of telling that story. It could have been made ten years ago. At least, to us, the look is standard, but maybe if you look at it 100

years from now it might stand out as its own unique thing. We were at this restaurant last night and the owners had a five-year-old daughter who told us she's seen *Brokeback Mountain*. So, we said, "Okay, tell us what it's about." Because we didn't believe her. She said, "It's about two cowboys who fall in love." We asked her all these questions about it, and she had really paid attention, then we asked her parents and they said, "Yeah, she just sat there glued to the screen." I thought, that's the power of *Brokeback Mountain*, a five-year-old could watch it. I mean, she was a smart five-year-old, but still.

So you think there is a universality to it.
Yes, a simplicity and universality that was always an intention of the producers, [the author] Annie Proulx, and [the co-screenwriter] Larry McMurtry. I think they always had that universality in mind. I worked on [the project] for a little while and that was kind of the idea. [Note: Van Sant was originally scheduled to direct *Brokeback Mountain*, but eventually dropped out of the project.]

Were you disappointed that it didn't end up in your hands but in Ang Lee's?
No, that was a decision that I made.

How did you first come across James Fogle's novel *Drugstore Cowboy*?
A friend of mine from Portland had a copy that was Xeroxed from a manual type-written manuscript. I think from the first time that I read it [I wanted to bring it to the big screen]. I was in Hollywood pitching stories after *Mala Noche*. I remember pitching *Drugstore Cowboy* to Sean Daniel and Jim Jacks at Universal and they said, "Well, we like that story, but you're going to have to write a script, the manuscript is not going to help us," because there were two stories in the book. Eventually I adapted both stories into the screenplay and Avenue Pictures picked it up [and released it in 1989].

What kinds of preparations did you make for the filming?
It sort of goes that every film has its own method of looking into the story. I had never read the Larry Clark book *Tulsa* but it was about similar types of people, about criminals and drug addicts, groups of people in a small town, and in our case it was Tacoma and parts of Portland, which is the Northwest version of Tulsa or

Oklahoma City. I had an idea of that lifestyle even though I didn't know it firsthand. I also had an idea from reading William Burroughs. I think Matt [Dillon] had even more information [about those types of characters] than myself because he lived in New York and knew people who had lived that life, although they were like rock-and-roll versions. He knew Rockets Red Glare, who was a famous actor and really out-of-control heroin addict. For his part, Matt went to the film library of the Museum of Modern Art and watched some films about addicts in New York, and he also hung around with this guy named Johnny, whom he knew for years, who'd been an addict. On my end, I looked at pictures of some of the real people that Fogle had hung out with [and based his novel on]. They were like any kind of group of friends, but they were petty criminals. Fogle himself had been in and out of jail since he was thirteen, and the drugs entered into his life early as a way of making money. He was in prison at one point in the 1950s and somebody told him to forget banks, that drugs in the drugstores were worth more money than some of those piles of bills, and that all he had to do is just jump over the counter and grab them.

Were there many improvisational scenes in _Drugstore Cowboy_?
Well, I think for all of the films that I've made there's always been a real hesitation to be glued to the screenplay. A lot of times, if [the actors] just say things the way they would normally say them, you can get a better reading than saying it exactly as it's written [in the script], which is unlike the way it is done in the theater. When we made _Mala Noche_ and _Drugstore Cowboy_, I was most interested in having the actors deliver a scene, not necessarily as it was written down. When the actors become aware of that, they're a little freed up. There is a stilted quality that goes with trying to do [a script] as it's written down. There was one improvised scene in _Drugstore_ with [William] Burroughs, where he and Matt walk through the park, but they were still following the idea of the scene in the script. Matt found a section of Fogle's book which became his character's speech in the rehab facility.

I understand that in _My Own Private Idaho_, the speech where River Phoenix sits in front of the campfire and talks about his feelings for Keanu Reeves is improvised.
No, but it was re-written. There is a version of the script that was

Matt Dillon in Drugstore Cowboy *(1989), Avenue Pictures/Photofest*

River Phoenix (as Mike Waters) and Keanu Reeves (as Scott Favor) in My Own Private Idaho *(1991), Fine Line/Photofest*

published by Faber and Faber. The speech is about a page-and-a-half long; River took that and made a three- or four-page scene out of it.

What led you to identify William Shakespeare as a point of inspiration for *My Own Private Idaho*?

I think it was just a way of showing that life on the street hadn't really changed since the days of Shakespeare.

And inspiration also came from some real-life hustlers you had met?

Yes, there are a couple of people that I had met in Portland. It's different today, but back in the 1980s there was a very active street in Portland, Third Street, where a lot of hustlers wandered around. I met a guy there named Mike Parker and drew the inspiration of the character Mike from him. In the film, he has a cameo, playing Digger. He's been in a lot of my films.

I've heard that some of the cast and crew of *My Own Private Idaho* moved into your house during filming and partied so much that you had to go and find another place to sleep.

The cast and crew lived in the house, but not all of them. River, Keanu, and the editor lived there, and the editing office was in the basement. The costumer and my assistant also lived there. It wasn't so much that people where partying, although they were partying when there was time off—just hanging out, drinking beer, or playing music. It was mostly that there were so many people in the house and that I needed some place more reclusive [after being on the set all day]. It was a time when I'd just bought the house and didn't even really have any furniture in it, or at least good furniture, so I went back and stayed at my apartment downtown.

Is it difficult to look back at that movie now and see River Phoenix?

It's always hard to think about losing River, but it's been a long time now and I've lived way more years with him gone than with him around, so I think I've gotten used to the legend of River Phoenix. When it happened, it was quite a catastrophe and I always felt like it was like Jimi Hendrix dying or something; it was like, why did that guy have to die? But he did.

From everything I've read, the two of you had become close friends.

He was a really close friend, he had a lot of close friends. He really spread himself far and wide; there might have been as many as thirty people that he was very, very close to. I remember when we lived at my house [during filming], he had his own phone installed just so that he could call all the people that he needed to be in touch with. [Afterward,] he would call me once a week just to keep in touch. So, I lost a really good friend as well as a really great actor. I hoped to make other films with him.

Even Cowgirls Get the Blues [1993] was not well received. How did its negative response affect you?

I was shooting *To Die For* [which was released in 1995] when *Even Cowgirls Get the Blues* came out. I think that was perhaps a good thing. It can make you kind of bummed out, but I think in each film, at least for me as a filmmaker, I can only see the design of the film and the intentions. *Drugstore Cowboy* and *Even Cowgirls Get the Blues* are very similar films, as far as I can see. I can see lots of faults with *Drugstore Cowboy*. I remember finishing shooting it and having this wave of dread creep over me. I wanted the cinematography to be similar to *Mala Noche*, but *Mala Noche* was shot with a small camera with a crew of two people, and we had a crew of eighty on *Drugstore Cowboy*. At the end, I just thought, I screwed it up. It's the same thing with *Cowgirls*: I could see all the good things but a lot of bad things too. In *Drugstore Cowboy's* case, the critics only saw the good things and in *Cowgirls'* case, they only saw the bad things, but to me they were virtually identical.

So many people are deeply affected by reviews.

Yeah, it can get to you. There are so many ways to listen to feedback. It's supposed to be an artistic presentation or statement, whether it's a gallery showing or a band performing, like how a band can get booed on different nights performing for different crowds. I believe what the critics say, but there is a seasonal quality to these things. I mean, whether or not [what they said about] *Cowgirls* was true, it is still playing, it has a life. I have faith that it does communicate to people. There are certain films in history that don't go over well that still have lives, and *Cowgirls* does have a life.

What was it like to collaborate with Allen Ginsberg on [the video for his poem "Ballad of the Skeletons"]?

I first met [William] Burroughs in 1975 when I was visiting New York and I had wanted to make a film based on one of his short stories. I called him up, he was in the phone book. He said it was fine, that short films didn't make any money. So over the years I kept in touch with him, and then he appeared in *Drugstore Cowboy*. By the time I met Allen, he was aware that Burroughs and I knew each other. I think I first met him over the phone to discuss the video adaptation of "Ballad of the Skeletons." It was always very educational to talk to him because you could ask him anything and he'd just tell you. He had virtually been [involved in] every scene from the Beatles, Bob Dylan, the Beats, and he was a character in the Ken Kesey San Francisco scene. So you could ask him, like, "What were the Chicago Riots like?" And he would just give you the whole story.

Your version of *Psycho* [1998] was another very interesting point in your career, because so many critics reacted negatively to it.

I think the hostility was based on the [fact] that we were copying it shot for shot. There was something about the way we were doing it that really angered film professors and critics. I remember Roger Ebert arguing on his television show that the film shouldn't be made even before the film was actually made. Which I thought was interesting, that somebody would say that something shouldn't be tried. The idea [to remake *Psycho*] came right after *Drugstore Cowboy*. I was having meetings with studios—they would have these general meetings where you would meet the president—because at that time I had become a director that [big-name] actors wanted to work with. At this particular meeting at Universal, there were about three or four other people, and one of them was in charge of the studio's film library. He said that he had old films and scripts, and if I wanted to remake one of my favorite films from the '50s, that would be possible. But when he said that, he meant a forgotten black-and-white noir film, not a well-known film [like *Psycho*]. The remakes were kind of a trend at the time; they had remade *The Big Easy* and *DOA*. I didn't like that trend because I felt that they would take old films like *The Big Heat*, which was so perfect in its original, and would make up new shots. They would use long lenses and deep focus, and bring it up to date, so to speak. In some ways, I thought the films were already so beautiful that they should just re-issue them, but the studios wanted new stars in them. So I thought, a way of reissuing [a classic like *Psycho*] would be to simply copy it, but with the new stars; and not change the angles, because the angles are what the film is. The executives sort of laughed and said, "We don't think we'll be doing that any time soon." So, every time I went back to Universal, which was every couple of years, I would say that I still wanted to do the *Psycho* remake. Again, they would laugh and say, "Well, we don't think that will happen." Every year in the weeks before the Oscars [after the nominations are an-nounced], the studios go around and call the agents of those who are nominated and they try and get them attached to [a new proj-ect]. They want to scoop them up from the other studios. [In the year when *Good Will Hunting* was nominated,] Universal called my agent [with this in mind]. I said, "Yeah, I want to remake *Psycho*, but I don't want to change it, just shoot it over again." They sud-denly thought it was great, that it was a brilliant idea because they wanted me there [at Universal], no matter what. So now I had to sit down and think about whether I really wanted to do it. It actually took me a couple of weeks of thinking, "They're saying yes to me, but do I actually want to follow through with this?" I remember telling [film composer] Danny Elfman and he just said, "They'll kill you, everybody will kill you, they will hate that." He was right. But it's interesting. I think the reason that [the critics] were angry wasn't because we remade *Psycho*. It was the way we did it.

Well, there are some key differences between the original and your version. In the original, Janet Leigh as Marion Crane is hor-rified that she has taken the money, but there is a moment in the remake when Anne Heche seems to take pleasure from taking it. Also, Vince Vaughn is masturbating as he spies on Heche; where-as in the original, Anthony Perkins is more repressed.

Yes, we changed a couple of things. When I looked at it recently, I was shocked at how many things we'd missed. Even though we were copying the camera movements, there were these odd dif-ferences that really stood out. It's an interesting example of how it's almost impossible to appropriate something, even though you're copying as if you're Xeroxing it. A film like that was what Hitchcock did best; everything that was part of his expertise was made up of existential elements of crime and shame, dark and light, black and white. Black and white was a main thing about the [original]. I just don't have that in my physiology, I'm not Catholic—there are just so many [differences between Hitchcock and I] that even if you copy them, you are left with an Episcopal version of the movie.

Do you regret not shooting it in black and white?
No, I think that it could have turned out in a lot of different ways. I mean, I always thought that movies would turn out different if I start them on the wrong date, for example. Sometimes the magic [of a film] works more onscreen than you thought it did while filming it and sometimes the opposite happens. The only explanation that I can offer, after doing so many films, is that it's unexplainable.

There are also films like *Titanic* (1997), which everyone raved about when it was first released, but now people say, "What was I thinking?"
I think people can be caught up in the enthusiasm for a film that is doing well. I think *Titanic* was a very successful movie in that it drew in people sentimentally, not because of the way the film was made. [The enthusiasm could also be attributed to] the spectacle of the Titanic itself. Then, the fact that it made more money than [any other film] had, was so invigorating.

You directed two traditional studio films in a row—*Good Will Hunting* [1997] and *Finding Forrester* [2000]—then returned to low-budget indie films with *Gerry* and *Elephant*. You have talked about the speed of working with small crews, and how it's so much harder with large crews. Was that a factor in going back to basics and doing a film like *Gerry*?
Gerry started out very small, budget-wise. There was an amount of money that came from Germany for an unnamed project. It was like we could deliver them anything so long as it was in color and it was in 35mm; that was the criteria. I was going to make the entire movie with that money we received, which at the time was a fifth of the budget that we had been advanced. I was prepared to get a digital camera and go out into the desert with Casey [Affleck] and Matt [Damon] while they were on their days off from shooting *Ocean's Eleven*. But it kind of morphed from that; we did it after *Ocean's Eleven* was [finished shooting] and had a 35mm camera,

which made a big difference. I was financing it myself, something I hadn't really done since *Mala Noche*. We had a small crew, deliberately so. That was one of our rules. Filmmaking can get boring after awhile because [by then] I had done maybe eight movies. It can be the same drill; you get a script, you get actors attached to it, you put together a crew—there's always these different things that you're saddled with; the movie ended up costing somewhere between $7 million and $25 million. [Jean Luc] Godard was always trying to get the camera to be really tiny for similar reasons because a big camera and a big crew will influence the way the actors behave. [The experience becomes] more of a circus. Plus, with a big-budget movie, everyone is looking over your shoulder because so much money is involved; the studio doesn't want to lose it so it expects you to follow the script. If you deviate at all, you're seen as breaking the contract. Big-budget films are packaged in such a strict way that having fun is not what is encouraged. So, with *Gerry* at least, we didn't have a legal department, we didn't have a script to check through the legal department, we didn't have a production design department, we didn't have a lighting department. We got rid of all of these aspects of making movies by just not having them. The other two films, *Elephant* and *Last Days* [2005], were similar. We got used to finding locations that were already dressed up in a certain way just so we could get rid of the element of production design. I guess it was partly inspired by my earlier stuff, and that was similar to the Dogma guys in Denmark. [Dogme 95 (or Dogma 95) is an avant-garde, naturalistic filmmaking movement started by Danish filmmakers Lars Von Trier, Thomas Vinterberg, Kristian Levring, and Søren Kragh-Jacobsen that refutes "gimmicky" filmmaking.]

So you were inspired by what the Dogma filmmakers were doing?
I was inspired by them because I thought, "Look, they're doing the thing that I always wanted to do." After *Drugstore Cowboy*, I just kept saying it would be interesting to see if I could go back to small-budget films. I still haven't quite gone back because each time a film starts up, including *Gerry*, the project just keeps getting bigger and bigger. With *Gerry*, we did end up having some trucks on the set and eight guys on the grip crew. Secretly I wanted to just shoot with three people—myself and two actors. I always want to go back to a simpler method [of filmmaking]. I think those meth-

ods produce a particular style. For *Mala Noche,* for instance, we only had three lights, and they were all spotlights. Having fewer choices contributes to the style of a film.

Elephant is so different from Michael Moore's *Bowling for Colum-bine* [2002], the previous year's hit documentary about the Columbine school shootings. Your film is remarkably open-ended.
There have been a lot of anti-gun activists who've written to me since seeing *Elephant* asking me to join the cry. Guns are their own issue, outside of school shootings. School shootings are some of the most dramatic examples of having so many guns around. A stronger issue, to me, is that of conformity. By conforming, I think kids are rewarded. The ones who aren't turning out as homogenous as everyone else tend to get the feeling that they won't fit in anywhere. Those kids may think of striking out, either by ending their lives, running away, or ending others' lives. I think it stems from this need to have everything alike. The guns are a last resort. It's not just their proximity that brings this about.

The cast of *Elephant* is phenomenal. I'm struck by that scene where the three girls go into the washroom after eating and purge. I know a great deal of the film was improvised. How much of what went on in scenes was the cast's idea and how much of it were things that you told them to do?
The whole idea of them bulimically throwing up didn't come from them, but from a story someone told me. Other than that, however, they were pretty much on their own. The things that they were talking about on camera were things that they had talked about during the casting session.

Were you upset by Todd McCarthy's review in *Variety* that accused you of being anti-American when *Elephant* won at the Cannes Film Festival?
[*Laughs.*] He charged a lot of people with being anti-American, including the French journalists. I think he thought they had too much sway in how [winning] films were chosen. He was accusing everyone! I don't travel outside of America that much. I suppose you could be exclusively American and still be anti-American.

He also said that the reason for the shootings in *Elephant* is that the killers were gay Nazis.

I didn't know this, but when we were making the film, apparently some of the rally cries around Columbine were that "Fags did this." In the movie, a Nazi film can be seen on a TV at one point, but they're not really watching it. They're just waiting for the guns at that point. On the History Channel, they often show films about Nazis or World War II, because people will tune in, unless you want to claim that anyone who watches a film about Hitler on the History Channel is a Nazi. I wouldn't.

And the gay part is clearly referring to the kiss in the shower. And the kiss in the shower is, I don't know ... I just thought that the film was about boys who were like that, boys who spent a year in the basement alone, and if they were on their way to commit suicide, something like that might happen. I didn't want to ignore that part of their personality that relates to each other in a sensual way. I didn't think of it as gay particularly, but I guess it is in that moment. I don't think I'd label these two kids gay. In some ways, it's that they just haven't ever kissed anyone. It's that they are inexperienced, innocent kids. They don't know what they're doing in the shower, and they don't know what they're doing on the way to the school with the guns.

I guess you don't have a lot of time for Vito Russo's [author of *The Celluloid Closet*] arguments for positive depictions of gays and lesbians on screen....

I think Vito was right about a lot of things. I don't think that if he saw *Elephant*, he would say it falls into that category though. I don't think he was a reactionary, if that's the right term. He tried to understand images rather than have knee-jerk reactions. The killers may be gay, but so are the kids in the gay-straight alliance in the film. That's the thing about high school, the gay kids aren't sure if they're gay and the straight kids aren't sure if they're straight. The film's not really saying that anyone's gay or straight. Just because one kid gets into the shower and kisses another kid, doesn't make him gay. I think that makes it a kiss.

FILMOGRAPHY

Gus Van Sant is director and writer of the following which are features unless otherwise noted:

Paranoid Park, 2007
Paris, je t'aime ("Le Marais" segment), 2006
Last Days, 2005
Elephant, 2003
Gerry, 2002
Finding Forrester (director only), 2000
Psycho (director only), 1998
Good Will Hunting (director only), 1997
Ballad of the Skeletons (short film), 1997
Four Boys in a Volvo (short film) (director only), 1996
To Die For (director only), (1995)
Even Cowgirls Get the Blues, 1993
My Own Private Idaho, 1991
Thanksgiving Prayer (short film), 1991
Drugstore Cowboy, 1989
Five Ways to Kill Yourself (short film) (director only), 1987
My New Friend (short film) (director only), 1987
Ken Death Gets Out of Jail (short film) (director only), 1987
Mala Noche (Bad Night), 1985
The Discipline of D.E. (short film), 1982

Rosa von Praunheim: Deep Threat

Rosa von Praunheim's career is astonishing for a number of reasons, among them his prolific work habits. The German director, who was born Holger Mischwitzky in Latvia in 1942, has created an unusual oeuvre of more than sixty films, including fiction features, short films, documentaries, and experimental hybrids.

Not surprisingly, von Praunheim renamed himself for queer political reasons, taking the name Rosa to honor those homosexuals who were detained by the Nazis during World War II and forced to wear "Rosa Winkel," or pink triangles. The choice also meant that the director has a name identified as feminine.

Von Praunheim first came to prevalence in 1971 when his landmark documentary, *It Is Not the Homosexual Who Is Perverse, But the Situation in Which He Lives*, made waves throughout West Germany. (Though born in Latvia, von Praunheim's family emigrated to West Germany when he was a child.) With it, von Praunheim challenged young German gays and lesbians to take action, asking them to confront their complacent bourgeois values and to think broadly about social change. In West Germany, the filmmaker saw a stagnant social and political order, one he insisted needed to be shattered. His film became as inspirational as it was wildly controversial, instigating the formation of over fifty gay political groups all over Germany.

Like German lesbian filmmaker Monika Treut, von Praunheim has spent a great deal of time in America. A number of his films indicate a fascination with American culture in general, and New York's sexual and cinema underground and the nation's gay, lesbian, and transgendered communities in particular. In 1979, he made *Army of Lovers or Revolution of the Perverts*, a documentary about the American gay and lesbian movement from the 1950s to the mid-1970s. In *Survival in New York* (1989), von Praunheim examined the lives of three German ex-pat women struggling to get by in Manhattan. And in 1992, von Praunheim made *I Am My Own Woman*, a documentary about notorious East German transvestite Charlotte von Mahlsdorf, a film that would win the International Film Critics Award at the Rotterdam Film Festival. (Von Mahlsdorf's life would also serve as an inspiration for *I Am My Own Wife*, Doug Wright's play that would win the Pulitzer Prize in 2004.) These films are prime examples of von Praunheim's fascination with outsiders and the marginalized.

Like virtually all gay men of his generation, AIDS had a profound

Rosa von Praunheim

impact on von Praunheim. In 1985, he made what is surely one of the most radical early responses to the international HIV crisis. *A Virus Knows No Morals* was risky and daring on two fronts: it was both a musical and a black comedy about AIDS. It was also an attack on bourgeois notions of good taste—a von Praunheim specialty—with graphic descriptions of any and all sexual practices. When considered in its original historical context—the height of hysterical homophobia in the early stages of the AIDS crisis—the film is as disturbing as it is hilariously audacious. Von Praunheim continued to address the AIDS crisis, often in documentary form, depicting the anti-government protests of American activist groups like ACT UP.

Given his outspokenness, von Praunheim has consistently been caught up in various controversies, with critics both gay and straight and from the right and left attacking him for his stances on numerous issues. In the early 1990s, von Praunheim found himself shut out by much of the German media after he outed a number of prominent national celebrities and was accused of unethically invading their privacy. His most recent films indicate that he has no intention of avoiding touchy issues: in 2005, he made *Men Heroes and Gay Nazis*, a feature-length documentary about gay neo-Nazis, and *Your Heart in My Head*, based on the true story of a German man who placed an ad on the Internet stating that he wanted to be killed and eaten by another man (a cannibal read the ad and followed through on the request).

The feisty von Praunheim has also won his share of admirers. Alice A. Kuzniar put it best in her 2000 book, *The Queer German Cinema*: "Although his enemies may be loathe to admit it, Rosa von Praunheim is unquestionably the most important figure in the Queer German Cinema as well as the most energetic spokesman for the gay movement in Germany in the last quarter century."

Rosa von Praunheim now teaches courses in directing at the Film and Television Academy at Babelsberg in Potsdam, Germany. He spoke with me by phone from his office in February of 2006.

Do you remember the first film that made an impression on you?
I wasn't allowed as a young boy to go to the movies. I remember once that I accompanied my mother who went to see a movie while I waited outside until she got out, so perhaps it was an age problem. [Later,] I was very impressed by early Fellini films. Giulietta Masina was my favorite actress when I was a teenager, and she actually came to Frankfurt because she had a part in a bad German film.

I stood in line to see her. Fellini's *Nights of Cabiria* [1957] with Giulietta Masina—that was a very important film. Sophia Loren also came to Frankfurt, and I waited a long time to get her autograph.

Nights of Cabiria is an upsetting film—Masina was very good in it.
She's good in all those Fellini films. I am very fond of expressionistic films, but I didn't know it when I first saw them. I am a fan of expressionism in general, especially painting, but also literature, poetry, and plays. It has been very influential on my work.

Then there were the American underground films of the late 1960s. In 1967, when I was about twenty-five, there was a major retrospective in Belgium of American underground film. Yoko Ono was there. The films of Gregory Markopoulos had a huge impact on me. Years later, I brought him to Germany and convinced some television producers there to hire him as a director of operas produced for television; I even assisted him. So I'd say early expressionistic art and then later the American underground were possibly my biggest influences.

In 1971, you released *It Is Not the Homosexual Who Is Perverse, But the Situation in Which He Lives*. Were you surprised by the widely varied responses to the film?
It was mostly left-wing gay students who lauded the film. Bourgeois audiences, gay or straight, hated it, because they were expecting a film that told them that gay people are wonderful or great, and that they are in trouble and we have to help them. I said listen, it's not just society in general that has to do something; homosexuals themselves have to be active. They have to step up and do something themselves, to fight for their rights. If they are attacked, they have to fight back, and not just find escape in glamor or movies or glossy magazines. So there was a political motive to attack my gay comrades. I was very angry for being forced into a gay subculture which was extremely repressed and hidden. At that time, it didn't offer many choices. Today, there are gay student groups, gay artist groups, but then there were mostly very bourgeois people going out at night to sleazy bars. It was exotic but I hated it. That is why I did the movie. It was an outrageous calling out to people, telling them to come out.

That film inspired a grassroots gay movement in West Germany.
Yes. The film was produced for television although in the end they
refused to show it. But the press reacted very positively to it, which
led us to show the film throughout West Germany. Whenever the
film ended, there was always an intense discussion afterward. We
wanted the film to inspire people, and we succeeded. Over several
years, more than fifty gay groups were founded as a result of the
film.

**So it was like a town hall, where you would show a film and then
have a discussion.**
I never allowed the film to be shown without a discussion afterward. After only a few of them, we saw that gay people were desperate to meet and discuss political matters and find ways to connect.
The first screening and discussion led to the formation of the first
gay group in West Berlin.

**It's interesting to think that you made this film without knowing
about growing gay activism in the US that was happening around
the same time; there was something obviously in the wind.**
In Germany, it was different because in 1969, the law changed so
that gay sex was no longer a criminal act, as long as you were over
twenty-one. This was so positive for gay people in Germany.

**It's funny to look at the film now because it seems that some of
the debates haven't changed much.**
Yes; look at Poland or Latvia now, where gays are just starting
to come out. The issue is relevant with every repressive government—look at countries in Asia or Africa. But a lot has changed
too; Germany is pretty progressive now. When we made the film,
we always looked up to the Netherlands which had very progressive
laws and where we as gay people could travel to and be open. Now,
the Netherlands is no longer the only country like that.

**You've said that at times you've felt at odds with Germany's gay
community. Do you still feel this way?**
My film was my first big achievement as a gay revolutionary. That,
and then helping to start up these gay groups, was my role for
many years. In the 1980s, AIDS came along, but because I had lived
in America for a long time, I already knew a lot about it. I decided
to become very active and provocative in the face of the AIDS cri-

sis in Germany; I wrote magazine articles, appeared on a lot of TV shows, and made films on the subject. I regularly called for safe sex practices, which caused a big political controversy. The left-wing groups were anti-American, and reacted negatively to safe-sex campaigns. They felt that Germany enjoyed a lot of freedom, and so did homosexuals, and that the campaigns were a way for the state to take away this freedom. This controversy, this disagreement between me and these left-wing groups escalated over a decade. In the early '90s, I started a big campaign to out famous German celebrities and politicians. That was the end of my being politically active, however. I was exhausted after so much fighting.

And there was a boycott of your work?
Yes, a boycott of my AIDS films. Also, there was a campaign to deny me film or television jobs. Eventually, I was exhausted, both from the AIDS fight and having lost a lot of friends. So around 1992, I started to become less active in the gay community. But I still did films about gay subjects, like transsexuals, such as *Transsexual Menace* [1996]. I also studied gay history, and made a film about Magnus Hirschfeld the sexologist, as well as one about 100 years in the history of the gay movement. More recently, I did a film on gay Nazis and on a gay cannibal. But, since 1992, I haven't really been active politically in gay groups.

You wrote controversial things about persons with AIDS in 1990 upon the release of your trilogy [*Feuer unterm Arsch, Die; Positive*; and *Silence = Death*] on the AIDS crisis. You criticized people for their complacency in the face of the epidemic and their refusal to adopt safe sexual practices. I believe that you've since said you regret writing them.
It Is Not the Homosexual was a film that was made with a lot of anger; this is very much a part of my character. My outing of celebrities and some of the things I wrote about the AIDS crisis reflect the same character. In the early 1970s, the reaction was positive in general, but in the '90s, it just was the opposite. I got a lot of criticism, but I was the same person who did it out of the same motivation. I think that if you work politically, you never know if you win or lose at the time.

Have attitudes changed in Germany about the practice of outing? In North America, some people now think it can be justified at times.

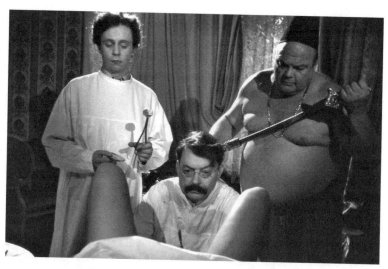

Tima die Göttliche (left) and Friedel von Wangenheim (center) in Der Einstein des Sex/The Einstein of Sex *(1999), courtesy Rosa von Praunheim*

Bernd Feuerhelm (right) in Nicht der Homosexuelle ist pervers, sondern die Situation, in der er lebt/It Is Not the Homosexual Who is Perverse, But the Society In Which He Lives *(1971), courtesy Rosa von Praunheim*

You know, over ten years later, some of the people I outed now say it was the best thing that could have happened to them. There was one talk show host who was very popular and who always refused to talk about my outing him, but recently he said it was good for him personally because nothing negative ever happened to him as a result.

When I watch your films, I think a lot about Bertolt Brecht. Would you say that he has been an influence on your work?
No, I wasn't really connected to Brecht, but some people thought so because *It Is Not the Homosexual* is a very theatrical film. You could possibly see connections, but I never intended them. I liked expressionism, and Brecht was too theoretical, too constructed.

I remember at one point in an interview you said, "I don't make films to make people feel comfortable, I make films to provoke and challenge and make people squirm in their seats." That's very much what Brecht argued: that artists are not supposed to make people feel comfortable when they come to the theater.
But in a way he did. Brecht always said the opposite of what he actually did. He pretended to be proletarian but he was not. He loved entertainment. His *Threepenny Opera* is entertainment; it's about poor people, but it's entertainment for the rich.

Some people said that in your film about famous gay rights pioneer Magnus Hirschfeld, *The Einstein of Sex: Life and Work of Dr. M. Hirschfeld* [1999], you gloss over his racist writings.
You have to see Hirschfeld as a man of his time. At that time, science was different. You can't judge it from our modern-day point of view; that's not fair. Of course, he was very involved in the phase of biology when there was hope of helping gay people by finding reasons in nature for it, and to prove that it was some kind of biological fact. He thought that would make it safer for gay people, and that's why he tried to prove it. But he more or less made a fool of himself with many experiments.

What do you think of the current gay marriage debates?
My views have changed a lot since I made *Army of Lovers* [1979], when I made fun of gay marriages, gay churches, gays in the military, and all of that. Now I think, as long as you live in a bourgeois society in which heterosexuals are free to marry and join the army

and be members of churches, then why not gay people? Most gay people are bourgeois; they want to be bourgeois and to be a part of mainstream society. You can't force them to be revolutionaries. But I don't see that many people taking part in gay marriage. I think that the gay community is very different from heterosexual communities. But as an option, it should be legal—why not? I think differently about it now. I see a lot of gay couples who stay together a long time. It is an act of solidarity. They are comfortable together, they want to protect themselves and get old together. I have been with a man, my American friend, for twenty-seven years. We broke up once after the first five years and he had relationships in between and I was always was very promiscuous, but I am very happy that we live together.

What were some of the things that shocked you the most when you did *Men Heroes and Gay Nazis* [2005], the documentary on gays on the far right?

I found it shocking in general. What I couldn't understand was that this could happen. Of course, I always knew that it existed. When the gay movement started in Germany, there were right-wing gays who attacked us. We always thought, "Oh, these crazy people," and we didn't care much about them. But when I studied gay history, I discovered that from early on, from the beginning of the twentieth century, there were right-wing gay groups and intellectuals, with a lot of manifestos and books written. We were too busy with our own emancipation to notice. And all of my earlier films were about left-wing gays whom I admired. *Men Heroes and Gay Nazis* started when I made several films of interviews with elderly Nazi victims, all of whom are now dead. I had trouble getting financing for the documentary, which gave me a long time to do research on the phenomenon of right-wing gays. I tried to understand the contradiction; it was very difficult for me to grasp.

Did you manage to make sense of it?

As a journalist conducting interviews, you shouldn't get into heated discussions with your subject; you have to take him as he is, however stupid his ideas are. You have to listen, find out what makes him tick. I really wanted to find out why these people ended up like this. Why did they have these ideas? Where did they come from? When they grew up, what were their first motives and influences? The more I found out, the more I understood what was happening. One thing was that they wanted to be considered special—some of them grew up in left-wing surroundings and wanted to stand out, some of them were very young. Some joined right-wing groups and then discovered that they were gay and managed to find others who were gay and right-wing. It's similar to being a gay Catholic priest; your life is a contradiction, and you are perhaps attracted to others with similar contradictions. It is the same with all sects, whether religious or political. In some neo-Nazi organizations, some who are gay say they will never go public. If they did, it can lead to murder, and it has.

Do you feel that your role has changed since you became a full-time professor at a university?
At first I thought so. I was afraid it would corrupt me as it was the first time that I got paid regularly. But the position will end this year; I will have been teaching for six years. I have no money to show for it and I won't have a pension. Actually, while I taught I continued to make films, and I'm going to have to again because I didn't make enough money from teaching to retire. But you know, I think I learned a lot from it. I think I learned more than my students.

FILMOGRAPHY

Rosa von Praunheim is director and writer of the following unless otherwise noted:

Men Heroes and Gay Nazis (feature documentary), 2005
Umsonst gelebt-Walter Schwarze (short documentary), 2005
Wer ist Helene Schwarz (feature documentary), 2005
Your Heart in My Head (feature), 2005
H.I.V. So Long! A Fairy Tale (short film), 2004
Charlotte in Schweden (short documentary), 2003
Cows Knocked Up by Fog (feature documentary), 2002
Phooey, Rosa! (TV feature documentary), 2002
Queens Don't Cry (feature documentary), 2002
Fassbinder's Women (feature documentary), 2000

Can I Be Your Bratwurst, Please? (short film) (director and co-writer with Lawrence Elbert and Lorenz Haarmann), 1999

The Einstein of Sex: Life and Work of Dr. M. Hirschfeld (feature) (director and co-writer with several writers), 1999

Wunderbares Wrodow (TV feature documentary), 1999

Gay Courage: 100 Years of the Gay Rights Movement in Germany and Beyond, 1998

Transsexual Menace (TV feature documentary), 1996

Neurosia: Who Shot Rosa von Praunheim? (feature) (director only), 1995

Meine Oma hatte einen Nazipuff (TV short film), 1994

I Am My Own Woman (feature) (director only), 1992

Mann namens Pis, Ein (short documentary), 1991

Stolz und schwul (short documentary), 1991

AIDS-Trilogie: Feuer unterm Arsch, Die (short documentary), 1990

AIDS Trilogy: Positive (feature documentary), 1990

AIDS Trilogy: Silence = Death (short documentary), 1990

Life is Like a Cucumber (feature documentary), 1990

Survival in New York (feature documentary), 1989

Anita: Dances of Vice (feature) (director and co-writer with several other screenwriters), 1987

Dolly, Lotte and Maria (feature documentary), 1987

A Virus Knows No Morals (feature), 1986

Horror Vacui (feature) (director and co-writer with Cecil Brown and Marianne Enzensberger), 1984

Berlin Blues (feature), 1983

Mein New York (TV short documentary), 1982

Red Love (short film), 1982

Our Corpses Still Live (feature) (director and co-writer with several writers), 1981

Rote Liebe – Wassilissa (feature), 1981

Grafin von Richthofen (short documentary), 1980

Army of Lovers or Revolution of the Perverts (feature documentary), 1979

Death Magazine: or How to Be a Flowerpot (feature documentary), 1979

24. Stock, Der (TV miniseries) (director and co-writer with Bert Schmidt and Dorothee von Meding), 1977

Fruhling fur Frankfurt (short film), 1977

Portrait George and Mike Kuchar (short documentary), 1977

Tally Brown, New York (feature documentary), 1977
I'm an Antistar (feature documentary), 1976
Porträt Marianne Rosenberg (short documentary), 1976
Underground and Emigrants (feature documentary), 1976
Berliner Bettwurst (feature), 1975
Monolog eines Stars (TV short film), 1975
Rosa von Praunheim zeigt (short documentary), 1975
Axel von Auersperg (TV short film), 1974
Passions (short documentary) 1972
Was die Rechte nicht sieht, kommt erst recht aus dem Ohr heraus
   (short film), 1972
Bettwurst, Die (feature), 1971
*It Is Not the Homosexual Who Is Perverse, But the Society In Which
   He Lives* (TV short film) (director and co-writer with Martin
   Dannecker and Sigurd Wurl), 1971
Homosexuelle in New York (short documentary), 1971
Macbeth Oper von Rosa von Praunheim (TV short film), 1971
Rosa Arbeiter auf goldener Straße – 2. Teil (short film), 1969
Samuel Beckett (short film) (director and co-writer with Dante
   Alighieri), 1969
Sisters of the Revolution (short film), 1969
Grotesk – Burlesk – Pittoresk (short film) (co-director and co-
   writer with Werner Schroeter), 1968
Rosa Arbeiter auf goldener Straße – 1. Teil (short film), 1968
Von Rosa von Praunheim (short film), 1968

John Waters: The Pope of Trash

For over thirty years, John Waters has been one of America's leading alternative filmmakers, but in more recent years, he has become one of its most visible cultural icons. He often appears on television talk shows as a sort of raunchy Oscar Wilde, offering sharp commentary on any and every topic imaginable. In a particularly memorable episode of *The Simpsons*, he basically plays himself, a gay man with a penchant for kitsch. As journalist Sarah Hampson writes in *The Globe and Mail*, Waters has become a self-acknowledged "parody of himself."

But then there are his films, in particular the classic early ones, which are impossible to dismiss. Sit down and watch what I would call Waters' quintessential trilogy, *Pink Flamingos* (1972), *Female Trouble* (1974), and *Desperate Living* (1977), and you'll see the astonishing and comically subversive power of his work. From Divine eating dog shit at the end of *Pink Flamingos* to the sheer insanity of Mink Stole, a woman then in her thirties playing an eight-year-old girl in *Female Trouble*, these films remain shocking, vulgar, and audacious to this day.

Aside from their crass appeal, Waters' films from this era can also be considered groundbreaking in their gleeful defiance of easy genre categorization. Though they've primarily been described as vulgar comedies, they are, I would argue, horror films; Waters has asserted that his early works stem from his own sense of anger at the time, expressed through repeated assaults on bourgeois notions of taste. My own (albeit anecdotal) evidence of this experience is worth recounting: on numerous occasions, I've introduced these films to friends whose cinematic tastes I've considered somewhat conservative, and overwhelmingly they have reacted to them with horror, describing how the films gave them nightmares, how they are often "full of overweight people and drag queens." It's for these reasons, among many others, that I have such respect for Waters. His films get under moviegoers' skin; if they are in on the joke, fantastic, if they aren't, even better. But Rex Reed, himself a famous gay film critic, clearly didn't like Waters' approach, at least in the 1970s. The 1983 book *Midnight Movies* includes Reed's reaction to *Female Trouble*, in which Reed described the film as "filthy, repellent, beyond coherence, and so amateurish it looks like it was shot with a Brownie Instamatic.... Where do these people come from? Where do they go when the sun comes down? Isn't there a law or something? This compost heap is even dedicated to a member of the Charles Manson gang!"

John Waters on the set of Hairspray *(1988), New Line Cinema/Photofest*

In more recent years, Waters has arguably become a less threatening filmmaker, yet his movies maintain a certain off-kilter charm. From his satire of a seemingly normal, suburban housewife/murderer, *Serial Mom* (1994), to his spoof of the film business, *Cecil B. DeMented* (2000), Waters continues to provoke unique reactions from audiences—alas, though, without help from most of his original entourage, many of whom died prematurely. Waters' most recent work, *A Dirty Shame* (2004), depicts a group of sex addicts taking over much of Baltimore, Waters' beloved hometown, and where all of his films take place. Critics were aghast by Waters' return to gross-out turf; Roger Ebert gave the film "a big thumbs down" and *Entertainment Weekly* went as far as to grant it an F grade. Waters, it appears, was back in the game.

I've interviewed Waters a few times over the years; he's always warm, friendly, and generous with his time. Here, I spoke with him about the DVD re-release of *Pink Flamingos* and his sense of himself as an "activist who is gay," rather than a gay activist.

When I heard news of the twenty-fifth anniversary DVD release of *Pink Flamingos* [originally released in 1972], I was pleasantly surprised. It seemed like something filmmakers like Coppola would do with *The Godfather*, with what people think of as high art. Was it your idea to do it?
Yes. In 1995, at the Cannes Film Festival, I pitched the idea to Fine Line [the original production company, now a subsidiary of New Line Cinema]. There were about four people working there then, and now of course it's a huge company. I told them I had this new footage, and at the time their only [DVD] re-release had been [the French film] *Belle de Jour*, and it had been a success, so I said let's do a low-rent *Belle de Jour*. And they said okay. [The re-release of *Pink Flamingos*] looks great. We blew it up [from 35mm], digitalized the sound, put the music back in. At the end, I fade in and show a few lost scenes with Divine and Edie [Edith Massey].

In 1986, as a university student, I had the opportunity to interview Divine [see interview at this chapter]. He was fantastic.
Did he fall asleep? Sometimes Divine would just fall asleep during interviews. It was nothing against the reporter, but if he sat down for too long, he would just fall asleep.

You know, it was strange to promote *Flamingos* twenty-five years after the initial release. But it's the only way Divine could star in a new movie [after his death]. His picture is everywhere again and I think he would like that because he's quite slim in *Pink Flamingos*.

You added an hour of extra footage of *Pink Flamingos* for the special edition. How did you decide what to use?
I just tried to choose the best [footage available]. I didn't really have any outtakes or bloopers. I had whole scenes that were edited together but [had been] left out [of the original].

I recall when *Hairspray* first came out in 1988, you said in interviews that there really weren't any great trashy movies any more.
I think what I meant at the time was that there aren't any really good exploitation films anymore because Hollywood makes them now. Things that you used to only find in exploitation films now routinely appear in Hollywood films. But there are still films that cause trouble. Certainly, [Bruce LaBruce's] *Hustler White*. There's always going to be kids who'll do it and thank God for that.

Since *Pink Flamingos*, many of the cast members have died: Divine, David Lochary, Edith Massey, Cookie Mueller. In your films, you often treat death outrageously: castration, people getting blown up, having their bowels blown out, and so on. How have the deaths of your friends and coworkers affected your work?
It's affected me way more in my personal life than in my professional life. I am missing out on growing old with these people. But one good thing about getting older is that [life] gets a lot easier. I miss them because they were really, really close friends. David Lochary [who played Raymond Marble] died so very long ago [1977] that unfortunately I'm very used to his death. David never really saw any real success we had, except underground success. Divine unfortunately had one week to enjoy what he'd spent his whole life trying to get at [Divine died in 1988, shortly after the release of *Hairspray*]. That stinks, but having one week to enjoy [*Hairspray's* release] is better than not having it at all. If Divine were still alive, I think he would have been in all my [subsequent] movies. The studios wouldn't have let him play Kathleen Turner's part in *Serial Mom* [1994], but he would have been the neighbor and the part would have been bigger. It would have been written differently.

Cookie [who played herself] was a really good writer, more than

Colleen Fitzpatrick (as Amber von Tussle), Debbie Harry (as Velma Von Tussle), Divine (as Edna Turnblad), and Ricki Lake (as Tracy Turnblad), in Hairspray *(1988), New Line Cinema/Photofest*

Divine (as Francine Fishpaw) and Tab Hunter (as Todd Tomorrow) in Polyester *(1981), New Line/Photofest*

she was an actor. She was sort of our Charo, and I mean that with respect. Edith [who played Edie] is the only one I don't know how you'd duplicate. She was a completely natural [actress]. You certainly couldn't replace Edith. I don't know how you could do that.

Do you still spend time with Mink Stole [who starred in many of your films]?
Oh yes, we're very close. We did an event together at Planet Hollywood in LA. She lives there and gets a lot of [film] work; she was in David Lynch's *Lost Highway*. She was with me when the Los Angeles County Museum did a retrospective of my work. It's funny that *Pink Flamingos* has been received with such respect now when all those years ago it would have gotten us arrested.

When *Pink Flamingos* was first released, it received many negative responses, but in the years since, it has impacted many audiences and filmmakers in a positive way.
It has been received with a certain kind of respect that makes me very happy, because the people who I would care if they liked it, generally do. What was even more important to me was that when this film came out, it had no critical support and completely became a hit through word of mouth—something that is impossible today. There were no ads, and I think audiences aren't so brave today [to attend films that are not widely marketed]. They need to be told something's good or be reinforced [of its validity] by advertising images. I like the idea that this film became huge not through money or marketing, or any of the things that run Hollywood today. It [was a success] because crazy people liked it, and lucky enough for me, there's crazy people in every city. And God bless 'em, people who have a similar sense of humor as mine, and there are people in every country like that.

In Danny Peary's book, *Cult Movies*, he states that you were irresponsible with *Pink Flamingos*.
I loved that! I think he was also the one who said it went beyond humor to pure pathology. I loved that too.

Do you ever have regrets about things you have depicted in your movies?
No. Oh, in *Mondo Trasho* [1969] we chopped off chickens' heads—I suppose I regret that. It was a joke that no one ever understood. I

wouldn't do that today, though I certainly don't lose any sleep over it. If I did regret anything it would be a scene that was too long, or that I didn't have more money [to make a film]. But I don't regret any of my films morally. I'm quite proud of them. The only reason I ever did any of this was to make people laugh, and if they can still laugh all these years later, then I did a good job.

You've been called the Pope of Trash, the King of Sleaze, the Prince of Puke. What's your favorite title?

There's more! Let me think: the Anal Ambassador, the Marquee de Sade, the Duke of Dirt. They're fun. Certainly the Pope of Trash is my favorite because William Burroughs said it. So to me, that's divine intervention. That's like the Pope giving you a title.

Do you consider yourself a gay activist?

I consider myself an activist, but an activist who's gay. Gay is not enough. All gay films aren't necessarily good. I don't define myself by my sexuality. However, I've always said that I was gay, although no one ever asked. I think they feared the answer was worse than gay. Only recently have they asked, and I think it's because of AIDS, which has made it a much more political issue. I don't think it makes me any worse or better to be gay. Obviously much of my audience has been gay, but not totally by any means. Gay people are the best audiences, actually, because they always like movies.

The episode of _The Simpsons_ in which you guest-star is considered one of the best they've ever done.

I was proud to do _The Simpsons_. When I was growing up there was no way the family could sit around and watch a cartoon like that in prime time that was so blatantly pro-gay. It just couldn't have happened. My ten-year-old nephew phoned up and said, "You were really good on the show." In some ways it's much braver to say that you're gay on _The Simpsons_ than it is to say it in _The Advocate_, because I don't know the sexuality of the person I buy my newspaper from, the person on the street. But they know mine, which is an odd thing. In a perfect world, when gay liberation is achieved [people's sexuality] won't be an issue anymore. That should be the goal of gay liberation: we shouldn't even have to talk about it anymore. I actually prefer it when crowds are mixed. Gay bars are boring to me.

Do you have an issue with gay people who place their sexuality above all else in terms of their identity?

To segregate yourself is the worst idea possible. I'm totally against isolation and segregation. I heard someone the other day say, "Me and five other bottoms went on vacation together." It staggered me that people could pick their friends that way. That's actually funny. Gay culture's actually become a lot hipper lately; it used to be a bunch of conservatives in gay bars in the 1960s. Thank God things have changed in forty years.

That's interesting, because many have also said that gay culture itself has recently become boring and conservative.

Did you read the book *Anti-Gay* [edited by Mark Simpson]? It's [a collection of essays] written by gay people who are mortified by gay culture. A few of the stories are very funny. Actually, I went to a club in New York on Gay Pride Day and they were having a Gay Shame Day. It was really funny. They didn't allow any muscle queens in and they didn't play any disco. To me, all the muscle queens seem to be trying to make up for something that happened to them in high school. I've never been to a gym. I've gotten laid because I could make people laugh.

Are you in a relationship?

No, not right now. And I don't feel the need to be living with some-one. My house is very much my own and I have a hard time seeing myself letting anyone say, "I'll hang this here." Generally, being by myself is a luxury. I certainly sleep with people, but I don't want to be married. People I go out with usually end up resenting my lifestyle anyway. Because when we go out, people tend to recognize just one of us all the time. I don't have any control over that. Gen-erally, it's hard. But anyone has a hard time in a relationship. I'm not whining, it's just an occupational hazard.

What do you see as the most significant aspect of those films you made in the 1970s?

Just how gloriously happy and joyous [the period] was—in ways that we could never understand, but that's half the reason the peo-ple who liked it, liked it so much. They were in on the conspiracy.

Are there any things you see in independent cinema today that strike you see as unsettling?

There's certainly stuff I don't like, but not really anything unsettling. If it were unsettling, it'd be good. That's what I'm waiting for, for this younger generation [of filmmakers] to come up with something more threatening than '70s revivals. They should be making movies that make me nervous.

How would you feel if Republicans started making movies?
That wouldn't make me nervous because I wouldn't go and see them. *Pink Flamingos* never made Republicans nervous because they never came to see it. It wasn't made for Republicans, it was made for hippies. We were hippies and the audience were hippies. It was a joke on what was politically correct then, which was peace and love and the hippie movement. I'm a liberal, God knows, a card-carrying ACLU [American Civil Liberties Union] member. And they're the easiest to shock, because everything's all right to them until it's in their house and then they get very nervous. I love to fuck with that.

FILMOGRAPHY

John Waters is director and writer of the following which are features unless otherwise noted:

A Dirty Shame, 2004
Cecil B. DeMented, 2000
Pecker, 1998
Serial Mom, 1994
Cry-Baby, 1990
Hairspray, 1988
Polyester, 1981
Desperate Living, 1977
Female Trouble, 1974
Pink Flamingos, 1972
Multiple Maniacs, 1970
The Diane Linkletter Story, 1969
Mondo Trasho, 1969
Eat Your Makeup (short film), 1968
Roman Candles (short film), 1966
Hag in a Black Leather Jacket (short film), 1964

Divine in Female Trouble *(1974), Fine Line Features/Photofest*

Postscript: A Conversation with Divine

*In 1986, at the age of twenty-one, I decided to interview Divine, John Waters'
leading "lady" in a number of his now-legendary films, for* The Gateway,
*the student paper at the University of Alberta in my hometown of Edmonton,
Canada. What follows is the first interview I ever conducted. Divine was in
town for two nights, playing at a club called Goose Loonies. (No, I'm not
making that up.) After the show on the first night, I left a note for his manager at the adjoining hotel asking if I could interview Divine the next day. It
worked—I got a call, and my heart pounded rapidly as I realized I'd landed
an interview with one of my idols.*

*The only recording device I had was a ghetto blaster—and an ugly yellow
one at that. But damn, was Divine ever sweet. He was just the best: warm
and funny, but full of star power. It was precisely the kind of experience a
starstruck student journalist like me dreamed of. Here's the article, as it appeared in the pages of the September 9, 1986 edition of* The Gateway.

In 1972, independent filmmaker John Waters released a film called
Pink Flamingos. The film featured a 300-pound star, then virtually unknown. The character was "Divine—the most disgusting person in the
world." The film played repertory cinemas across North America and
Europe and Waters and Divine both gained notoriety for their work.
The final scene was particularly noteworthy: in order to prove his title
as the most disgusting person in the world, Divine picks up still-steam-
ing dog feces and eats it. A star is born.

Divine continued to make films with Waters, the last one being *Polyester* (1980), which co-starred Tab Hunter. *Polyester* was filmed using a
brand new cinematic device: Odorama. Audience members were given
scratch-and-sniff cards, allowing them to "smell along" with the action. Divine then worked with director Paul Bartel on *Lust in the Dust*
[1985], starring again opposite Hunter.

In 1978, Divine began his singing career. He has since recorded such
pop disco hits as "Love Reaction" and "You Think You're a Man." His
records sell well internationally—in fact, he has several gold and platinum albums. He has toured virtually everywhere to sell-out crowds,
including Israel and Japan, as well as across Europe. In 1984, he appeared on the British TV series *Top of the Pops*. After the program aired,
the TV station was flooded with 12,000 calls, all protesting his appearance. The producers of *Top of the Pops* decided Divine could not appear
again on their show.

Divine's latest film is *Trouble in Mind* [1985], directed by Alan Rudolph, in which Divine has his first male role, playing a gangster. The film has received excellent reviews, as has Divine for his performance.

Divine was performing his nightclub act at Goose Loonies last summer. I interviewed him in his hotel room. As I spoke to him, it struck me that everything I'd ever read in a Divine interview was true. Divine was charming, witty, polite, and above all, candid. We discussed his film work and rumours of a network TV series.

After coming out of a screening of *Trouble in Mind*, someone said to me that you stole the film.

One reviewer from *The Hollywood Reporter* said that too. I was quite flattered.

In the film you play a mob leader. Did Alan Rudolph write this part with you in mind?

Yes. This part was written for me. I was his first choice. He came to Bernard's [Bernard Jay, Divine's personal manager] office, and sort of plopped this thing on my lap.

He had seen your work with John Waters and Paul Bartel.

Yes, and was a fan of that work, and he said he thought I'd be good in this man's part. I've been looking for a man's part for about eight years.

You'd had a male role in *Female Trouble*, though—playing a man who raped yourself, or the female character you played.

Yeah, but this was just a few seconds. I really didn't get to do any acting or dialogue besides humping someone—a stand-in—which wasn't that enjoyable, this 400-pound monster. She wasn't the prettiest woman.

Will a sequel to *Pink Flamingos* ever be made? I read John Waters' article in *American Film* magazine about his attempts to get someone to financially back the sequel.

I think it was scrapped after Edith Massey died. John said he would never try to find a replacement for her or me or for anyone. As far as he's concerned, there aren't any.

Certainly not for Edith Massey.

Or *me*. [*Laughs*.] You're talking to me! No, that's true. There aren't any other Ediths around. But really, it wasn't my favorite script. We did enough with dog shit.

You've had a lot of press about the shit.
Yes. Whether it was real or not, I'm not going to say, but the scene stuck in people's minds … stuck in my throat.

I've heard that scene estranged you from your parents.
For about nine years, we didn't speak. We're great now, though.

I was happy to read that you'd reconciled.
It's real good now. They're fans. Which makes me feel so much better because I'm an only child, and of course we were very close and spent a lot of time together. Then all of a sudden we didn't speak, and as far as I was concerned it was for no reason at all. I think they finally realized that too, because I'm just doing what I love and do best, which is being a comedian and an actor and making people laugh.

How did you and John Waters meet and how was it that you established a professional relationship?
We were neighbors. We grew up in Lutherville, Maryland. John was quite a movie buff, as I was too. John just always wanted to make movies. He had a Brownie Super 8 camera that his parents bought him as a present, and we used to get together on Sunday afternoons, about ten or twelve of us. He would write scripts for us during the week and we would act them out on Sundays. Actually, we did it out of sheer boredom. When I was a teenager, we didn't have discos or anything to go to. Sounds like I came out of a covered wagon or something!

There were teen centers, but they were for the nerds, no one really wanted to go to them. On Wednesday night we would get together and have Coke and chips—Coca-Cola, that is—and watch the rushes. We thought we were the hottest thing since sliced bread. Finally, someone said, "You should show these to other people. These films are funny!" There's a spring festival in Baltimore, and John rented a hall and showed the film. He charged forty-nine cents to get in. Some people from the University of Maryland filmmaking school saw the film and thought it was fabulous. They asked John and I if we would come to the school to show the movie and to give the kids there incentive to make movies because ours was made for about $250.

I went all done up, and John came onstage first and gave a long speech about movie-making, and then he introduced me as the "most beautiful woman in the world almost"—almost because I'm a man—and I came out having a modelling fit and then answered questions about acting, which I thought took a lot of balls. That was our routine.

John also helped me with my first club act in San Francisco. I would push out a shopping cart onstage, and there was ground beef and fish and a telephone book. I would spin the fish around and rub them all over my body and then throw them into the audience, which would splatter all over people. It was a horrible mess. Then I'd throw ground beef at the people, and rip the telephone book in half. Three guys all dressed in black would come out and lie down head to foot, I would walk over top of them and squat over their faces and flashbulbs would go off. Then I would answer questions from the audience. This was my nightclub act at the time.

This must have been very racy then, years ago, versus today [1986].
> Yes, it's come around now. People used to sit there with their mouths just open—especially if they got hit by a fish. When I did my first play in New York, I played a dyke matron in a women's prison. One convict had a pet chicken, I find the chicken and in the next scene I go into my office with a cooked chicken on my finger and I pull its leg off and eat it, then throw the chicken into the audience. One night, it hit a man with a suede coat on, and the producers had to buy him a new coat—$500!

So you were well-received off-Broadway and on the London stage?
> Oh yeah. I got rave reviews in London. I used to have them memorized. But I've had better ones since!

Do you have any plans to work with Waters again soon?
> It all depends on the script. If he's going to do a *Pink Flamingos 2*, then no, I'm not really interested. I think it'd be going backwards. I can't speak for John, but for me I don't really feel it's the right

thing to do at this particular time in my career. I think John's a brilliant writer. He's one of my favorite screenwriters and directors, and one of my dearest friends.

Is the rumor about a television series true?
All these rumors! I'd love to do a TV series. There are some people in Hollywood who are quite interested in me. But at this point that's as far as it goes.

I wonder how any of the major television networks would ever have the guts to put Divine in a series.
Oh, you'd be surprised. I've been up for major TV shows. They've usually been killed by the head of the individual network at the last minute. This is the same problem I've had throughout my career. But now, many of the studio heads have changed and are young men and women who were in fact big fans of *Pink Flamingos*. Which is great for me! There are in fact quite a few shows I could get on at present.

A *Dynasty* appearance, perhaps?
[*Laughs.*] I'm not going to name them.

I recall your well-publicized ban from *Top of the Pops* in London. Have you appeared on that show since your first time?
No. But one of my records was on the charts and they did cover it. They just showed parts of the video.

I was surprised by the producers' decision. You just sang the song, and didn't make any suggestive gestures. Boy George had appeared on the show in drag, and no one protested. It seems people were offended by fat.
That's what I said too. But I thought, "Some of the people who watch it are fatter than I am and sit home on their fat asses watching television." They're the very ones who complain! They had 12,000 complaints and they say about 10 million people watch the show. That's not a very big ratio. However, my record sales doubled the next day! The only people who were ever banned from *Top of the Pops* were the Sex Pistols, Frankie Goes to Hollywood, the Beatles, and myself. So I felt this wasn't bad company to keep, when it goes down in history.

You travel a lot. Do foreign customs agents ever give you hassles?
Only in Canada. Once in Germany, and another time in Sweden.

You're riding a wave of popularity right now. Where do you see yourself in ten years?
I'm going for it. Right to the top. Why not? All I can do is not make it.

One could say you already have. You're quite a cult phenomenon.
Oh, but I want more than that. I want Oscars, Golden Globes, Grammys. I mean, why not? If somebody had told me five or six years ago that I'd have gold and platinum records, I'd have said they were crazy because I didn't sing. But now I've got them on the wall. And if someone had said that I'd make a movie with Kris Kristofferson or Geneviève Bujold I'd have told them they were crazy. These are big stars. My final scene [in *Trouble in Mind*] was with Kris—I got to get shot by him.

I'd like to see you get an Oscar.
So would I. And I will, if I have anything to say about it. It's been a dream of mine since I was a kid.

As an outsider, what do you think of Edmonton? It's one of Canada's most conservative cities.
You wouldn't have thought so from the crowd last night! I haven't had a chance to see much of Edmonton. I'm going out to that big shopping mall today [West Edmonton Mall, at the time the world's largest shopping center]. I've heard so much about it.

Some people are offended by your act. They consider you a bit of a freak—a novelty only because you're overweight and obviously homosexual. How do you react?
They're assholes. [*Laughs.*] These are people who are uptight about their sexuality. Not everyone's going to like me, but I'm not doing my act for everyone, I'm doing it for those who like it. Some people don't like Diana Ross, and all she does is get up and sing pop songs. I don't think I'm a freak, I'm just another entertainer who happened to do something no one else had. People don't know how to label me. Unfortunately, it seems everything has to have a label. I've always said that I'm a character actor, I play different characters. It just so happens that the characters that I was given to play

were women. I don't knock these roles—they've given me a large
following.

**Boy George has made a few negative remarks about you to the
press, which surprised me.**
Especially when he'd be sitting in every show I did in London.
Then he'd go on TV and say that he couldn't stand me—well, then
why did he buy a ticket for my show? I've heard through people
that he's actually a big fan. Basically, he just said those things to
protect his image.

BIBLIOGRAPHY

Allinson, Mark. *A Spanish Labyrinth: The Films of Pedro Almodóvar.* London: Tauris, 2001.

Anger, Kenneth. *Hollywood Babylon.* New York: Dell, 1975.

Aviv, Caryn and Shneer, David. *Queer Jews.* New York and London: Routledge, 2000.

Baker, Rob. *The Art of AIDS.* New York: Continuum, 1994.

Baker, Roger. *Drag: A History of Female Impersonation in the Performing Arts.* New York: New York University Press, 1994.

Barrios, Richard. *Screened Out: Playing Gay in Hollywood from Edison to Stonewall.* New York and London: Routledge, 2003.

Beard, William, and White, Jerry. *North of Everything: English-Canadian Cinema Since 1980.* Edmonton: University of Alberta Press, 2002.

Benshoff, Harry, and Griffin, Sean. *Queer Cinema: The* Film *Reader.* New York and London: Routledge, 2004.

Benshoff, Harry M. *Monsters in the Closet: Homosexuality and the Horror Film.* Manchester: Manchester University Press, 1997.

———. *Queer Images: A History of Gay and Lesbian Film in America.* Lanham, Md.: Rowman & Littlefield, 2006.

Biskind, Peter. "Girls Gotta Dream." *Vanity Fair,* January 2007: 93–99,142–144.

Creekmur, Corey K., and Doty, Alexander, eds. *Out in Culture: Gay, Lesbian, and Queer Essays on Popular Culture.* Durham and London: Duke University Press, 1995.

Crimp, Douglas, ed. *AIDS: Cultural Analysis/Cultural Activism.* Cambridge, MA: MIT Press, 1988.

Doty, Alexander. *Flaming Classics: Queering the Film Canon.* New York and London: Routledge, 2000.

———. *Making Things Perfectly Queer: Interpreting Mass Culture.* Minneapolis: University of Minnesota Press, 1993.

Dundjerovich, Aleksandar. *The Cinema of Robert Lepage: The Poetics of Memory.* London: Wallflower Press, 2003.

Dyer, Richard. *The Culture of Queers.* London and New York: Routledge, 2002.

———. *The Matter of Images: Essays on Representations.* London and New York: Routledge, 1993.

———. *Only Entertainment.* London: Routledge, 1992.

⸺, ed. *Gays and Film.* New York: Zoetrope, 1984.

Dyer, Richard with Pidduck, Julianne. *Now You See It: Studies in Lesbian and Gay Film.* London and New York: Routledge, 2003.

Ebert, Roger. "The Doom Generation review." *Chicago Sun-Times,* Nov. 10, 1995. http://rogerebert.suntimes.com/apps/pbcs.dll/article?AID=/19951110/REVIEWS/511100301/1023

Esther, John. "Gregg Araki: Tackling the Tough Ones on Film." *Gay & Lesbian Review,* Sept–Oct 2005: 44–45.

Falsetto, Mario. *Personal Visions: Conversations with Contemporary Film Directors.* Los Angeles: Silman-James, 2000.

Farber, Jim. "The Wizard of Sleaze." *Soho News,* May 27, 1981.

Feil, Ken. *Dying for a Laugh: Disaster Movies and the Camp Imagination.* Middletown, CT: Wesleyan University Press, 2005.

Fernie, Lynne, Forbes, Dinah and Mason, Joyce, eds. *Sight Specific: Lesbians and Representation.* Toronto: A Space, 1988.

Fields, Danny, and Lebowitz, Fran. "*Pink Flamingos* and the Filthiest People Alive?" *Interview,* May 1973.

Gamson, Joshua. *Freaks Talk Back: Tabloid Talk Shows and Sexual Nonconformity.* Chicago: University of Chicago Press, 1998.

Giulano, Mike. "Slimy Waters: An Interview with the Cesspool Cineaste of Baltimore." *L.A. Reader,* May 25, 1979: 36.

Goldie, Terry, ed. *In a Queer Country: Gay & Lesbian Studies in the Canadian Context.* Vancouver: Arsenal Pulp Press, 2001.

Greyson, John. *Urinal and Other Stories.* Toronto: Art Metropole and The Power Plant, 1993.

Hadleigh, Boze. *Conversations with My Elders.* New York: St. Martin's Press, 1986.

⸺. *The Lavender Screen: The Gay and Lesbian Films: Their Stars, Makers, Characters, and Critics.* New York: Citadel Press, 2001.

Hampson, Sarah. "King of the Golden Age of Trash." *The Globe and Mail,* April 5, 2003.

Hays, Matthew. "Make Art, Not Politics: Gregg Araki on Going *Nowhere.*" *Montreal Mirror,* July 17, 1997. http://www.montrealmirror.com/ARCHIVES/1997/071797/film1.html

Hoberman, J. and Rosenbaum, Jonathan. *Midnight Movies.* New York: Harper & Row, 1983.

Holden, Stephen. "'Didn't Do It for Love': Too Much Frenetic Change." Review of Monika Treut film. *New York Times,* May 1, 1998. http://www.nytimes.com/library/film/050198love-film-review.html

Ives, John G. *John Waters*. New York: Thunder's Mouth Press, 1992.

Jay, Bernard. *Not Simply Divine*. New York: Fireside, 1993.

Kramer, Gary M. *Independent Queer Cinema: Reviews and Interviews*. Binghamton, NY: Southern Tier Editions, 2006.

Kuzniar, Alice A. *The Queer German Cinema*. Stanford: Stanford University Press, 2000.

LaBruce, Bruce. *The Reluctant Pornographer*. Toronto: Gutter Press, 1997.

Monk, Katherine. *Weird Sex and Snowshoes and Other Canadian Film Phenomena*. Vancouver: Raincoast Books, 2001.

Morris, George. "Just Folks: John Waters." *Take One*, March 1978.

Murray, Raymond. *Images in the Dark: An Encyclopedia of Gay and Lesbian Film and Video*. New York: Plume, 1996.

Musto, Michael. "Desperate Living: Not a Pretty Picture." *Soho Weekly News*, October 20, 1977.

O'Brien, Glenn. "I Call on John Waters (and also Divine)." *Village Voice*, March 3, 1975.

Onstad, Katrina. "A Life of Anger." Interview with Kenneth Anger. *Guardian Unlimited*, Oct. 27, 2006. http://film.guardian.co.uk/interview/interviewpages/0,,1933260,00.html

Peary, Danny. *Cult Movies*. New York: Delta Books, 1981.

———. *Cult Movies 2*. New York: Delta Books, 1983.

Pevere, Geoff, and Wise, Wyndham. *Take One Special Edition: Interviews and Essays*. Toronto: *Take One* Magazine, 2004.

Poole, Wakefield. *Dirty Poole: The Autobiography of a Gay Porn Pioneer*. New York: Alyson Books, 2000.

Porter, Ryan. "Like Alice in Wonderland." Interviews with John Cameron Mitchell and *Shortbus* cast. *fab style quarterly*, 2, Fall 2006: 46-49.

Rich, B. Ruby. *Chick Flicks: Theories and Memories of the Feminist Film Movement*. Durham, N.C.: Duke University Press, 1998.

Russo, Vito. *The Celluloid Closet: Homosexuality in the Movies*. New York: Harper & Row, 1981.

Scott, Jay. *Great Scott: The Best of Jay Scott's Movie Reviews*. Toronto: McClelland & Stewart, 1994.

Shilts, Randy. *And the Band Played On: Politics, People and the AIDS Epidemic*. New York: St. Martin's Press, 1987.

Skal, David J. *The Monster Show*. New York: Penguin, 1993.

Smith, Jack. "'Pink Flamingos' Formulas in Focus." *Village Voice*, July 19, 1973.

Smith, Paul Julian. *Desire Unlimited: The Cinema of Pedro Almodóvar* New York: Verso, 1994.

Sprinkle, Annie. *Hardcore from the Heart: The Pleasures, Profits and Politics of Sex in Performance.* New York: Continuum, 2001.

Suarez, Juan Antonio. *Bike Boys, Drag Queens & Superstars: Avant-Garde, Mass Culture, and Gay Identities in the 1960s Underground Cinema.* Bloomington: Indiana University Press, 1996.

Trebay, Guy, "John Waters Smells Success." *Village Voice,* May 20–26, 1981.

Tyler, Parker. *Screening the Sexes: Homosexuality in the Movies.* New York: Da Capo Press, 1993.

Van Sant, Gus. *Pink.* New York: Anchor, 1998.

Varnier, Greg. "Arthur Dong: Lens on Homophobic America." *Gay & Lesbian Review,* July–August 2005: 30–31.

Vogel, Amos. *Film as a Subversive Art.* New York: Random House, 1974.

Waters, John. *Shock Value: A Tasteful Book about Bad Taste* New York: Delta, 1981.

Waugh, Thomas. *The Fruit Machine: 20 Years of Writings on Queer Cinema.* Durham and London: Duke University Press, 2000.

———. *Hard to Imagine: Gay Male Eroticism in Photography and Film from Their Beginnings to Stonewall.* New York: Columbia University Press, 1996.

———. *The Romance of Transgression in Canada: Queering Sexualities, Nations, Cinemas.* Montreal: McGill-Queen's University Press, 2006.

Wise, Wyndham, ed. *Take One's Essential Guide to Canadian Cinema.* Toronto: University of Toronto Press, 2001.

Wood, Robin. *Sexual Politics & Narrative Film: Hollywood and Beyond.* New York: Columbia University Press, 1998.

Yosef, Raz. *Beyond Flesh: Queer Masculinities and Nationalism in Israeli Cinema.* New Brunswick, NJ: Rutgers University Press, 2004.

Zucker, Carole. *In the Company of Actors: Reflections on the Craft of Acting.* New York: Theater Arts Books/Routledge, 1999.

Websites:
www.anniesprinkle.org
www.bookrags.com
www.imdb.com
www.nfb.ca
www.rosavonpraunheim.de

Index

Matthew Hays with Joan Collins, photographed by Jan Thijs

MATTHEW HAYS has been a film critic and reporter for the weekly *Montreal Mirror* since 1993. His articles on popular culture and politics have also appeared in *The Globe and Mail*, *The New York Times*, *The Guardian*, *The Advocate*, CBC Arts Online, *Gay Times*, *Frontiers*, *The Toronto Star*, *This Magazine*, *The Gay and Lesbian Review*, *Genre*, *The Hollywood Reporter*, *Montage*, *Cineaction!*, *Cinema Scope*, *Xtra* and *fab*. He is a contributing editor for the national Canadian film magazine *POV*, and is the Montreal correspondent for *Playback*, Canada's film and TV industry publication. A 2006 nominee for a National Magazine Award, he is the recipient of the Concordia University Alumni Association Teaching Excellence Award for 2007. Hays received his MA in communication studies from Concordia University in Montreal, where he now teaches courses in film studies, communication studies, and journalism.